THE LAST WORD AND
THE WORD AFTER THAT

*A Tale of Faith, Doubt,
and a New Kind of Christianity*

Brian D. McLaren

○

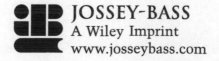

JOSSEY-BASS
A Wiley Imprint
www.josseybass.com

Published by Jossey-Bass
A Wiley Imprint
989 Market Street, San Francisco, CA 94103   www.josseybass.com

Jossey-Bass books and products are available through most bookstores. To contact Jossey-Bass directly, call our Customer Care Department within the United States at 800-956-7739, outside the United States at 317-572-3986 or, fax 317-572-4002.

Jossey-Bass also publishes its books in a variety of electronic formats. Some content that appears in print may not be available in electronic books.

Library of Congress Cataloging-in-Publication Data

McLaren, Brian D.
　　The last word and the word after that : a tale of faith, doubt, and a new kind of Christianity / Brian D. McLaren.
　　　　p. cm.
　　Includes bibliographical references.
　　ISBN 0-7879-7592-3 (alk. paper)
　　1. Belief and doubt—Fiction. I. Title.
　　PS3613.C569L37 2005
　　813'.6—dc22   2004027032

Printed in the United States of America
FIRST EDITION
HB Printing   10 9 8 7 6 5 4 3 2 1

CONTENTS

*This book is dedicated to the many people who love God
or want to love God or are seeking for a God to love but have
been repulsed by ugly, unworthy images of a cruel, capricious,
merciless, tyrannical deity.*

*It is also dedicated to people who love God but have a nagging
fear that God may turn out to be less than good or kind or loving
in the end. This doubt makes their hearts uneasy, their worship
forced and fake, and their commitment conflicted or half-hearted.*

*Along with them, it is dedicated to those who used to believe
but for similar reasons have lost faith and grown spiritually
apathetic or cynical.*

*Finally, it is dedicated to pastors, parents, friends, teachers,
and neighbors who love all these people, listen to their questions
with gentleness and respect, and want to help them find honest
answers they can live with. Although this book will not answer
all their questions, it will let them know that they are not wrong
or alone in asking their questions, and it may help them find
a place where they can in good faith have faith. That is my
pursuit as well.*

ACKNOWLEDGMENTS

GRACE, THANK YOU for Italianizing me a bit, believing in me, encouraging me, and making me laugh. Thanks also for reading drafts of everything I write and giving me intelligent, honest feedback. I've never felt more supported or more blessed to have you as my partner in life, marriage, parenthood, ministry, and all the other crazy things we do together.

Jodi, thanks for caring about our relationship and for being generous with me when I'm traveling too much or holed up in my office writing. I'm going to miss you so much when you go to college! I hope you know how special you are to me and how deep you are in my heart. Rachel, Brett, and Trevor—thanks for becoming friends whom I respect so much. The only thing better than being your father is being your father *and* your friend. Thanks for all you've contributed to this book.

Cedar Ridge, thanks for another season of growth, joy, learning, and adventure together. Thanks for the freedom you give me—to think, to travel, to write, and to be a human being, not just to play a religious role. I am honored to be part of this community.

Sheryl Fullerton, thanks for being exactly the kind of editor I need. I feel I'm being inaccurate if I refer to "my" books; they're really "ours." Thanks also to the whole crew at Jossey-Bass. You take pride in your work, and I'm proud to be associated with you.

Four friends read this manuscript and gave me extensive feedback: Leif Hansen, Ken Archer (theologicalthinking.com), Mike Morrell (zoecarnate.com), and Dr. Stanley Grenz. Your insights and suggestions have made the finished product so much better than it would have been otherwise. Thank you.

To the people of the emergent community (www.emergentvillage.com), thanks for being courageous catalysts in my life and in the lives of thousands of people. I have learned to "know with you" in ways that have enriched my life profoundly.

To my critics, thanks for the times you offer your feedback with kindness, because you help me learn things I wouldn't learn without you. And thanks for the times you offer your critique without kindness, because then you challenge me to grow in character. Speaking of critics, none of them should assume that real people mentioned in these acknowledgments or elsewhere in this book agree with anything said by the fictional characters of this book or by its author.

Thanks for all who encourage me with kind words, notes, letters, and e-mails. I hope this book will encourage you in return.

B.D.M.

INTRODUCTION

THIS INTRODUCTION FRAMES *The Last Word and the Word After That.* If you want to encounter the story without my thoughts about it, you may want to read this last, after you've finished the rest of the book.

○

I BELIEVE THAT GOD is good. No thought I have ever had of God is better than God actually is. True, my thoughts—including my assumptions about what *good* means—are always more or less inaccurate, limited, and unworthy, but still I am confident of this: I have never overestimated how good God is because God's goodness overflows far beyond the limits of human understanding. That conviction gave birth to this book.

Now if you believe everything is pretty much fine in the Christian church and its theology, if you believe that only small cosmetic or methodological tweaks are needed in a basically sound enterprise, then there's no need to read this book. If, however, you believe that our common images and understandings of God are generally too small and even mean, then this book may help you—and us.

On the surface, this book appears to be largely about hell. But it isn't really. Those who read it and react to it as such will have missed the point. True, the subject of hell is worth talking about. In researching the evolution of the conventional doctrine of hell for this book, I discovered that the story is truly fascinating, putting its horror aside for a moment. In Christian theology, hell (which a character in this series calls the tail that first wagged and then became the dog) is catalytic; too little attention has been paid to the practical effects various formulations of the doctrine of hell have had on Christian thought, worship, behavior, and practice. But the subject has all but disappeared, at least overtly, from most contemporary preaching—whether liberal or evangelical—although fundamentalist preaching is in many a place still quite spicy with it. As Martin Marty quipped, "Hell has disappeared and no one noticed."[1] The widespread

---

1. *U.S. News and World Report,* January 31, 2000, p 44.

suppression, cooling, civilizing, and now near-disappearance of hell deserves some notice and reflection from serious scholars and professional theologians. As a mediocre pastor, former scholar, and amateur theologian, I can't claim to be sufficient for that task. I can only raise questions here that I feel need to be raised and hope that better scholars and professional theologians will provide better answers than I've been able to discover or construct.

As I see it, more significant than any doctrine of hell itself is the view of God to which one's doctrine of hell contributes. William Temple once said that if your concept of God is radically false, the more devoted you are, the worse off you will be.[2] So this book is in the end more about our view of God than it is about our understandings of hell. What kind of God do we believe exists? What kind of life should we live in response? How does our view of God affect the way we see and treat other people? And how does the way we see and treat other people affect our view of God?

When the brilliant and influential American theologian Jonathan Edwards etched the image of an angry God upon our minds in a famous sermon in the eighteenth century, was he helping us or hurting us, telling the truth straight or slanting it?

> The God that holds you over the pit of hell, much as one holds a spider or some loathsome insect over the fire, abhors you and is dreadfully provoked: his wrath towards you burns like fire; he looks upon you as worthy of nothing else, but to be cast into the fire.[3]

Whatever you think of Edwards's sermon, the conventional doctrine of hell has too often engendered a view of a deity who suffers from borderline personality disorder or some worse sociopathic diagnosis. *God loves you and has a wonderful plan for your life, and if you don't love God back and cooperate with God's plans in exactly the prescribed way, God will torture you with unimaginable abuse, forever*—that sort of thing. Human parents who "love" their children with these kinds of implied ultimatums tend to produce the most dysfunctional families, and perhaps the dysfunctions of the Christian religion can be traced not to God as God really is but to views of God that are not easy for people swallow while remaining sane and functional.

2. Thanks to Dr. Dallas Willard and Dr. Keith Matthews for the William Temple reference, which was included in class notes from a Fuller Seminary class they team-teach.
3. Jonathan Edwards, "Sinners in the Hands of an Angry God," 1741.

With this situation in mind, it is no wonder that many theologians and preachers like myself have downplayed or entirely dropped the idea of hell in our writing and preaching. Perhaps intuitively, we have known that something is wrong and so we've backed off until we figure out the problem—or until some foolhardy person ventures to do so for us.

Meanwhile, the popular reaction against the mean-spirited God distortion often creates an equally distorted and distorting view of God: the divine doting Auntie in Heaven, full of sweetness and smiles, who sees war and corruption and violence and racism and says, "Well, boys will be boys. Would you care for another blessing, dearie?" Along with our doting Auntie in Heaven, we have God the chum, God the cheerleader, God the mascot (denominational or national), God the genie, God the positive force, God the copilot, God the romantic sweetheart, God the sugar daddy, God the rich uncle, God the sentimental feeling, God the watchdog, God the absentee landlord. All of these distortions probably, in some way, flow from an understandable but unhealthful overreaction against God the eternal torturer. Perhaps the consequences of these distortions are not as serious as those of the traditional approach; perhaps they're more serious. But either way, they are scary for their own reasons, as I hope the book will make clear. Is there a better alternative to either of these polarities: a just God without mercy for all or a merciful God without justice for all? Could our views of hell (whichever extreme you choose) be the symptoms of a deeper set of problems—misunderstandings about what God's justice is, misunderstandings about God's purpose in creating the world, deep misunderstandings about what kind of person God is?[4]

Those are the kind of questions I'm pursuing in this book. No doubt, many readers will dislike the answers given by various characters in this book; I hope they won't blame me for raising the questions and playing out through these characters conversations that many of us have silently in our own minds or in tense whispers among trusted friends in parking lots or dimly lit restaurant booths. Other people will read this book and wonder, *why the fuss?* For them, everything in this book will seem so patently obvious and noncontroversial, they won't be able to imagine anyone needing it, much less arguing against it. The whole subject seems rather medieval to them. I hope they'll realize that a great many people do, in fact, need this conversation—very, very much.

Many conservative religious people I know complain about "political correctness," which they associate with left-wing restrictions on freedom

---

4. I'm using this anthropomorphic language intentionally, realizing that it could be misunderstood and hoping it won't be.

of speech. I hope they will not impose a conservative P.C. restriction on people who want to bring these kinds of questions and conversations out into the light. (Yesterday someone told me that the pastor of a large church had banned his staff from reading and discussing the first book of this trilogy, so freedom of speech is on my mind today.)

At any rate, at heart this book is about the goodness of God and life with God. This means it is about the gospel and about justice and mercy and a new way of understanding their relationship—suggesting that God's justice is always merciful and God's mercy is always just. This book flows from the hunch that the heart disease afflicting the Christian community is chronic and serious rather than cosmetic: deep in our hearts, we don't fully love God because we are not fully confident that God is fully good.

Of all my books so far, *A New Kind of Christian* has sold most strongly, elicited the warmest response, and engendered the most controversy.[5] Meanwhile, I feel its sequel, *The Story We Find Ourselves In,* is actually a more radical book, although its more subtle tone disguises that fact. This final volume, which rounds out the trilogy, will probably be judged both radical and controversial. I am not proud of this and actually wish it weren't so. I am not a fan of controversy. As a pastor, "the unity of the Spirit in the bond of peace" is a precious thing to me; no one should disturb the peace unadvisedly or lightly. I would much prefer that my books be banned than have them cause destructive conflict in churches or trouble for pastors, who face enough problems without needless controversies being stirred. I would not go down this road at all if I did not feel, deep in my soul, that the issues raised here need to be raised for at least some people to consider, for the good of individuals who seek God, for the good of the church in all its forms, and for the good of the world at large. It is my belief, hope, and prayer that any short-term controversy will lead to long-term benefits that are truly worthwhile.

I am tempted to beg for mercy in this introduction, knowing that some conventional religious leaders take on an attack-dog affect when conventional formulations—of hell, God, or justice and mercy—are questioned. With that in mind, the biblical character I identify with most these days is Balaam's ass, whose story is recounted in Numbers 22 (well worth reading before you continue). As a voice in the ongoing conversation about God and the world, I am, like my equine counterpart, both an unlikely candidate and a last resort. And if I, like the donkey, seem to be veering uncooperatively from the conventional path, it's because I see something

---

5. As I write this introduction, it's too early to tell how *A Generous Orthodoxy* (Emergent/YS/Zondervan, 2004) will be received.

ahead that others might not see. Balaam's poor beast was beaten three times, but eventually his message was heard and Balaam stopped long enough to reconsider and see what he needed to see. If I can have similar results, any beatings I get will be well worth it.

I can imagine some impassioned critic of this book concluding a review with a statement something like this: "It's bad enough that McLaren has undermined conventional understandings of hell, but in its place what has he offered? No clear alternative. One cannot even tell for sure, after a careful reading of this book, whether McLaren is an inclusivist, conditionalist, or universalist. All one can say is that he is clearly not an orthodox exclusivist." In response, I might offer, as I have often suggested elsewhere, that clarity is good, but sometimes intrigue may be even more precious; clarity tends to put an end to further thinking, whereas intrigue makes one think more intensely, broadly, and deeply. Jesus' teaching on the kingdom of God is a case in point; his parables don't score too well on clarity, but they excel in intrigue.

Even more, I might add that like some politicians, we often seek clarity at the expense of truth: we would rather have something simple and clear than continue to search beyond convention for a truth that won't resolve to a neat formula, label, category, or pat answer. Or I might reply that asking me—as people often do—whether I'm an inclusivist or a universalist is like asking a vegetarian whether she prefers steak, pork, or venison. The question that yields these answers as options is a question I have no taste for asking. My intentional avoidance of this question does not spring from fear of saying what I really believe; a fearful writer wouldn't even begin a book like this. Rather, I am more interested in generating conversation than argument, believing that conversations have the potential to form us, inform us, and educate us far more than arguments. So this book is presented as a conversation, with multiple points of view, not as an argument pushing only mine.

Three disclaimers need to be made in this regard. First, this is not a "fair" book. It is not an attempt to give equal time to all views. It intentionally underrepresents the conventional view on the grounds that it is already widely known and defended. Second, while it intends to privilege new voices and minority reports as alternatives to the conventional view, it doesn't even promote the best-known alternatives but rather explores a less traveled path. Finally, even this path is not very original, depending heavily on seminal ideas presented by Bishop N. T. Wright, Lesslie Newbigin, and others.

Rather than claiming the last word on hell, then, I consider this sketch an accomplishment more suitable to my modest talents: to make a largely secret, forbidden conversation about hell more overt, public, and accessible. That's not everything, but neither is it nothing. I look forward with eagerness to see what creative Christian leaders—especially young ones, previously unheard ones, and ones from the global South—might do in taking the ideas and questions raised in this book and working with them further so that we all will see and celebrate the ultimate goodness of God more clearly and so that we may more joyfully and fully do justice, love kindness, and walk humbly with God.

Too few people read introductions like this, and as a result, I regularly have people contacting me asking for a phone number or an address for the fictional character Neil Edward Oliver so that they can invite him to speak at an event or ask him to become their mentor. They're disappointed, and sometimes even a little angry, to find out that Neil (a.k.a. Neo), Dan Poole, and their circle of friends don't really exist outside our shared imagination. So once again I say, as I said in the first two volumes: all of these characters are fictional. I'm honored and gratified that the characters have seemed so real to many readers.

Some people have been concerned that Dan Poole's precarious professional career is in some way my own, but I'm glad to report that that is not the case. However, Dan's experiences reflect those of too many of my colleagues—including many pastors who have written me heartbreaking letters in response to the first two volumes in this series; their pain should be a deep concern for church members everywhere.

Also, as I've said before, I do not think these books can be called novels, at least not very good ones. Instead, I'd recommend they be categorized as "creative nonfiction" or fictional theological-philosophical dialogues in a long tradition that runs (with varying degrees of quality) from Plato through Galileo to *Ishmael, Tuesdays with Morrie,* and *Calvin and Hobbes.* Ideas and issues drive the dialogue here, not plot and character as would be the case with a bona fide novel.

I recently heard Dr. Walter Brueggemann say that theological educators should follow the same two guidelines that responsible sex educators follow:

1. Don't tell students more than they are ready for or can handle.

2. Don't tell them anything they'll have to unlearn later on.

In that spirit, I hope that readers will treat the concepts found in this book with appropriate care; presented to the wrong people at the wrong time and in the wrong way, they could do harm—to individuals and communities, both of which are precious, even sacred, in my view. In this regard, Plato's Socrates reflects on the disadvantages of written communication when compared to face-to-face conversation in *Phaedrus:*

> The fact is, Phaedrus, that writing involves a similar disadvantage to painting. The productions of painting look like living beings, but if you ask them a question they maintain a solemn silence. The same holds true of written words; you might suppose that they understand what they are saying, but if you ask them what they mean by anything they simply return the same answer over and over again. Besides, once a thing is committed to writing it circulates equally among those who understand the subject and those who have no business with it; a writing cannot distinguish between suitable and unsuitable readers. And if it is ill-treated or unfairly abused it always needs its parent to come to its rescue; it is quite incapable of defending or helping itself.[6]

You may be an unsuitable reader for this book, and if so, because I care about you, I would rather you reward some other author with a book royalty, not me. Again, if that's the case, you might wonder why I would risk presenting these potentially hurtful or divisive ideas. As I said before, there can be only one answer: I believe that leaving religious status quo unquestioned is potentially even more destructive.

The word *destructive* is often associated with the word *deconstructive,* but the association is erroneous. Deconstruction is not destruction; it is hope. It arises from the belief that sometimes, our constructed laws get in the way of unseen justice, our undeconstructed words get in the way of communication, our institutions get in the way of the purposes for which they were constructed, our formulations get in the way of meaning, our curricula get in the way of learning. In those cases, one must deconstruct laws, words, institutions, formulations, or curricula in the hope that something better will appear once the constructions-become-obstructions have been taken apart. The love of what is hidden, as yet unseen, and hoped for gives one courage to deconstruct what is seen and familiar.[7] This book, in a sense, attempts to deconstruct our conventional concepts of hell in the sincere hope that a better vision of the gospel of Jesus Christ will appear.

Is anything undeconstructable? someone is asking. Obviously, while God and God's mysteries would be beyond human deconstruction, it makes sense that anything constructed by humans would also be deconstructable by them—including human formulations about God and God's

---

6. Thanks to Ken Archer for this delightful quote, which may be found in Plato, *Phaedrus and Letters VII and VIII,* translated and introduced by Walter Hamilton (New York: Penguin, 1973), p. 97.

7. Thanks to Jack Caputo for this understanding of deconstruction. See his *Deconstruction in a Nutshell* (Fordham University Press, 1997).

mysteries. Perhaps deconstruction, then, could be seen as the search for God and God's mysteries when human constructions may be obscuring them: it is an endeavor hoping eventually to fail, for when it fails and reaches the Undeconstructable, it has reached the goal of its pursuit.

It has been said that the best way to deconstruct something is to write an honest, detailed history of it. I pursue that task in these pages with regard to hell. What will appear beyond the deconstruction remains to be seen. Perhaps something better will emerge—that is my hope and prayer, but the outcome is by no means certain even now that I have finished writing this book. The task begun in these pages must enlist readers like you to help complete it.

Walker Percy used to say that he wrote his novels without plot outlines and other tools of planning. Instead, he created a character in a predicament, and as he wrote, he watched to see how the character would find a way out of the predicament. Again, admitting that this is something less than a full-fledged novel, I should admit that this book developed along lines similar to Percy's work. If the story line seems to meander and turn back on itself from time to time, this reflects my sense of how characters in real life might actually learn and grow—characters, I mean, like you and me, in predicaments like ours.

At the end of the book, you'll find some commentary on each chapter, giving what would normally be included in footnotes along with additional reflections. Those pages are an essential part of this book, and it is not complete without them.

I've tried to make this a stand-alone work; if you're joining the trilogy in part three, you should be able to get your bearings just fine. Yet I hope that after you begin here, you'll also go back and read the first two books in the series. Together, I think, they can immerse readers in many of the critical issues facing our faith communities, especially our biblically rooted Christian faith communities, as we venture deeper into the twenty-first century and an emerging global culture and as we emerge from the modern world with its comforts (for some) and its discontents.

OK: when you turn the page, it's fiction.

Laurel, Maryland   Brian D. McLaren
January 2005

BOOK ONE

THE LAST WORD

SOMETHING SERIOUS

From centre unto rim, from rim to centre,
In a round vase the water moves itself,
As from without 'tis struck or from within.

—*Paradiso*, XIV.1–3

ONE COLD AND SNOWY NIGHT in January 2003, I wrote these words in my journal:

> I am midway in my journey through life and I seem to have lost my way. I find myself in a dark place walking, walking, not sure if dawn will ever come. As on a winter night, when black ice forms on every sidewalk and stairway, I can find no firm footing anywhere, and every moment when I am not splayed out on the ice, I am afraid that I am about to slip. A Christian, not to mention a Christian pastor, should not hate. Nor should he feel despair. But here I am, in my early forties, and I find myself filled with hatred as a closed basement closet is filled with darkness, and my limbs are heavy with despair. Every step is hard. To lift my hand to my face is laborious. Even standing makes me feel how strong gravity is. I hate this.

As I read those words now, they sound melodramatic, but that's how despair is: grave, cosmic, weighty, epic. This is the story of how I came into that heavy darkness and sought to emerge from it. Whether or not I have fully emerged even now, you will be the judge.

It's hard to pinpoint exactly when this whole episode began. I guess I could go way back to 1999, when I stood for several months on a different ledge of despair and considered jumping out of the ministry. With the help of my wife, Carol, and a good friend named Neil Edward Oliver, I pulled back from the ledge in 1999 and began to feel a renewed sense of call in ministry, but just as my enthusiasm returned, hard times also returned in late September 2002. A faction on my church council had raised questions about my doctrinal orthodoxy, so I had been placed on administrative leave until they could conduct a hearing and determine a plan of action. For me, that meant no preaching, no pastoral duties—it was like a paid vacation, really, except that I awoke every morning with a vague feeling of static anxiety; the first words that formed in my mind as I emerged from sleep were "Oh, no."

My closest friend on the council, and the only one who stayed in frequent contact with me, was Ky Lang. He had confidentiality commitments to observe, so he couldn't say much about the council's plans and progress, but he did tell me not to expect anything definitive until after the new year. "You've got a few months of paid leave, Dan. Try to enjoy it." I did try—by spending as much time as I could reading, going out for coffee nearly every morning with Carol, taking long midday walks, kicking a soccer ball with my two sons, Corey and Trent, and reading some more. But it wasn't easy to enjoy my freedom, knowing what was at stake in my life. "Oh, no" kept echoing in my thoughts.

I prayed a lot during this time, especially on my walks. As beautiful October gave way to a mild November and an unusually cold December here in the Washington, D.C., area, a strange kind of peace at first coexisted with the anxiety and then gradually overshadowed it, much of the time at least. The Christmas season came and went—my first Christmas in many years without sermons to prepare.

Ky was faithful to his confidentiality commitments. He said little, beyond the fact that the council was having meetings—"death by meetings," he called it, and he gave me signals that the council was divided on what to do about me—though I never knew whether the division was four to four or seven to one.

Through these many weeks, I had surprisingly little contact from church members. They had been encouraged by the council to respect my privacy and the council's process by not interfering with my administrative leave. I'm sure people were curious, but through September and October there were only a few phone calls, some suspicious, with a "What are they doing to you?" kind of tone. Others, perhaps assuming the worst—which would mean that my problems were actually of a sexual rather than doctrinal nature—would call and tell us they were praying for us, assuring us they were available if we needed anything. By December, you would have thought we had moved to a new state where we didn't know anyone except Ky and his wife, Leticia, who called and visited often. After years in the spotlight, so to speak, it was actually a relief to have some privacy.

My sense of equilibrium was shaken on a snowy Saturday afternoon in late January 2003.

My daughter, Jess, a second-semester freshman at College Park, Maryland, had come home from college for the weekend. She said she wanted to do her laundry and enjoy some of Carol's home cooking. College food, she said, was boring and was making her fat. But on Saturday afternoon, she made it clear that she had another reason for the early-semester visit. She sat down at the dining room table where I was working on a puzzle, a favorite hobby of mine since childhood and a hobby to which I had turned on Saturdays since I didn't have a sermon waiting to be touched up. "What's up, Jess?" I asked, not looking up from my welter of pieces.

"Can we talk for a minute, Dad?" she asked. "It's something serious."

At "serious," my head snapped up; I felt a rush of internal alarm and my thoughts raced from pregnancy to drugs to depression to bad grades. I nodded, feigning calm. You would think I might feel relieved when she said, "It's about God, Dad, and my ability to keep believing in him, or her, or whatever. It's my faith—I think I'm losing it." The internal panic that flushed through my soul at that moment was no less strong than it would have been if she had said, "I'm pregnant," or "It's cocaine," or "I can't stop thinking about driving off a bridge," or whatever.

I swallowed, nodded again: "OK. Tell me more," those four words being the best summary of what I've learned about both parenting and pastoral counseling through the years.

"Here's the problem," she said. "If Christianity is true, then all the people I love except for a few will burn in hell forever. But if Christianity is not true, then life doesn't seem to have much meaning or hope. I wish I could find a better option. How do you deal with this?"

My daughter's question stabbed me more painfully than I can adequately explain. She had found the Achilles' heel, so to speak, of my own theology, and with that one simple question, I felt something snap in me. No, it didn't snap: it softened, like a floor joist weakened by termites or dry rot. It sagged and crumbled and broke in stages over the days and weeks to come.

I had generally avoided the subject of hell in my preaching over the years, touching on it only when necessary and even then doing so as gently as possible. Whenever anyone asked me about hell, I'd give my best, most orthodox answer, but I'd secretly think, "I'll bet they won't buy it." If they did, I was surprised, because if I were on their side of the table, investigating orthodoxy from the outside instead of defending it from within, my answers would not have sufficed.

Anyway, as parents learn to do—and pastors too—I hid my panic and smiled with a kind of reassuring parental smile.

I tried to help Jess that Saturday afternoon by telling her about "inclusivism," an alternative to the "exclusivist" view she was unhappy with. While exclusivism limited eternal life in heaven to bona fide, confessing Christians, inclusivism kept the door open that others could be saved through Christ even if they never identified as Christians. That seemed to help. After maybe twenty minutes of conversation, the buzzer on the dryer sounded, and she thanked me and went off to pack her warm, dry clothes in her duffel bag while I sat there pretending to keep working on my puzzle. I had a feeling she'd be back with more questions before long.

She was—later that night. "Can I ask you another theological question?" she asked, plopping down on the couch next to me. I hit the mute button on the TV remote, and she said that she still wasn't satisfied with inclusivism. It might get a few more people into heaven than exclusivism, but how did I deal with the fact that even one person could be tortured for an infinity of time for a finite number of sins? I again put on my parental face, and this time I told her how a finite being's offense against an infinite God is an infinite offense, which she didn't buy and I didn't push because I myself couldn't imagine a biblical writer using that kind of argument. Then I told her about "conditionalism," the idea that hell is temporary and leads to extinction rather than eternal torment, another minority opinion in Christian theology regarding hell, which helped her a bit more, but only until the next morning.

When I came downstairs for breakfast at about 7 A.M., she was brewing some coffee and picked up the conversation as if neither of us had ever left it.

"So Dad," she said, pouring a cup for each of us, "I still couldn't sleep with your answer. It kept churning in my mind all night. I keep asking myself, what's the point of God even making the world if so much goes to waste? And do you think God planned to have some people tortured forever from the very beginning? Or was hell a kind of unexpected plan B that God couldn't anticipate and is now stuck with? Neither of those sounds very good, you know?"

This time, I had nothing to offer. Exclusivism was my starting point, inclusivism was my fall-back, and conditionalism was my last resort. She continued, "So since I couldn't sleep, I went on the Internet last night—well, really it was early this morning—and I was reading about universalism. It sounded pretty cool. What do you think about that?"

In my theological circles, universalism is one small step removed from atheism. It is probably more feared than committing adultery, and to be labeled universalist ends one's career. Decisively. So I again had to hide my shock that my little girl was not only asking questions: now she was flirting with a dangerous heresy. But I didn't know what to say, so I made a joke about not answering theological questions before 9 A.M. on Sundays, and she let me off the hook. She seemed cheerful enough when her boyfriend, Kincaid, picked her up that afternoon to drive her back to campus. Maybe just considering the option of universalism had a calming effect on her, but it had the opposite effect on her dad.

I had been taught exclusivism since childhood: everyone was excluded from heaven after death unless they were included among the personally, individually, consciously "born again" or "saved." In college, through the writings of C. S. Lewis, I encountered a kinder, gentler modification of exclusivism that acknowledges that it is possible to be saved by Christ without ever having "prayed to receive Christ." Somewhere in *Mere Christianity*, Lewis had written a few simple lines that comforted many of my friends, even though they made me a little nervous:

> The world does not consist of 100 per cent Christians and 100 per cent non-Christians. There are people who are slowly ceasing to be Christians but who still call themselves by that name. . . . There are other people who are slowly becoming Christians though they do not yet call themselves so. There are people who do not accept the full Christian doctrine about Christ but who are so strongly attracted by him that they are his in a much deeper sense than they themselves understand. There are people in other religions who are being led by God's secret influence to concentrate on those parts of their religion which are in agreement with Christianity and who thus belong to Christ without knowing it.

His words "led by God's secret influence" always reminded me of Paul's words in Romans 8—"Those who are led by the Spirit of God are children of God"—and that always kept the inclusivist back door secretly open for me, even though most of my colleagues and nearly all of my parishioners considered me an orthodox exclusivist.

Also growing in popularity was conditionalism, or conditional immortality—exclusivism or inclusivism minus the idea of "eternal conscious torment" (abbreviated ECT by its critics), which meant that the unredeemed would be punished for their wrongs and then would cease to exist or that only the redeemed would be resurrected from the unconscious sleep of death. I guess you could say that I was, in reputation, at least, an exclusivist who had secret inclusivist leanings and who could tolerate conditionalists. But universalism was another story. It went further than I was willing to go. It asserted that everyone would ultimately be reconciled to God through Christ, so hell would ultimately be empty, which is tantamount to saying it wouldn't exist, at least not for humans. There were many variations on how and when and so on, but the happy ending, it seemed to me, was too good to be true. Or was it too good *not* to be true? When such questions came to mind, I'd wave them away as quickly as I could, like a cloud of bees.

"Well," I thought, trying to console myself as Jess and Kincaid backed out of the driveway later that day, "if Jess becomes a universalist, at least she'll still be a Christian. That's better than her giving up her whole faith." But then I thought, "But she won't be able to be a member of Potomac Community Church." Our church's doctrinal statement, which I couldn't remember verbatim, may have allowed wiggle room for a mild case of inclusivism, but universalism? No way. The idea that my daughter could be a Christian but not be welcome in my own church stuck like a thorn in my thoughts. I couldn't shake the unacceptability of that. Of course, then it dawned on me that my own status there was far from secure. I'm not sure if that realization made me feel better or worse.

I leaned against the door frame, watching through the storm door as Kincaid's faded red Honda putted up the hill and passed over the crest and out of sight, leaving a bit of blue smoke in its wake. For several minutes, I just stared at the road at the summit of the hill, watched the blue smoke rise, fade, and disappear, and noticed as a few snowflakes began to fall from the blank gray sky. I felt a pang in my soul, something painful and dangerous, hard to define, but something I couldn't ignore. The pang formed into words: "If Jess isn't welcome at PCC, I don't want to be welcome either."

From those moments on, the subject of hell snowballed (pardon the pun) into something close to an obsession. Alien questions kept landing in my mind, abducting my attention. Should the purpose of Christianity be reduced to this: to increase the population of heaven and decrease the crowdedness of hell? Was the message of Jesus and the apostles, at the root, information on how to get your personal soul into heaven after you die? Is that what it all boiled down to? Were billions really going to burn in endless torment because they didn't believe in Jesus? What real purpose did that serve? Was that good enough news to be called gospel? Was human life that despicable, that expendable? Was God that cruel or heartless? Was God's kindness that frail? Was God's justice that severe? Was that kind of severe justice even just?

In the months that followed, my daughter's questions became my own: Did God, from the beginning, have two purposes in mind—one, to have some people eternally in torment, and two, to have others eternally in joy? Would a good Being ever conceive of such a plan? Or was God's original purpose to have only one ending—a happy one—but then accidents or disasters occurred that God couldn't see or prevent so that now the two ultimate destinations were an unwanted necessity? Or is it possible that God has only one end in mind, the same one God has had from the beginning: to banish and eradicate all that is evil and save all that can possibly be saved?

These questions were generally followed by an avalanche of more immediate questions: What if I modified or jettisoned my orthodox idea of hell? What would go with it? Would any sense of ultimate justice or accountability remain? Could and would people be good without hell looming beyond death? Was hell a necessary deterrent to evil behavior? Would people assume that Jesus, church, the Bible, and Christianity itself are expendable, only marginally important when hell becomes less threatening? Would God evolve into our kind, doting, benign Grandmother in Heaven, so anything goes, so everything's OK, so all is groovy, have a nice day, whatever? Without the backbone of hell, would Christian faith become a kind of jellyfish religion, soft, spongy, transparent, negligible?

Questions like these can energize, but they had the opposite effect on me as I stared out at the empty blacktop, the brown winter lawns, the oak across the street still holding its old, dead leaves, the other trees looking naked and sad, the flurries falling randomly and melting on the driveway, the sidewalk, the front step. I felt completely drained by the uncertainty, the doubt, the nagging, nattering questions. I despaired of ever finding adequate answers to them; there were too many, and they were too hard. And something else happened as I stood at my storm door, my breath creating a slow pulse of fog against the glass. A hot, seething feeling I had hardly ever experienced started to form deep in me. It was so unfamiliar, I didn't know what it was it at first. It felt like it came from my gut and rose like heat through my heart and lungs. Then it rose further and lodged in my throat, and then it ached in my head with a feverish sentence I never expected, never could have predicted: *I hate Gil Zeamer. I hate that guy.*

When I realized what I was saying to myself, I literally shook my head and placed my forehead against the cold glass. *What's happening to me? I shouldn't hate anybody, even Gil. Where is this coming from?* A chill tightened my shoulders, and I stepped away from the glass storm door, closed the wooden front door, and went and sat on the sofa in the living room. *What's going on? I shouldn't hate. But I do—I hate Gil Zeamer.* I prayed—"God, don't let me become bitter. Help me understand Gil, forgive him, love him. Don't let me hate. Teach me to process this in some other way." And gradually the feeling passed, and I thought I was over it for good. I put on a sweater and went into the dining room to work on my puzzle, hoping it would distract me from morbid and troubling thoughts of hell and hatred. That night, though, the feelings came back, and I wrote that melodramatic entry in my journal.

FLARE-UP

*This mount is such, that ever
At the beginning down below 'tis tiresome,
And aye the more one climbs, the less it hurts.*

—*Purgatorio*, IV.88–90

GIL ZEAMER, HUSBAND of our church council chair, Nancy, was the instigator behind the doctrinal investigation that had put me on administrative leave. He had once been someone I considered a friend but over the previous year or so had become convinced that I was a budding heretic or at least "doctrinally soft," and our relationship, though cordial, became more and more coolly so.

I suppose you could best describe Potomac Community Church with the "moderate Evangelical" label, and Gil represented the most conservative end of our church's spectrum. His little clique was vocal, and his influence was strong among them, although anyone outside the group didn't take him too seriously—his argumentative nature put them off. He was one of those people that pastors learn to accept as a trial that builds character, a critic who keeps you on your toes but generally does so more or less good-naturedly: annoying, a little draining, but not vicious. He was happy for me to be a bit more progressive than he, as long as he could bark and nip at my shins whenever he felt I was drifting too far to the left.

"It's that Neil Oliver friend of yours," Gil said to me one Sunday after church, back in early September. "He's a bad influence. You've got to stay close to the center. He's way over on the liberal side. That's why you need me on the conservative side, keeping you honest. I'm your watchdog."

In this case, whether or not his centrist prescription was wrong, he was partly right in his diagnosis, as critics often are: my friend Neil had indeed been an influence on me. Anyway, Gil and some friends from his little clique had typed up transcripts of a dozen or so of my sermons, and then they had taken out selected sentences and put them in a table: sermon quote on the left side under the column heading "Dan Says," item from our church doctrinal statement on the right side, under the column heading "PCC Says." Through all of this, Gil was very businesslike, as if he were an enthusiastic referee who loved his job and I were a basketball player who just double-dribbled or stepped out of bounds. It was his job to blow the whistle and to do so with gusto. Nothing personal.

I had tried to keep my composure regarding Gil and his faction, but Carol, I knew, was struggling. She felt worried and maybe even a little ashamed when I was put on leave. "When people hear about this, you know exactly the first thing they'll think, darlin'. They'll wonder who she was and when it happened and what I am going to do about it. You know how church people can be," she said. Her anxiety made me all the more careful to try to stay calm. Even so, sometimes in my dreams I'd find myself arguing with Gil, long and intense arguments about theology and church matters, and I'd awaken with a start from a shouting match with him, my heart pounding, muscles twitching and tense.

The feeling of Gil-focused hatred flared up again a few days after my conversation with Jess, on Wednesday night, when Ky Lang came over after a council meeting. Ky was about thirty, the youngest member of the council. He was Vietnamese; his parents were among the "boat people" of the early 1980s. He was tallish, lanky, stylish. He wore those black-rimmed glasses that looked nerdy years ago but then became very cool. Ky had a striking haircut too—Carol called it odd—short on the sides with a shock of unruly black hair on top that flopped down to his eyebrows. He was always brushing it back with his fingers. He was an environmental lawyer, a pleasant, cheerful guy, really bright, impossible not to like.

That night, Ky had been outvoted in a major decision—unprecedented in PCC history: to become associate members of the Biblical Evangelical Fellowship, a group known as the watchdogs of conservative Evangelical doctrine. He was livid when he came in, sat at our kitchen table, and told us what had happened.

PCC had always welcomed conservatives, but we took some pains not to be pulled into the more neofundamentalist orbit of the religious right. We tended to put adjectives other than *conservative* in front of our evangelical label: *open, mainstream,* even *progressive.* The fact that we had women on our council and had even elected a female chair tended to scare away the more fundamentalist folk who visited but never really settled in long enough to become voting members and swing us back in their direction.

So Ky was shocked, and I even more so, at the news that night, that Nancy—no doubt under Gil's influence—had introduced a motion to join the Biblical Evangelical Fellowship pseudodenomination. Ky objected and Nancy countered by saying they *needed* to make the move because the BEF offered "confidential in-church consultation" to help churches deal with "doctrinal matters and pastoral issues." In other words, it was my fault the church needed to take this step. It appeared to Ky that Nancy had already conferred with everyone else on the council except Ky; they were silent, he said, perhaps a little embarrassed, until it came time for a voice vote, when all but Ky said, "Aye." "This is an organized plan to get you out, Dan," Ky said, slapping his palm on the table, causing a little tremor among the spoons and forks. "This is wrong. I can't believe Nancy has become Gil's puppet."

At that moment, a surge of fury rose in me, rage about what was happening to me, to Carol, to PCC, and to Nancy—and I took the coffee mug I was cradling in my hands—fortunately it was empty—and I threw it against the wall; it hit with a bang and thudded down onto the vinyl floor. "That idiot!" I shouted, as the mug spun a few times before coming to rest under the edge of the dishwasher. It didn't even give me the satisfaction of shattering. Only the handle broke off. "God, this is my life they're jerking around!" I said, half-cursing, half-praying. I stormed out of the kitchen and out the front door and just paced for a minute or so outside on our front porch step, very literally to cool off in the January night air. Gradually my breathing slowed and my hands stopped shaking; beginning to feel cold, I came back in, apologized, picked up the mug and handle, which were still lying on the floor, and sat down again.

Ky and Carol seemed to have been sitting in silence since I left. I broke the silence and recounted how the council had elected Nancy as our chair because she seemed like a peacemaker—gentle, not pushy or opinionated. Deep down, we knew we were growing polarized on our church council, and we hoped she could keep us from splitting apart. We never anticipated how her gentleness would make her vulnerable to her husband's behind the-scenes manipulation and pressure. Nancy herself was a pastor's kid, and I actually felt sorry for her, stuck as she was between her traditionalist husband and her reluctantly progressive pastor. "We elected Nancy, but we got Gil," Ky Lang said. "This situation is so full of crap." That's about as profane as PCC folk get.

He wanted to organize some sort of congregational meeting to stop the process. I was grateful for the sentiment, but I dissuaded him. I was tired of church squabbles. Carol took my hand as I said, "No, Ky. I won't fight.

I'm just going to quit. I'm sick of this whole business. I'm drained, and if I'm not careful, I'm going to start hating someone." Of course, I knew it was already beyond that.

"No, Dan, you can't quit. Not yet, anyway," he said. "Remember, a lot of us are at PCC because of you. We didn't join a BEF church; we joined a community church that isn't anybody's clone. This is really a hostile takeover. You can't just roll over and play dead. It's not fair that the majority of us who love your leadership should suffer because of—"

"It's not that simple," I broke in. "It's not like I stayed the same and they changed. They're reacting to changes they've perceived in me. And they're right. I have changed. And I'm not done changing yet. I can't blame them for being alarmed. Even Carol worries about me sometimes." She smiled and squeezed my hand.

"But what do they expect?" Ky asked. "Do they really expect that a pastor comes out of seminary at twenty-six or whatever and has all the answers? Do they really expect a pastor to never change or grow or rethink things? That's so unrealistic. It's worse than that—it's unhealthy. Gosh, when lawyers learn and change, they call it professional development, but when pastors change, they call it . . ." Ky couldn't find the right word, but Carol supplied it: "Heresy."

That launched us into a long discussion about churches, pastors, the spiritual life, and Neil Oliver, whom Ky had also gotten to know. Neil was in his late fifties, about fifteen years older than me. Born in Jamaica and raised in New Jersey, he still carried the delightful accent of the Caribbean. He had left the Episcopal priesthood after a divorce, years before I met him. He never remarried but went back to graduate school (to study philosophy and science, of all things) and eventually became a high school science teacher and girls' soccer coach. His friends began calling him "Neo" back in college, a nickname that was based on his initials. He begged us to stop using the nickname when the *Matrix* movies came out, especially the second and third ones, which, he said, were so bad that "they single-handedly stank up Western civilization, man!" Once he jokingly got down on his knees and said, "Daniel, I'm *kneeling* to beg you to start calling me *Neil*!" But the nickname was a habit none of his friends could completely break, even though we tried.

I once commented to him that the prefix *neo-* meant new, and he had certainly brought new insights to me. He put up his finger and said, "No, Daniel, *neo-* means a renewal of the old—you know: neoclassical, neoconservative, Neolithic. If I've done anything for you, I've helped you see old things in a fresh way."

As I said, I originally met Neil at a low time in my ministry, back in the late '90s, when I was thinking about quitting. As a former clergyman himself, he understood my predicament and became my guide and friend as I went through a deep rethinking of my faith. Among other things, he helped me understand how faith must engage with the culture in which it finds itself but how it can become so excessively enmeshed with that culture that its power is neutralized—actually, *neutered* was his word. If a faith becomes enmeshed, not just engaged, with a culture, Neil said, people hardly notice—until a wave of cultural change hits. Then, when people want to move on from that fading culture, when they want to be part of the new wave, they feel they must leave behind their faith as well. Their only alternative is to try to disengage their faith from the fading culture, but this is one of the most painful things a person can do—mentally painful, spiritually painful, he said. In times of profound cultural change, he explained—such as our current transition from a modern colonial culture, with its emphasis on rational certainty and conquest and control, to a postmodern and postcolonial culture, which distrusts rational certainty because of the violence that confident people have inflicted on others in their striving to conquer and control them. In times like these, people, thousands at the same time, face this agonizing task of disengaging their faith from the culture it has grown with, like two trees whose roots are intertwined. The transition isn't easy for anyone, but it's especially hard for leaders.

For me, this meant I had to figure out which parts of my faith I needed to uproot, or *disembed,* as he put it, from modern culture and colonial thought patterns so that they could reroot in the new "soil" of the emerging postmodern world. At first, I had hoped that Neil could show me some kind of rootless faith that hovered timeless and pristine above any cultural engagement, but he told me that such a faith didn't exist.

"From beginning to end," he said to me one day that first fall when we met, "our faith is *situated.* It's an unfolding story, and every story requires a setting. It's news—and not just news that happened but news that's still happening, and that means it requires a context. It's an ongoing movement and message that always take place in a medium. It's all about incarnation—about God entering and embracing our story. So if you want to abandon the story, if you want to get out of time and culture and into some timeless neutral zone above the fray, you're trying to get out of the very thing God is deeply into. Maybe some other religion or philosophy can deal with timelessness, but not real Christianity. It's forever timely, not timeless." The difference between the two wasn't immediately clear to me, but as time went on, I found the distinction quite significant.

Neil's impromptu lectures—which he could launch into at a moment's notice—tended to leave my head spinning. Sometimes they bordered on annoying, unless you realize he's an educator not just by profession but in his soul. It's not something he can turn off.

Over the previous eighteen months or so, through some intense experiences I've written about elsewhere, Neil had helped me rediscover my faith not as a set of doctrines or an outline of propositions but rather as a story that he liked to call "the story we find ourselves in." We don't just hear the story or believe it, he said, but it *enters* us, and we *enter* it: "The story of your life is taken up into this larger story, so you inhabit it, become part of it, experience it, and extend it," he said. "It becomes your way of life, your life story." This story-oriented approach (*narrative,* he called it) to Christian faith had taken root in me and was transforming my whole understanding of what it meant to be a Christian—and a Christian pastor.

These changes in my thinking meant that I had a choice: to hide them from my congregation or to figure out how to express them, communicate them. I had chosen to be more overt than covert, knowing that it was a little risky for a "play it safe" guy like me in a setting like mine: my congregation by and large preferred the standard mainstream way of thinking, which Neil disparagingly called "radio orthodoxy," since it was bolstered by religious broadcasting.

This gradual but real transformation in my theology had been intriguing to many people in my congregation—among them Ky Lee and his Salvadoran wife, Leticia (typical of people in our D.C. area, also a lawyer). But to others—a majority or a minority, I never knew—my ongoing transformation was scary, unsettling. For people like Gil (an engineer, not a lawyer), faith was meant to be solid, bolted down tight, static, secured; in the midst of a turbulent world, it was one unchanging reference point, something from the past that we keep going back to, a place to escape the chaos. Christianity was a Sousa march, completely charted, with a strong downbeat, great for military maneuvers, not jazz, with all its swing and syncopation and improvisation and blues notes.

Ky, Carol, and I sat at the kitchen table, recounting what had brought us to this point. Then the conversation reached a lull, broken after a minute or so by Carol: "So Dan, Gil thinks you're skiing down the 'slippery slope' of the left, so he wants to jerk the congregation to the right through the BEF, as if there's no slippery slope on that side of the mountain. Here comes the chaos."

"Yes," Ky replied, shaking his head sadly but smiling at the same time. "I never liked the slippery slope analogy anyway. To me, we're starting at the bottom of the mountain, not the top. Dan's not sliding: he's trying to climb. Oh, well. Inquisitions happen."

Carol said, "Ky, do you think there's any hope? Maybe Dan *should* just resign now and not waste any more time. I reckon you're taking a lot of heat for being Dan's advocate."

"No, Carol, please don't think that. You're right—I think some of the council members are hoping that if the process drags on long enough that you'll . . . that you'll get the message and start looking elsewhere. Nobody has said that, but this thing is progressing at a slug's pace, and the lack of urgency tells me a lot, and then, of course, this BEF thing is a really big load of crap. But so many people in the church—not council members but people at the heart and soul of PCC—they're calling me and telling me they want you back. We've got to think about them. I'm certain that Gil's faction is a small minority—less than twenty percent. The only problem is that the twenty percent might include ninety percent of the council. But please, don't give up. Not yet. Not yet." With that, Ky got up, gave us both a hug, and put on his coat. At the door, he added, "I think two opposite things are happening at once. Some people are opening up, moving beyond old ways of thinking, asking new questions. They're restless, and they have hope that there are new and better answers out there. At the same time, a lot of people are tightening up, entrenching, backing into old corners where they feel safe. I guess that kind of drama is playing out all over the place."

"Including here," Carol said. "Now you drive carefully." Ky gave us each a hug and ventured outside. It was snowing again.

Our conversation lingered in my thoughts. I reflected on it in my journal later that night before going to sleep:

> Lord, shouldn't faith be a way *through* the chaos, something calling us forward into the chaos, not back into some safe zone behind it? Shouldn't faith give us courage to climb the mountain, even though the climb is hard? Faith should be a dynamic force in the midst of the turbulence. It beckons, calls, guides us through the turbulence, toward something ahead of us and above us, calling us higher up and deeper in and farther on into the ongoing adventure of life. Faith keeps us from turning back or digging in or giving up or breaking down. This is what your whole message seems to be about: a dynamic revolutionary force in history called "the Kingdom of God." It is always "at hand," always available, always coming to us from the future, always keeping us moving onward, straining forward, leaning, reaching, stretching ahead to touch it, receive it, enter it. So I face this chaos and seek to keep faith and climb. But tonight it is hard, very hard. And hate is crouching in the shadows, stalking me. God help me.

3

POET IN A TRENCH COAT

I thought the universe
was thrilled with love.

Inferno, XII.41–42

OVER THE NEXT FEW DAYS, my feeling of hatred subsided, temporarily at least, but not my preoccupation with hell. The dark subject became like a vexing scientific problem that a researcher fiddles with even deep in dreams. The problem feels intractable, but the scientist still hopes: *If I don't give up, if I just hang on and keep wrestling with the problem, an insight or solution will eventually show itself.*

I tried to talk to Carol about it, but she had worries enough. I considered talking with my friend Neil, but we had talked about the subject several times over the years, and I think he had grown impatient with my intractability: I couldn't be comfortable with the exclusivist position I inherited on the one hand, nor could I accept any alternatives on the other. Neil himself had gotten some kind of resolution on the subject, but I couldn't pin him down to understand what that resolution was. Besides, I knew he was busy with school, and Kincaid, my daughter's boyfriend and Neil's housemate, had told me that Neil was dating someone, which was quite a surprise. So I postponed contacting him for several days. Finally I could think of no one else to talk with, and my need for a conversation partner was intensifying, so I shot him a short e-mail: "Neil—I'm struggling with the hell question again. So is Jess. Can we talk?—Dan."

The next day, I had four e-mails waiting, the first two bearing the same subject line, "Re: From DP." The first one said, "Would love to talk but schedule is shot this week. Next?—Neil." The second one said, "Try history first, not doctrine.—Neil." That was it. I loved the guy, but he drove me crazy sometimes. When you wanted a sentence, you got a treatise. When you wanted a treatise, you got five lousy words.

The third e-mail was also from Neil, the subject line reading, "P.S." It was even shorter than the first two: "Check out Bonda. One purpose." What in the world was Bonda?

There was one more message waiting in my inbox.

TO: DanPoole@backhandspring.com
FROM: Sappho@mac.com
SUBJECT: Inquiry about a visit
DATE: February 22, 2003

Dear Reverend Poole:
My nephew, George Kyriacos, attends your church, and I occasionally visit with him. Although I am not a regular churchgoer, I enjoy your services, and your sermons make an impression on me. George recently told me of your problems at the church, and I wondered if I could visit you with a gift. I will not stay long. Would there be a day I could stop by soon? I live in Bethesda and would need directions to your home in Gaithersburg. If this is presumptuous of me to ask, please disregard this e-mail. May God bless you.
Pat Murray

I knew George but not Pat. George was a nice Greek boy, or half-Greek anyway. His Baptist mother and Orthodox father had never been able to agree on a church, so George grew up with no religion at all. While in college, he had been invited to PCC and had come to faith in Christ during his sophomore year. He stayed involved in the church through his college years and now worked at the National Institute of Science and Technology in Gaithersburg. He was a faithful guy: quiet, well-mannered, dedicated, dependable—there every Sunday. Pat, I deduced, must be his mother's sister. She hadn't been asked to "respect the privacy of the process" with us since she wasn't a member of PCC. Although I had little desire to have a stranger come by, still, I felt I should oblige Pat's request, partly because I wondered what kind of gift she wanted to bring us. So I replied with directions and recommended that she come by the following Tuesday afternoon, any time after 2 P.M.

It was about 2:05 P.M. when I heard a knock at the door. When I answered it, the person standing there with a large manila envelope in hand wasn't George's aunt, or anybody's aunt for that matter. Pat was a man, or at least appeared to be—short, angular, with close-cropped salt-and-pepper hair, dressed in jeans, hiking boots, and a gray trench coat. In his hand was a large manila envelope. Two things immediately struck me about Pat's sixtyish face: weathered, wrinkled skin and a sincere smile that seemed to be more about the eyes than the mouth.

"Reverend Poole, I presume?" When Pat spoke up, his—her?—voice sounded too high, like that of an older woman who has smoked too many cigarettes for too long: a little edgy, raspy, rough, but somewhat feminine. In a second, I saw Pat as a woman, then as a man, then as I wasn't sure what, which was reflected in my awkward question: "You are . . . ?" I asked, obviously looking confused.

"I'm Pat, Pat Murray," he or she replied, not helping me by continuing, "George is my nephew." I welcomed Pat in, took the trench coat and hung it on the coatrack in our foyer, and encouraged Pat to sit down in the living room. I noticed that Pat was wearing a silver stud earring—indeterminate sexually—and a tailored blue Oxford shirt that was just baggy enough to hide any hint of a figure. I offered Pat coffee or tea, and Pat asked if I had any fruit or vegetable juice instead, which I did have. Before returning with the drinks, I found Carol and asked her to join us. I'm not sure why I wanted her there.

I brought back three glasses of tomato juice, my head still spinning over my inability to assign Pat to a gender, and introduced Pat and Carol. Pat sat on the sofa, and I was on the loveseat angled just to Pat's left, with Carol beside me.

"Reverend Poole," Pat began, but I interrupted and said just to call me Dan, after which Pat continued: "Dan, George has told me what you two wonderful people have been going through. As I may have told you in my e-mail, I'm not much of a churchgoer, but I do believe in God, and I love God. When I attended your church with George and my partner, you struck me as a kind man. Many clergy aren't, you know. My nephew thinks very highly of you, and ever since he told me about your situation, I've been praying for you."

The word *partner* must have made me flinch, and Pat noticed. "You probably caught that I mentioned my partner, Chloe. Yes, we're lesbians, although I'm a rather strange case. You see, I was born intersexual—do you know what that means?" I nodded, somehow made shy and awkward by her candor, and she continued, "Hermaphrodites, as they were called back in the '40s, were an embarrassment. Our situation is still little understood. I was born—I hope you don't mind my being so frank—with one ovary and one testicle, along with female genitalia and something called a semipenis, which means a malformed male organ. Back in those days, doctors quickly cut off anything male and rendered all intersexuals female. I suppose it was easier surgically, and it belied their assumption that females were basic human beings and males were base-model females with important added features."

I expected Carol to be more uncomfortable than I with all this, but she seemed completely nonplussed and natural. "I saw a TV show on the Discovery Channel about intersexuality. But you're the first intersexual person I've ever met."

"Knowingly anyway," Pat said, smiling. "The condition of intersexuality is more common than many people realize—I've read that about one in two thousand live births requires attention from a specialist in sexuality. So you may have met many of us before but just didn't know it, especially since most of us are, as I said, rendered female. Anyway, I was rendered female, but all through childhood, I was a complete tomboy—you know, climbing trees, playing army with the boys, preferring football to girly sports—and my parents worried that the doctors had made a mistake. When I reached puberty, they explained my condition, and I began taking hormones to make me . . . manifest as a woman. But unfortunately, my brain seemed less plastic than my glands had been, and I felt more manly than womanly even when I grew breasts. By then, though, the hormones had halted the development of a male voice, so my voice never dropped. The result is . . . that I am what I am: an intersexual. In my twenties, I stopped trying to be something I wasn't, and I simply decided to dress and act the way I feel, which is neither completely male nor female. I hope that doesn't make you too uncomfortable."

"No, not at all, but . . . uh, well, no, no, that's very clear," I said. "Thank you for your candor because, well, I, ah . . ."

"You were wondering what I was as soon as you saw me, right?" Pat asked with a wink. Then she—I guessed I should think of Pat as a she, since Pat used the word lesbian—reached over and touched me on the knee. "One thing I didn't tell you, Dan. My father was a pastor like you. He was licensed with the Nazarenes. Imagine how it felt for him to have to face the fact that God—or life, or whatever—had made me different. It was such a struggle for him, but he was a great father. Chloe and I have been together for many years, and Dad has always been most kind to both of us, although he never could bear to refer to Chloe as my partner. He always called her my friend or my housemate. It was quite cute, really."

I smiled, nodded, and had no idea what to say. Pat continued, "Kindness is what I appreciate most in a person, Dan. My dad was kind, even if he didn't know what to do about me. And when I heard you preach, I knew you were kind too. People like me . . . we appreciate kindness, with all we go through. That's what makes it all the more sad to hear what your church is putting you through. To think that your opinions on some minor matters of dogma could be more important than kindness . . . that's why I had to come and see you. And Mrs. Poole—Carol?—we've never met, but George says the nicest things about you, and I'm sure this is a very difficult trial, to see your husband being questioned like this."

"Yes, Pat, yes, it is. I reckon this is the hardest thing I've faced in my life so far. I've had a kind of charmed life up to now. So I guess it's my turn. I've never had anything to deal with like you have." Carol shocked me with how comfortable she was talking with Pat. As far as I know, Carol had never talked with a homosexual, much less an intersexual lesbian, but she couldn't have seemed more natural: "Tell us about Chloe."

"Well, at our age, sexuality isn't the main thing anymore, you know? When people think of lesbians or homosexuals in general, that's what they think about—sex fiends, sex maniacs. And of course, there are plenty of sex-obsessed gay folk just as there are heterosexual folk, which is understandable because the loneliness and isolation for gays can be crushing. Rejection causes people to act out, you know? But my dad wasn't far off: Chloe is my best friend, my life partner. She retired early a few years back— retired from a career as a forensic pathologist. She spent her working years studying crime scenes and gleaning evidence from cadavers—a little chilling, I know, but it was important work and she helped bring a lot of violent people to justice—rapists, serial killers. Now, though, she's quite ill. She's—to put it quite bluntly—she's very obese, and she's diabetic. Her diabetes has left her unable to walk without a cane—you know, foot problems, leg problems—so I support her and I care for her, which I feel honored to do. She's the most wonderful person I've ever known."

"She sounds like a sweetheart," Carol said. "Do you have any children?" I immediately blushed, thinking Carol had said something stupid.

"Why, yes," Pat replied. "Chloe had been married and divorced before we met. You know, it's quite common really, gay folks trying marriage to cure their condition, which is not to say that some people can't be reoriented, because I've met some, and I know that some can and do change. Anyway, Chloe has a son, Dexter, whom we raised together. And now Dexter is married, and he and his wife just had a beautiful baby boy. Here, let me . . ." And as Pat reached into her back pocket for her wallet to get a picture, Carol got up to sit beside her.

"Oh, he's gorgeous!" Carol said. "Look, Dan!" And soon I was looking at an intersexual lesbian step-grandmother's photograph of a beautiful bald baby.

We talked a bit more about Pat's family, and then Pat turned to me. "Dan, people like me find it hard to get involved in churches. Of course, many Christians think we're an abomination and should be burned at the stake or something. Others think we're just being rebellious and perverted by choice, and if we'd just repent, our 'problem' would go away. Or they believe we've got some sort of sickness that needs to be treated before other people catch it. Lots—probably the good people of your church would be like this—lots of people say they want to love the sinner but hate the sin, which sounds tolerant and loving to them but strikes people like me as ghastly and cruel—as if what we are is a sin. I would have loved to get involved at your lovely congregation, but it was . . . too risky. Anyway, a lot of people like Chloe and me are very close to God even though churches won't have us. I make my living as a freelance editor and writer, but my real passion, my real gift, is to be a spiritual poet. And that's why I wanted to come see you."

Pat handed me the manila envelope that had been wedged between her and the arm of the sofa. "When George told me what was going on at Potomac Community Church, and when he told me how badly he felt for you, I . . . I felt inspired to write some poems. People usually deprecate their own work, but I'm not like that. I'll tell you what I really think: I think they're darn good!"

At that she laughed, and Carol laughed, but I didn't, maybe because I was on the verge of being overwhelmed with emotion. I stared at the simple brown envelope and for some reason it moved me deeply. I'd never received an original poem from anyone, much less a stranger. Pat said, "I hope they'll bring some encouragement to a kind man like yourself, whether they're great literature or my version of a greeting card. Lord knows every word was written with love and prayer." She touched my knee again and this time gave it a squeeze. "You're in my prayers, young man."

"Keep that 'young man' stuff coming," Carol said, putting her hand on Pat's shoulder. "You'll make him feel great." As I opened the envelope, Pat rose to leave. "I promised I wouldn't stay too long," she said. "I'll let you read those on your own."

"No, no," I said, beckoning for her to sit down. "No, please stay." I pulled out five sheets of paper, each with a poem. "Pat, I wonder . . . would you read these aloud for me? I'm not an expert in poetry, but I know . . ."

"Yes," Pat said, taking the pages, "poetry is to be read aloud. And I'd be honored," and then Pat's gruff voice grew as tender as it could. "You do remind me of my father, Dan. If he had been born forty years later, I might have been able to read him the poetry I wrote for him too. I'll bet I wrote a hundred poems for him, but he never was comfortable—"

Pat coughed, leaned forward, placed her elbows on her knees, and began to read in a raspy voice.

HARVEST

I will die one day and from
My life, God will harvest some
Good fruit. Much God will discard:
Husks, leaves, stems, purpose fulfilled,
All be torn away and burned
Or left to rot and nourish
Seeds unborn. All judged good will
Flourish; to God be returned,
All that ripened sweet and strong.
Good fruit saved, forgotten wrong.
How much good harvest will from
My uncertain status come?
This mistake of me, caught in
Between two genders, unsure.
Can that harvest truly be
Worth our pain, yours, mine, also
That of all the earth? Can it?
You are like me. You are not
This or that. You have fought to
Find a place where you are free,
Not stuck, boxed, not cut to fit
What others may expect. So,
Your pain is great. You wonder:
What will your harvest be?
I tell you, it will be good.
I know.

After a pause, Pat explained, "I've developed this rather odd form for some of my poems, like that one, and the next one. Each line has seven syllables, except the last. This next one is called 'Boxes.'"

BOXES

We like things boxed. Cereal,
Candy, soap, gifts, and corpses.
They seem safe when boxed, as are
We. As is God and other

Potential dangers. So we
Sleep in a box, awake in
A box, shower in a box,
Refrigerate food, store knives,
Drive to work, work for hours, where
We stare each day at boxes,
In boxed lives. Boxed-in we live.
Through boxed windows we look out, in.
God, once boxed, broke out, broke free.
But we keep pushing God back,
Our Jack, popping out on cue,
To music, though it's not fair.
Nests have birds. Dens have foxes.
God will have none of our small
Boxes. God is free, and we
Are too.

"That's beautiful," Carol said. "And so true. A lot of poetry goes right over my head, but I can understand your poems quite well." Pat smiled: "This next one is a little more personal. I call it 'Curse.'"

CURSE

When I was a young child, boys laughed at me.
Queer, dyke, freak, jerk, they said.
Girls mocked me too, and worse:
They avoided me, told me no secrets, never laughed
With me around, wished me gone, dead, I suppose.
My curse: I was not one of them.
They never saw my scarred heart, my stained, strained face.
Their religion was the same; I was ever neither one or another,
Always an outsider, I.
Their religion grew strong by excluding,
Mine, meeker, would embrace the other.
You are of my religion. You are my brother.

I closed my eyes as Pat said those last lines. I took off my glasses and wiped my eyes, then held the bridge of my nose between my thumb and forefinger for a few seconds, eyes still closed. "Thank, you, Pat," I said, my breath catching awkwardly. "That touched me." Pat continued, "This next one is very short, very simple really, and I call it 'Advice.'"

ADVICE

If they are cruel, be kind.
If they are mean, don't mind.
If they reject, don't fret.
If they insult, forget.
If they exclude, love still.
If you cannot, God will.
If you lose hope, just wait.
Don't hate.

In light of all I'd been going through, those last two words seized me. Carol, who didn't know about my internal struggle with Gil, said she liked that one best. "Well, there's one more," Pat said. I should have guessed what the title would be.

HELL

Hell is not my condition or my destiny.
Hell is not my present uncomfortable location.
Hell is neither state of mind nor lake of literal fire.
Hell is no vacation from salvation.
Hell is a warning, and like all warnings, issues
From love, from wisdom, from better judgment—
Whether God's or from our own best selves,
It does not matter. Its purpose, not its substance, is the point.
For all who listen, hell will tell:
Flee justice, hate kindness, walk proudly without God,
And life will burn, waste, scar, erase, deface, disgrace, and pull
Your soul deep down a dark hole.
You will grind your teeth.
It will not be pleasant. You have been forewarned. But
Do justice, love kindness, walk humbly with your God,
And hell has done
Its best good work, like Nineveh's threatened destruction,
Which upset Jonah when it didn't occur. Anyway, you
Can forget about it.

I thanked Pat for the poems, and Carol did too, and then I thanked her again. She told us she had promised not to stay long and so we walked her out to her car. As we walked back to the house, Carol gave me a squeeze and said, "She's right, you know. You're a kind man. She's quite a poet, isn't she?"

"Maybe a prophet too," I said, spooked by the relevance of this stranger's words, spooked also by how warmly Carol responded to her. What was happening to my conservative wife? Was she changing her views on homosexuality, or was her kindness—Southern or Christian—making those views irrelevant? *It's a strange, unpredictable world,* I said to myself later that day as I thumbtacked Pat's poems to the wood rafters of my attic office. A bit yellowed, they're still there now, as I write these words.

4

PARTY IN THE LIVING ROOM, TORTURE IN THE BASEMENT

Therefore springs up, in fashion of a shoot,
Doubt at the foot of truth; and this is nature,
Which to the top from height to height impels us.

—*Paradiso*, IV.130–131

IT SNOWED A LOT that February. We broke a lot of records, and the kids were out of school quite a bit. I think it was during the second or third major snowfall of the season that Nancy Zeamer called, maybe two weeks, maybe three, after my first conversation with Jess about hell and a few days after our memorable visit with Pat. I was out shoveling the driveway, so Carol took the call. Before all this trouble began, Nancy and Carol had been close friends, but they hadn't spoken even once since September.

When I came inside, Carol looked upset. I asked her what was wrong, and she told me that Nancy had just called to tell us to be looking for an official letter from the council. "She was obviously calling for you and was uncomfortable getting me. I asked her what it was about, and she just told me I should wait for the letter and hung up quickly," Carol said. "She was so . . . so distant and businesslike and cold. Like ice. I reckon it's going to be bad news." She looked like she was about to cry.

Carol did cry as we fell asleep later that night. "How many friends am I going to lose through this, Dan?" she asked. I said nothing but pulled her next to me and felt her tears on my bare shoulder. She cried, then sniffled, and then I felt her breathing change. Soon I was asleep too, deep in a restless dream I remember only vaguely.

Somewhere in my dream, I was shouting at Gil Zeamer. Through our yelling, I heard an alarm sounding, louder, louder, and I knew I should attend to it. I walked away from Gil and suddenly I was half awake, jumping out of bed to answer the ringing phone. I stumbled out of bed, tried to steady myself by focusing on the digital clock flashing 12:25, 12:25, 12:26, . . . and then moved unsteadily across the room to fumble the cordless phone from its stand and find the OK button. "Daddy," Jess said, sniffling, "I'm sorry I'm calling so late. Did I wake you up?"

"What's wrong, Jess? Are you OK?"

"Oh, Dad," she said, "I need to talk. I know it's late." Carol had turned on the light and was sitting up in the bed. I cupped the receiver and whispered, "She's OK—just needs to talk," and then spoke to Jess: "No problem, no problem. Let me take the phone into another room so your mom can get back to sleep."

When I got settled downstairs, Jess began. "Dad, I went to campus fellowship tonight. I don't like it that much, but I'm trying to get involved. The staff worker is great, but some of the students—well, here's what happened. They have this sharing time where you're supposed to get up and tell what God is doing in your life. So I got up and told them about our talk last month, you know, about hell. You've always told me I'm a pretty good storyteller, and the students were laughing and all when I told them my dad was a pastor, but I never thought of a question to ask him until I moved away to college. So I told them the whole thing about my questions about hell and God. And then I told them—like what you told me— about exclusivism and inclusivism and conditionalism. Then I told them how I had really prayed about it and felt good about being a universalist. I guess it was kind of naive, but I thought they'd be happy, you know, that God had answered my prayer and that I feel so much better now, but when I finished, there was this long dead silence. Like usually, people clap after somebody shares something, but there was this long drawn-out nothing. Kincaid was with me, and he started to clap, but he was the only one, and it was so embarrassing, like I'd farted in public or something."

At her sniffling converted into a laugh, and I laughed too. Then I told her how sorry I was that this happened and that I understood that it must have been really embarrassing. "But Dad," she interrupted, "that's not the bad part yet. It gets worse. When the meeting was over, this girl, she's actually Clarissa Zeamer's roommate—you know, Clarissa who goes to our church—this girl named Joanna comes up and asks if 'Caid and I want to go out for coffee. I was so relieved because it seemed as if nobody knew what to say to me after my faux pas. So we go down to Route 1 to Starbucks, and it was just starting to snow, and while we're walking there, she's really friendly, just getting to know us and stuff. But when we get there . . . Dad, it was so weird.

"She tells me that universalism is one of the worst heresies in Christian history, and it was totally inappropriate of me to say anything about it, especially because I'm a *pastor's daughter*—like that exempts me from having my own brain and opinions, you know?

"Anyway, then I apologize for making her feel uncomfortable and I ask her to tell me how she deals with the whole hell issue, and she starts telling me that she believes a whole bunch of stuff that completely blows my mind."

I had a feeling I knew what was coming, and my hunch was right.

"She tells me that before God ever created the universe, he decided to create some people who would be blessed forever and others who would be damned forever. Then I say that sounds cruel, and she tells me it had to be that way, because the blessed would never have any idea of how blessed they are unless they had something to compare it to. I said that sounded crazy and sick, and she told me to look up the words *election* and *predestination* in the Bible and I'd be convinced.

"Then, Daddy, maybe I shouldn't have said this, but I said if that's what the Bible teaches, then I don't believe the Bible anymore, and if God is going to send all my friends to hell, then he can send me right along with them, because I love them, and I'd rather be loyal to them than save my own skin, but I didn't exactly say *skin,* if you know what I mean, Daddy, which shocked her and really got her mad. I said I could never be happy in a party upstairs in the heavenly living room knowing that so many people were being tortured in the basement, and I thought it was pretty heartless of her to think that she could be happy under those circumstances. In fact, I told her I thought God would be disgusted to have people like that at his party and that I thought God himself would go down into the basement to help the people there.

"So she says that I feel that way because I'm looking from a human point of view, and I don't understand God's holiness and justice, and God's ways are higher than our ways and whatever, and I was like totally appalled at this, and I told her that didn't sound holy and just, it sounded sadistic, and my Dad didn't teach me a sadistic version of Christianity. So she said that you weren't teaching the truth anyway, which is what Clarissa Zeamer had told her, and now she knew Clarissa was right.

"At that point, 'Caid speaks up and says, real serious, 'Hey, Joanna, I've got a question for you. You seem very knowledgeable about hell and all, and I've always wondered: Who's more likely to go to hell—homosexuals or those dudes who carry the "God hates fags" signs? I mean, is it more serious to fool around with the wrong gender or to portray God as an ignorant, hateful bigot?'

"At first it looks like Joanna is going to answer, and then she realizes that 'Caid is kind of making fun of her, and she says something about hell not being a laughing matter. Then 'Caid says that insulting his pastor and his girlfriend's father isn't too cool either. He says you're the person who helped him become a follower of Jesus, and she shouldn't criticize someone she's never met, and then she says she's just saying what the 'Word-a-God' says, and don't argue with her, argue with the 'Word-a-God.' Then she goes, 'Remember, God gave us the Ten Commandments, not the Ten Suggestions.' I think she thought we would find that very clever.

"Anyway, then she says that maybe the saints in heaven are actually glad when they realize that the unsaved are getting what they deserve, because the saints rejoice with righteousness, and God is a holy God and any offense against God is an infinite offense and deserves infinite punishment, and since the redeemed saints love God so much, they're happy with whatever God decrees. And if we knew the holiness of God, we would agree, but we must have accepted a man-centered gospel, to which I said I happen to be a woman, and of course that didn't help things at all.

"Finally, Kincaid says that he's pretty new to all this, and now he wonders if he made a mistake because this sounds like some sort of wacky cult for psychopaths, and maybe he made a mistake even becoming a Christian. Up to that point, I was mad—you know how I can be, Dad—but then suddenly I was scared, like this girl is making my boyfriend turn away from God, and I burst out in tears, right there in Starbucks.

"Then Joanna starts to feel bad, and she sort of apologizes, but it sounds so condescending, like she still knows she's right, but we just can't handle the truth, so maybe she shouldn't have told us. Then she tries to invite us to her church, which she says is Reformed *and* Spirit-filled, which means it has the very best of the old and new, and then 'Caid said something he shouldn't have, which I don't really want to quote, but it had to do with being filled with something other than the Spirit. So then we try to calm down a little bit, and then Kincaid says, 'Look, Joanna. I wasn't brought up in all this stuff. I just know that last year when my Mom died, she found this peace and this love, and she said it came from Jesus. I saw something real in her, and in all of Jess's family and friends too, and I wanted it, and it started happening to me. What you represent is exactly what I didn't want. I wanted Jesus, not Christianity. I think you've got Christianity, but I'm not sure you've got Jesus. I don't mean to judge, but the little I know about Jesus—I don't think he would want to sit up in the living room, like Jess said, having a big party with his Father and all his friends, while some of his other friends are frying in the basement. Everything I know about Jesus tells me he would go down there and get them out. So I can pretty much tell you that you'll never convince me you're right. I think you'd better leave now, 'cause Jess and I need to talk.' Actually, at that moment, I was so proud of Kincaid.

"Then I expected Joanna to give us another little sermon before she left, but she didn't. She just kind of looked confused and sad and said she hoped we'd come back to campus fellowship next week, even if we didn't want to visit her church, and she was sorry if she said anything that was wrong, because she wasn't inerrant, only the 'Word-a-God' was. Anyway, I said, 'We'll think about everything you said, and maybe we'll come to campus fellowship next week,' but frankly, Dad, I think I'm through with the whole business until I get this thing sorted out in my own mind."

I told her how sorry I was that she had this run-in with Joanna, and she asked me what I thought of what she had said, and to my complete shock, I said, "Jess, you said you were proud of Kincaid. Well, I'm proud of you, sweetheart. I'm really proud of you, and I'm proud of everything you said. And you can tell Kincaid that I'm proud of him too." And for some reason, right there on the phone with my daughter, this little sob erupted, more like a cough than a cry. I could hear Jess sniffling on the other end of the line, and we just kind of breathed together for a long time until she said, "I love you, Daddy. Thanks for listening," and I said, "I love you too, Jess. Thanks for . . . thanks for helping me. You really helped me tonight. More than you'll know."

"What's the answer, Daddy?" Jess asked. "Was I right in what I said?"

"I don't know exactly," I answered, "but something tells me whether your words were right, your heart was right, and I think that's what matters most."

When I went back to bed, Carol turned over and asked me, "Is everything OK?"

"I think so," I said. "She just needed to talk. It was good. It was good." She nestled up beside me, and for the second time that night, we fell asleep in each other's arms.

5

PLAYING HARDBALL

Solve for me that knot
which has entangled my conceptions here.

—*Inferno*, X.95–96

I RECEIVED THE LETTER from our church council that Friday, signed by Nancy.

February 14, 2003

Dear Dan,

Thank you for your cooperation during this time of assessment and doctrinal investigation. We continue to pray that God will lead us to determine whether your changing theological views are consistent with the beliefs and direction of Potomac Community Church.

As you have heard, we have become provisional members of the Biblical Evangelical Fellowship, largely to secure its support in difficult matters like this. The BEF has assigned a consultant, Chip Griffin, to help us work through this process. Here is what is planned.

1. We have put together a list of questions (included with this letter) that we would like you to carefully and prayerfully answer. Chip suggested that you feel free to answer in whatever detail you feel is appropriate, but we'd prefer your answers not exceed twenty pages, double-spaced. We would like you to complete these questions by February 28, 2003.
2. Between March 1 and March 15, the church council will meet in private to review your answers.

3. Between March 15 and 31, we will schedule one or more meetings with you (Nora will be in touch about this by phone) to discuss your answers and any questions we have. Chip Griffin will
moderate this meeting.

4. By April 15, we will make a decision about your continuing em-
ployment here at Potomac. You will either be reinstated or released from ministry here effective May 1.

5. You will remain on paid leave through this period, unless you
wish to resign sooner. If you wish to resign sooner, you will also
receive severance pay through June 30, 2003. If you are released
from ministry on April 15, your paid leave now through April 30
will constitute your complete severance package.

Please contact me by phone if you have any questions.

Prayerfully,
Nancy Zeamer
Chair, PCC Church Council

When Carol read the letter, she pursed her lips and whistled as she pointed to point 5. "Sounds to me like a recommendation that you resign right
away, darlin'. It's a pretty big risk to work the process and then be dis-
missed. Kind of like two weeks' notice, I'd say. Bless their hearts, they're
playin' hardball," she said.

I had already turned to the next page and read the list of questions. It
was the first one that jumped out at me thanks to my recent conversations
with Jess.

QUESTIONS FOR DAN POOLE
1. Describe in detail your doctrine of hell.
2. Briefly explain the gospel as you understand it.
3. What is your doctrine of Scripture?
4. Where do you stand in relation to the "openness of God"?
5. What school or stream of theology do you now feel most comfortable with?
6. What is your view on the scope of salvation?
7. See the BEF doctrinal statement below. Can you fully affirm all
the statements, and if not, please explain.

Nancy had forgotten to include the BEF doctrinal statement, but I hardly
noticed. *So Lord, you were using Jess's questions to prepare me for this,* I
silently prayed, focusing on question 1, but then added, *or maybe you're
using this to prepare me to help Jess.*

I sat with the letter on my lap, reading and rereading it, while Carol warmed up some leftovers for supper. The other questions seemed insignificant: only the hell question mattered. Had I lied to Jess when I told her I was proud of her and what she had said? If I was telling the truth, was I now rejecting the clear teaching of the Bible? How would this affect my job? The questions circled and landed and took flight again like planes on a runway.

Deep in my heart, I acknowledged that I felt *stuck* with the traditional view of hell. It bothered me to use *exclusive* and *Jesus* in the same sentence. Everything about Jesus' life and message seemed to be about inclusion, not exclusion. I couldn't figure out how anything with "eternal conscious torment" in it could be called "Good News." I wished there could be a better view. But then again, I was uneasy whenever anyone actually proposed an alternate view—as Jess had done and as my friend Neil did from time to time in our conversations. So oddly, if others attacked the traditional view, I defended it, even though in my own thoughts I disliked it, questioned it, and wished, like my daughter, that it weren't the only option.

Back in my early years in ministry, I often said to myself, *Someday I'm going to do a deep study of all this,* "this" meaning hell. I hoped that maybe if I really grappled with the biblical texts, I'd find some way of being faithful to the Bible but not stuck with the traditional view. But hell is one of those subjects that's more pleasant to defer than engage, so years had passed without my finding time to do the research. Now with these questions from the council before me, along with Jess's need for guidance, I had no option but to grapple with it.

In early February, Carol and I began renting out a room in our home to a young woman named Casey Curtis, a friend of Neil's whom we had gotten to know. Casey was African American and wore her hair in braids with little plastic beads in them, so when she was around, there was always the sound of the tinkling of her beads. Actually, there were a lot of other sounds too when Casey was around—especially joking and laughter. With Jess away at college, we had two empty rooms, so we could rent one to Casey and still have Jess's room for when she came home, and it could double as our guest room when she was at school. I was kind of enjoying the increased quiet around the house with Jess away and with the boys out of the house more with sports and school activities, but Carol exudes southern hospitality. "Besides," she said, "the rent might help us a bit if . . ." She didn't need to finish the sentence; I knew she was worrying about finances.

Our twin thirteen-year-olds, Cory and Trent, were especially thrilled to have Casey with us because Casey was perpetually fun and upbeat,

whereas their parents were subdued on good days and downright depressed on others. Looking back, I think she was a real godsend, kind of
like a human vitamin for our family, or a strong cup of coffee.

Casey had gone to seminary (with Neil's encouragement and financial
support) and then worked in youth ministry for a few years. Born in Baltimore, she had been living elsewhere (including Europe) for several years.
Now back in our area, she was serving as a "youth consultant," helping
several Episcopal churches in the area start or improve their youth pro-
grams. The job was only three-quarter time, though, so she had some free
time. The afternoon I received the questionnaire from the council, she was
doing aerobics in the basement. I heard the music stop, and then she bound-
ed up the stairs, her beads bustling, her gray T-shirt patchy with sweat.

"Hey, Reverend Dan," she said, coming over to exchange a sliding handshake that she had taught me—hoping to "coolify" me a bit. "What's up?
Whoa, you look upset." I showed her the letter and the questions, and she
sat down on an easy chair across from me, her eyebrows rising higher as
her eyes moved down the page. She finished, looked up, and asked, "Dude,
how can I help?"

I wasn't one to ask for help, but an idea came to mind. She had gone
to seminary in northern Virginia, less than an hour away. I asked her if
she would go to the library there and check out any books she found on
the subject of hell. "I'm especially interested in books about the history
of the concept of hell," I said, recalling Neil's advice.

"Sure, Rev.," she said, "and I'll do a lit review and photocopy the best
articles I can find too. And if they don't have enough resources, they're
part of a consortium, so as an alum I'm allowed to use the other libraries
too. I'll hook you up. This is major."

A day or two later, I got a call from Neil. "So it has begun. Casey told
me about the Inquisition," he began, his Jamaican accent lilting. "Sounds
like you've got quite a challenge on your hands, my friend. Want to talk?
My schedule is much better for the next couple weeks. Especially if we get
some more snow days."

When Neil asked about talking, it usually meant either hiking or drinking beer. I wasn't much of an outdoorsman, especially in winter, and even
less of a beer drinker, but Neil had tried to introduce me to both over the
years without much success on either account. "Where would you like to
go?" I asked, deciding some exercise would do me more good than some
alcohol.

"I've been wanting to go downtown to see the Holocaust Museum,"
he answered. "All these years living here and I've never seen it, and I'm
supposed to lead a field trip there in a couple weeks, so I need to famil-

iarize myself with it. Why don't you ride down with me on the Metro this Saturday? We can talk on the way down and back."

My boys had a Saturday indoor soccer game that I didn't want to miss, since I'd missed so many through the years. So I asked about Monday instead, which was Presidents' Day, so schools were out. Neil wondered if the museum would be open on the holiday. He checked its Web site and called me back. We were on for Monday morning.

6

I DON'T KNOW

Began I, with desire of being certain
of that faith which o'ercometh every error.

—*Inferno*, IV.47–48

SUNDAY CAME AND WENT, and even after nearly six months, it still felt a little strange to be doing anything other than preaching at PCC. Carol and the boys had begun attending a Baptist church nearby during my administrative leave. We had been asked not to attend PCC until the council had finished the evaluation process, and Carol took comfort, I think, in the familiar hymns and vocabulary of her childhood denomination. No offense to Southern Baptists, but I just couldn't bring myself to go, so each Sunday since September I found something else to do—including crossword puzzles, watching political news shows, and of course, reading. I know the boys felt strange leaving for church services with Carol while I stayed home, but these were strange times.

Monday morning, I got up early and made some sandwiches. I packed two lunches in my backpack and also threw in a book Casey had brought me from the seminary library on the history of hell. I had been up late the night before reading it and wanted to know what Neil thought of it.

I picked up Neil a little after nine. We rode down to the Shady Grove Station and made our way from the nearly empty parking lot, lined with ugly gray piles of snow, to the fare-card machines, through the turnstiles, up the escalators, and into an empty train car, just in time to hear the familiar *ding-dong* and feel the doors swoosh shut behind us. We took off our coats and found a seat facing forward (the backward-facing seats upset my stomach), and I moved our conversation from small talk—about Neil's classes, about a woman he had met (a doctor from a local hospital), about my daughter Jess and her budding romance with Neil's roommate, Kincaid Ellison—to more serious matters.

"So Neil, can you help me with the hell question? I'm taking your advice and reading about the history of hell. As long as I've known you, I've never been able to get a straight answer from you on the subject. And this book—" which I began to pull out, but then decided not to.

"Is that what would help you most, Daniel, to get a straight answer from me? I mean, does it really matter what I think? I'll be glad to oblige, but . . ."

I knew that *but* was coming, so I finished the thought: "But you'd rather hear what I'm thinking?"

"Learning isn't a consequence of teaching or listening," he said, and I waited for him to complete the saying, which was one of his oft-repeated favorites: "*but a consequence of thinking.*" I shook my head and he laughed and put his fist on my knee, suddenly switching to a serious tone: "Daniel, this won't be easy. This is the issue that will change everything for you. I've seen this coming since I first met you, man."

"Deep down," Neil said, "I know you don't feel good about your traditional view on this subject. But you're afraid to let it go. You're afraid to even question it."

"No, it's not that I'm afraid. I certainly am questioning it now," I said, turning in my seat to face Neil. "But, well, maybe I am afraid, I guess, but I think I should be afraid. There's a lot at stake. I guess I've always felt that it's so tempting to soften your view of hell, you know, like the . . ."

"Like those dirty, stinking liberals," Neil said, playing with me, stretching out *liberals* into three very distinct syllables as he always did.

"Well," I said, trying to regain my train of thought, "it's not just about being loyal to my conservative roots. It's about being loyal to the Bible and to God. I don't want to rewrite the Bible to suit my own tastes. I don't want to smooth off all the sharp edges so everything is ambiguous and palatable and soft . . ."

"That's something I love and respect about you, Daniel," Neil said with a wink, and before I could respond, he continued, "and that's a good thing. The truth does have sharp edges, and one can't try to make everything sugary and smooth. It's very tempting indeed to rewrite the gospel in our image, which many of my liberal friends have done."

I was a little surprised that he said this, and so I looked out the window to the right as we passed the Takoma Park Station and headed toward downtown, just gathering my thoughts for a few seconds. Neil spoke first:

"But that's the same problem conservatives have, I think. The traditional view casts God too much in the image of *Homo conservativo*." I didn't turn toward him, but I made a face that he could see, and he continued. "Daniel, do you really think God is like a petty human being, full of anger and revenge? Do you think God wants to inflict torture on people to retaliate for their wrongs? Do you think God would require us to forgive and then be unwilling to do the same?"

I'd heard this sort of argument before. "Of course not, Neil. I'm sure if God sends people to hell, it's not because he gets any pleasure in it."

"Ah, you've learned the 'hell's door is locked from the inside' argument. It's certainly a step in the right direction, but poor God. Isn't he in a tough situation?" Then Neil paused, baiting me, I knew, with his irony, but just before I was going to respond, he added, "You don't think he's stuck in some higher mechanism, do you?"

"What's that supposed to mean?" I asked.

"A lot of modern people forget that our talk of God as judge is metaphorical. In other words, to call God a judge is to make use of a figure of speech, a metaphor, which requires that there be a physical thing to which God is being compared. I think we talked about this before, years ago. Modern Christians assume that the kinds of judges back in biblical times are equivalent to the kinds of judges there are in today's world, but that's a terribly mistaken assumption." I looked at him and lifted my head slightly, signaling him to keep talking. "In early biblical times, there was no such thing as a complex court system or jury or constitution or annotated legal code or judicial precedent or nation-state. The judge was—one hoped—a wise, honest, and brave person who helped people resolve disputes and seek justice. It's true, certain kings like Hammurabi tried to raise the standard of 'judgemanship' by promoting standardized codes with standardized punishments, and in a way, the Jewish Torah is a further elaboration on this theme. But modern judges are so different. They're really mid-level bureaucrats, accountable to mechanisms of the court. This is the only way modern conservative Christians can keep believing in both a loving God and horrific hell. God is a decent judge stuck in a rigid, heartless system."

Now I made another face, and he continued. "You have to say that God doesn't want people to go to hell, but he's forced to do so against his will by the mechanisms of the court or the requirements of some higher abstraction called justice or something like that. He's a nice guy caught in a tough fix. He wants to forgive us, but he has to play by the rules of the court. It's the only way you can save God from seeming like a monster, visiting infinite punishment on poor little finite creatures who have no choice about being born into this high-risk, no-win game called life. Of course, when you solve the hell problem that way, you have the new problem of creating a higher authority than God. You know, the court mechanisms or the law to which God is subject or whatever. Where did those mechanisms come from—some higher, sterner Senior God above the kindly Junior God? Why not worship the Senior God, then, if Junior is having trouble handling both justice and mercy? Of course, that's exactly what some of your brothers do. They worship the Senior God, who actually does enjoy inflicting punishment without mercy on some while giving mercy without judgment to others, making distinctions for reasons we are never going to understand, in this life anyway."

In an instant, I turned toward him, took in a breath, furrowed my brow, and was about to say something—something angry, I think, but I didn't know what. So I let out a sigh instead, a sigh that ended in half a laugh. "Neil, you kill me. You really kill me. And you're still not going to give me a straight answer about how you see your way through this, are you?"

Neil replied, "I could if you want, but let me ask you a question, my friend. What are your nonnegotiables as you try to think this through?"

"Good question," I said, and thought for a minute. I hooked my left index finger over my right little finger to start counting my nonnegotiables: "First, I want to be honest to Scripture. I want to look at all the evidence and not throw anything out, not ignore anything. Second," now grasping my little and ring fingers, "hmm, second, I want to be . . . logical. I mean, I want to find an answer that makes sense. Third," by now I had taken three of my right fingers in my left hand, "I want to take into account what the best theologians have said through history."

Neil interrupted. "I think you'll have a problem there, depending on how you define best."

"Yes, I see your point," I said. "If best means those who agree with my position, I'm kind of predeciding. So I'll have to include minority reports. OK, I will. Then fourth, I want to be faithful to . . . I don't know how to say it—to my heart. I need to see what effects my conclusions have on my life, my relating to God and other people, to see if they produce better results in my character and ministry. If they don't, I'll need to reevaluate."

"Very wise, my friend, very wise—and very Anglican too!" Neil added with a wink. "You've just identified Richard Hooker's theological method: consult Scripture, tradition, and reason. That's part of what we call the via media—a middle way between Catholic and Reformed. The Methodists added a fourth element—experience—and called it the quadrilateral." Now he started using his fingers to count off his own points. "Scripture is a given. It's the norming norm for Christian thinking. You can throw it out when it bothers you if you want to, but then you have no guarantee that what you'll end up with can truly be called Christian. So Scripture must never be thrown out, never minimized; it must be a respected member of any conversation. Or perhaps it actually brings many voices to the table.

"Anyway, Scripture can't self-interpret, so that brings reason in. You have to try to make sense of the texts with intellectual integrity. And your reason has to deal fairly with tradition and experience too. Chesterton used to say that tradition is the democracy of the dead. It reminds us not to be prejudiced against voices just because they're not here anymore."

I'd heard that before and nodded, then added something I'd heard Neil say before—what I guessed he was about to say next: "But I know that the voice of tradition has usually been a baritone voice, as you say, white European male. That's why tradition has to extend to hear minority reports—what do you always call them?"

"Voices from the margins," Neil said, "the voices of the other. Voices from the poor and weak and oppressed and forgotten. And all of this has to be integrated with our own experience, with how our beliefs work out in our daily lives, with what kind of fruit they bear."

I was nodding: "Well, that's it. Those are my nonnegotiables too. I'm glad you approve."

"What will you do if you can't reconcile them?" Neil asked, now with some gentleness in his voice. "My liberal brothers and sisters generally jettison Scripture or tradition first when we get in trouble. Your conservative brothers tend to throw out—or at least, they tend to straitjacket—reason and experience, or else they narrow tradition down to an agreeable subset by including only voices from the past who agree with them. It's not easy to hold all four together. There will be a lot of pressure to negotiate one or more of your nonnegotiables."

"Then, then I'll say I don't know. I'll suspend judgment and live with the ambiguity. If I can't reconcile all four, *I'll say I don't know*," I said, as if I were stating a firm conclusion.

Neil spoke very softly, facing me directly: "Is that what you say now, Daniel? Why don't you say that now?"

His question hit me. Why *didn't* I say I didn't know? Why *did* I keep affirming the traditional view when it neither seemed right logically nor resonated with my experience of God? It was a moment I won't forget when I turned to him, speeding along on the Metro, and said, "Neil, I don't know." Then I realized I had said those same words to Jess a few nights before, and I suddenly felt—lighthearted, free.

It's funny how "I don't know" can feel like a revelation, a liberation, when you've been pretending to know something you didn't, which is a lot like pretending not to know something you do.

7

THE ARCHITECTURE
OF THE BIBLE

. . . talking we went bravely on,
Even as a vessel urged by a good wind.

—*Purgatorio,* XXIV.1–3

I DON'T KNOW. I kept repeating those words as if they were a mantra or an incantation. I had been pretending to know something when deep inside I didn't. It was like I had been sick with a cold for a couple of weeks and suddenly realized I could breathe freely.

When I unbolted my pretended certainty, another thought rushed in. My problem hadn't been that Scripture uniformly and unequivocally portrayed my traditional doctrine of hell; rather, it was that I had adopted a rationale—a work or construction of reason, logic, interpretation—for weaving the many voices of Scripture together into a tight cord. I had suppressed some voices and favored others. Others, lib-er-als—who rejected the traditional view—weren't necessarily rejecting Scripture; they were rejecting our traditional rationale, our conventional construction, our preferred way of weaving or binding together the many relevant passages of Scripture. They wanted to favor the voices we suppressed, and the reverse as well. Perhaps, I thought, if I could unweave the strands, they could be rewoven in some new, coherent way, some different way. Perhaps. Hope hid in that *perhaps*.

Why did I feel so relieved as we disembarked from the train, hastily buttoned our coats and put on our hats and gloves, and made our way up an escalator, across a platform, through turnstiles, and then up another long escalator into the morning light of the Capitol Mall? Why did I feel so relieved repeating those three words as we crunched over ice and snow?

Neil loves to walk. "How about we swing down by the Vietnam Veterans' Memorial and stop to say hello to Abe? Then we can curve back toward L'Enfant Plaza and be at the Holocaust Museum by eleven." The February morning was clear and bright, and Carol had been constantly nagging me to get more exercise lately, so I said OK. We set off—the stately old red sandstone Smithsonian office buildings ahead to our left, the newer Smithsonian museums on our right, the Capitol rising behind us, the spire of the Washington Monument directly ahead of us. There were a few tourists walking along, bundled up in their winter coats, and a few cars driving between the dirty snowbanks in the brisk winter sunlight.

"Casey told me she's been checking out books and photocopying articles for you," Neil said, setting the pace a bit fast for my aerobic ability.

"Yeah," I said, panting a bit. "I started reading one of the books already, on the history of hell. It's fascinating. I can't believe they never taught me any of this in seminary. Maybe they were afraid that if we knew the history, we'd question the dogma."

"Maybe, but I'll bet many of your professors didn't know the history themselves. The problem was modernity, Daniel. You know, the assumption that analysis is the essence of knowing." I remembered him saying something about this at some point in the past but needed him to refresh my memory. "Analysis means knowing things by breaking them down into smaller pieces. So we break the Bible down into testaments, and testaments into books, and books into chapters, and chapters into verses, sentences, clauses, phrases, words, roots, prefixes, and suffixes. Then, through our dissection, we think we've gained knowledge of the text, but one small detail is missing."

"Which is . . . ?" I asked, but he was answering the question before I even asked it.

"Which is all the larger realities in which the Bible exists, especially the larger story that carries each biblical statement. We lift statements out of their historical and narrative context, as if the Bible were some kind of timeless textbook or encyclopedia with no context, no history. So we read Genesis without knowing about a larger historical genre called sacred creation narrative, or we read Revelation without knowing about its contexts of Jewish apocalyptic literature or the literature of the oppressed. Or we read prophecies without knowing the larger genre of prophetic literature. We act as if the Bible is a codebook, and all one needs is the Bible, as if truth were hermetically sealed inside it. But even a codebook requires a key, so you know how to interpret the symbols. And the code is full-bodied literacy: metaphor, simile, hyperbole, understatement, mystification, rhetorical question, parallelism, irony, sarcasm, symbolism, reductio ad absurdum, pun, mockery, invective, exclamation, stream of consciousness, dream language, hortatory language, performative language—we need sensitivity to language with all its richness, diversity, variety, delight, and evolution."

I guess it's my background, but I always wince inside when I hear the word *evolution*. I tried not to flinch visibly. Neil realized, I think, that he had launched into another lecture and had lost me somewhere in it, so he stopped talking for several minutes. I didn't speak either. I could feel the gears turning, but I couldn't wrestle anything into words.

We were passing the White House to our right when he continued: "You could never understand or appreciate the architecture of the White House without knowing something about Greek columns and European castles and the Revolutionary War and democracy. In fact, this whole city was laid out by a French architect, Pierre L'Enfant. Its very design is an expression of the French Enlightenment. To walk these streets with your eyes open is to be in conversation with all those historical and philosophical elements and a lot more, whether you know it or not. And the Bible is a thousand times richer than all this," he said, expanding his arms and turning to embrace the whole city.

"That's what I'm realizing about hell," I said. "It's fascinating. It sounds terrible to say that—it's the history I'm talking about, not hell itself." Neil waited for me to say more, but I wasn't sure what to say, so we just walked on a bit farther, with only the sound of our footsteps crunching patches of snow and the occasional rush of a passing car breaking the silence. We crossed Fifteenth Street, and Neil asked me to summarize what I'd been reading so far. I had brought the book along in my pack hoping that we might get to talk about it, so I stopped at a bench to take out the book, which required first pulling off my gloves. With the book retrieved and my gloves back on my hands, I hoisted the pack back on my shoulders and we started walking again.

One thing was clear to me, I explained: hell was not "revealed" in the Old Testament. Nowhere did a Hebrew prophet have a vision or dream that revealed the reality of hell. It's never mentioned once in the whole Hebrew Bible. Even the latest books of the Old Testament, thought to have been written about 450 B.C., have no reference to hell. Instead, the idea appears suddenly—to us, anyway—in the Gospels, on the lips of Jesus. That's why it's such a thorny issue for Christians. Jesus is the first in all biblical literature to talk about hell, and he talks the most about it.

As I was summarizing all this, Neil was nodding his head, looking down at the sidewalk as we moved past the Washington Monument on our left. Neil is a long-legged guy, a good four inches taller than I, and I was getting pretty winded trying to keep up with his brisk pace. I motioned that I wanted to stop to retie my bootlace. When we started walking again, he picked up the conversation.

"Yes, I think we've talked about this a few years back," Neil said. "About how the Hebrew word *Sheol* was translated as *hell* in the King James Version. But that was a mistake. *Sheol* simply meant the place of the dead, the grave. There was no idea of an immortal soul involved and certainly no idea of different destinations for the good and the evil."

Neil went on to recount how the idea of an afterlife was probably not much of a part of the ancient Jewish worldview at all. The ancient Jews seemed to be focused on remaining part of God's blessing or covenant on their land in this history, not on achieving life after death beyond history. They wanted to stay reconciled to God so that neither they nor their descendents would lose their land or their status as God's special and chosen people. The Jewish sacrificial system was *not* instituted so that Jews could go to heaven rather than hell after they died, with a clean slate so to speak. Rather, it was instituted to help the people deal with the gap between God's law and their failure to fulfill it. Sacrifices allowed them to hold the high moral standard to which they had been called and to acknowledge their failure to fulfill it. They expressed repentance and a desire to return to fidelity to God through an act of good faith: giving of their best (a lamb, a goat, a bull, or other agricultural products) to God, eating a meal with God. The persistent Jewish disinterest in afterlife was all the more significant because their neighbors were fixated on a life after death, Neil said.

As he was speaking, I immediately thought of Old Testament passages I had frequently used in funeral services. "But what about when Job says something about knowing that his redeemer lives and asserting that he will see God in his flesh?"

Neil replied, "I think Job is saying that he believes he'll recover from his terrible illness and be vindicated—not as a soul in heaven but in this life, in his own body. At least that's how I see it."

"OK, but what about David, when Bathsheba's baby died and he said something about going to be with the baby?"

Neil didn't miss a beat: "He wasn't talking about heaven; he was talking about the grave. 'Of course the baby isn't going to be raised to life,' he was saying. 'But instead I'll die and be buried like the baby.'"

I was a little surprised. "What about that line from Psalm 23—I will dwell in the house of the Lord forever?"

"David is saying the same thing as Job had said: I might walk in the shadow of death, but I'll pull through and stay in the land of the living. I know—you're going to ask about forever, but forever doesn't necessarily mean for an unending succession of moments. It can also mean *without stopping*. Lovers use the word all the time—'I'll love you forever,' and so on—you know, meaning I won't stop."

I thought of mentioning the story of Enoch going to be with God without dying but then realized that that was a subversion of death, not a life after death. Then the story of King Saul consulting a medium and speaking to the prophet Samuel's ghost came to mind, but I quickly realized that even if it was a counterexample to Neil's point, it didn't fit in my theology either. It was just plain strange. Besides, the whole point of the story was that people were not supposed to take an interest in communicating with the dead.

So I was running out of funeral quotations but then thought of Ezekiel's vision of dry bones coming back to life. Wasn't that some kind of life after death?

"Daniel, don't you think those skeletons represent the Jewish people being delivered from exile? Isn't the rather macabre vision an image that simultaneously rebukes the people for their spiritual deadness and yet affirms God's faithfulness and power to rescue them?"

We stopped for a couple of minutes to look up at the Washington Monument, Neil pointing out the place partway up the structure where the color of the stone changed. He told me when and why construction stopped, which explained the change in stone color, but I was only half-listening and can't remember the details. I said, "It's kind of like the construction of this idea of hell. It seems to have evolv—I mean, developed—over a long history, and materials from different cultures were combined in the process. In this book . . ."—I was still holding the book I had taken from my backpack.

"Why don't you show me what you're learning?" Neil said. "Let's sit down for a few minutes . . . over there, at that bench down by the water."

We walked over next to the partially frozen Reflecting Pool and sat down. A few ducks paddled and dipped in the open water at the center. One tried to climb up on the ice that ringed the pool, but the ice wouldn't hold his weight, so he turned and rejoined the others, dipping, splashing, circling, quacking in a kind of mumble. I was afraid Neil would start telling me about what species the ducks were or where they migrate to and from or something similar, so I quickly opened the book and started trying to summarize what I had read so far about the history of hell.

"It seems like there were three or four main streams, maybe five. OK," I said, finding the appropriate chapter in the book to refresh my memory, "first is the Babylonian stream, which rises about 2000 B.C."

8

THE FIRST TWO THREADS

For 'tis no enterprise to take in jest,
To sketch the bottom of all the universe.

—*Inferno,* XXXII.7–8

"YOUR BOOK MUST BE USING *Babylonian* in an inclusive way," Neil said. "Because Babylonian civilization comes along quite late—well into the first millennium B.C., right?"

"I guess you're right," I said, looking up a timeline in the book. "There were Sumerian, Akkadian, and Assyrian cultures that rose to power in the Tigris-Euphrates valley. Then the Babylonians dominated in the same area, so this author uses the term *Babylonian* to cover them all. They had the same basic stories, although they changed the names of some of the gods, as the Romans did with Greek gods."

"I think they'd be better off using the term *Mesopotamian* to avoid confusion," Neil said. "But I'm acting like such a know-it-all, when really, I've never read this book of yours, and I'm mainly acquainted with what's directly related to the biblical story. Tell me more."

I leafed through my book to refresh my memory of what I had read the night before: "Nearly all the cultures of the Tigris-Euphrates valley had stories of the underworld, or the place of the dead, which was a kind of shadowy place, dry, barren, gloomy," I began. "Two goddesses were dominant in the stories. The first one, Inana, was the queen of the earth and sky, and she was also known as Ishtar, Astarte, and Ashtoreth (who turns up in the Bible too). The second one, Ereshkigal, was queen of the underworld, and was also called Allatu. A lot of the Babylonians' stories had to do with people from the land of the living descending to visit the underworld—kind of a morbid curiosity, I guess—not my idea of a great vacation destination. Going to the underworld, one had to pass through seven gates, as if one were moving toward the center of an ancient walled city, and at each gate, the traveler had to give up an article of jewelry or clothing, kind of like a gradual death tax, I guess.

"Once down there, Ereshkigal wouldn't let you leave, so you would have to promise to send someone back in your place as a substitute—weird resonances with some Christian atonement theology, I know. Interestingly, nearly all the stories involved certain common features—a mountain barrier, a river, a boatman and boat to get you across the river, and a sacred tree. In one story, a man is given permission to leave for six months every year, but his sister has to take his place for those six months. I think there's some resonance with the cycle of the seasons—dying and rebirth, that sort of thing."

Neil asked if this was the context for the epic of Gilgamesh. "Yes. The Gilgamesh stories really intrigued me," I said. "At one point, his friend Enkidu dies and Gilgamesh goes searching for him. He's allowed to speak to Enkidu through a hole in the earth or something like that, and Gilgamesh asks what being dead is like. Enkidu says it's so horrible he can't even explain it. His body is full of dirt, and vermin are gnawing on his body. But what's striking is that this isn't hell—this isn't a place especially designed for bad people. Enkidu is a hero, and he's here along with everybody else. It's very . . . egalitarian. And depressing. There seems to be no purpose in it. I can't imagine why anyone would tell stories like this, especially to children generation after generation. At least the story of hell is supposed to scare you into being good, but this is . . . this is unavoidable and pointless."

"Maybe," Neil said, "it's like going to horror movies today or even an amusement park or extreme sports. There's something in us that wants to face our fears."

"Maybe so," I said, "and I get the sense that this underworld also serves to keep the dead separated from the living. It's almost as if we who are living need to know that the dead won't come back to haunt us, to know that the land of the living is safe from encroachment by those from the past." Then I recounted another Gilgamesh story, about his visit with the Babylonian version of Noah, named Utnapishtim, who guides Gilgamesh to a plant that will give him immortality. But a snake steals the plant, and Gilgamesh's quest ends in failure. That reminded me of still another story, which I found and read to Neil, this one about a magical tree that is discovered by the goddess Inana and planted in her garden. But it is invaded by some demons—one of them, notably, in the form of a snake. She starts to cry and calls Gilgamesh. He comes to her aid and uses his ax to defeat the demons. Then he cuts down the tree and makes a bed and throne for Inana—symbolic, I guessed, of sex, fertility, and power. "Pretty weird," I said in summary.

"What do you mean?" Neil asked.

"Just that this is all so similar to the stories in the beginning of Genesis," I answered. "You know—snakes, trees."

"That bothers you?" Neil asked. "Does it bother you that the stories of Genesis are told in Hebrew?"

"What do you mean?" I replied.

"Obviously, if the Jews are going to tell a story, even if the story is somehow warranted or inspired by God, they have to use what's given to them as raw materials—language, for starters. Then, if they're going to use metaphorical language, they need to use what's around them, since metaphors help you learn by building a bridge to the unknown and unfamiliar from the known and familiar. Even in what I just said—I used the metaphor of a bridge, something known and familiar. I could have said 'you make a connection between the unknown and the known,' but even then you'd have another image in your mind from daily life, of plugging an appliance into a power source or something like that. We swim in metaphors. And that was another one."

"So," I replied, "you're saying that if the Jews are going to articulate their own beliefs, they'd naturally work with the language that was a given for them and draw from their cultural experience, and that would include the metaphors borrowed from these neighboring cultures and religions."

"Exactly. So the borrowings are just what you'd expect, and you find lots of them in the Bible. What you look for aren't just the similarities but the discontinuities. Do you see any major differences in how the borrowed elements are used?" Neil asked. I couldn't tell if he had something in mind or was just prodding me to think.

"Only what I said before," I replied, "that this underworld is kind of arbitrary. There's no segregation of the good and evil. But I guess that's the same as Sheol, not different. Hmmm. Oh—there are multiple gods instead of one supreme being. And then there's the whole issue of obeying God's commands and knowing good from evil, which is so crucial in the Genesis story. And it seems like humans are given more dignity . . . more dignity and more responsibility . . . in the Genesis story; they aren't just pawns or playthings. So I guess those are significant differences, aren't they . . . and they're all the more significant when you contrast them with the similarities: human beings who are perplexed by death and wonder where it comes from and how to cope with it and maybe beat it."

Neil nodded and asked what the second thread was.

"It's the Egyptian thread," I said, flipping ahead in my book. "In the Old Kingdom of Egypt, which lasted from, let's see, about 3000 to 2200 B.C., there was a concept of life after death but only for morally upright nobles. Everyone else died and that was it. But over time, between 2200 and about 1000, the idea of afterlife really keeps developing and gets quite complex. I had heard of the Egyptian Book of the Dead before, but I never knew what it was. It was a kind of survival guide—something you'd study so you'd know what to do after you died so you could avoid pitfalls and get to the best parts of the land of the dead.

"For the Egyptians," I continued, "the land of the dead, called the Tuat, is less like a Mesopotamian walled city and more like the Egyptian countryside. And it seems to be on another part of our world, not underneath— I guess to the west, past where the sun sets. There are two major gods who have power in it, Amon-Re and Osiris, and then there are lots of lesser deities or demons who control various territories—again, kind of paralleling the politics of Egypt with its basic hierarchy. When you die, you go along a river or a path, and you have to settle down in someone's territory—hopefully that of a god you honored through all the necessary rites during your life; otherwise you'll be living in the territory of a god who doesn't particularly like you. So it's clear that piety is important in setting you up for a good life in the Tuat.

"One of the innovations in this Egyptian scenario is that there is a kind of last judgment when you arrive in the Tuat. Osiris requires that individuals be judged according to *maat*, which seems to be a kind of code of honor or just behavior. Someone takes out your heart, which stands for your conscience, I think, and puts it in on a scale—you know, one of those balance scales with a pan hanging on either end of a crossbar. Then, in the other pan, they put a feather, representing *maat*. If your heart is heavier than the feather, you are allowed a life in the Tuat, into which you then travel until you find, or get stuck in, a particular zone or neighborhood. But if the feather is heavier, your heart is eaten by this fellow with a crocodile head, and I guess that's it for you: annihilation not in hell but a crocodile's jaws."

Right at that moment, Neil jumped up off the bench and started jogging over toward a nearby street corner. "Be back in a minute!" he said, turning back momentarily. I couldn't imagine what he was doing. A couple of minutes later he came back, walking this time, with two cups of hot chocolate and a pretzel dangling from a finger of each hand.

"All that talk of eating hearts got me hungry," he said. I groaned at the disgusting joke but was happy for the hot chocolate in the cold.

Neil sat back down on the bench, leaning forward with his elbows on his knees, and tried to put together what I'd been saying. "So you were saying that the Babylonian underworld is a kind of undifferentiated storehouse or prison territory, and the Egyptian Tuat is more like a mapped-out region with ethical subdivisions."

"Yes," I said, "but there were passages in some of the ancient Egyptian writings that sound a lot like hell—lakes of fire that people are thrown into, that sort of thing. But even then, they weren't tortured forever. They would be consumed by the flames and then be gone. It feels like a step above the Babylonian concept of afterlife since it involves some kind of ethical judgment, but still, it's none too appealing. I can see why the Jewish people wouldn't be interested in borrowing either concept."

Neil had finished his hot chocolate and was feeding pieces of the pretzels to some cooing pigeons that had flown in as we talked. I'm not a great animal lover, but Neil seemed completely engrossed. Eventually, he had a pigeon sitting on his knee taking pretzel fragments from his hand. Then a fellow with a big black dog came jogging by, and the pigeons scattered. Neil motioned for us to continue on our walk. I kept my finger in the book to keep my place.

"Well," Neil said, "we've got the Babylonian thread and the Egyptian thread. What's next?"

9

THE THIRD AND FOURTH
THREADS

New torments I behold, and new tormented.

—*Inferno*, VI.4–5

"NEXT IS THE ZOROASTRIAN thread. You probably know about Zoroaster already—the little there is to know, that is. I was surprised to learn
that we don't even know exactly when he lived. It could have been as long
ago as 1000 B.C. Apparently there was an ancient religion that was the
precursor to Hinduism and Buddhism, and this religion had a huge number of gods. But Zoroaster said there were really only two supreme gods,
a good one named Ahura Mazda or Ohrmazd, and his evil archrival, Angra
Mainyu or Ahriman."

"Basic dualism," Neil commented.

"Well, I think it's pretty complex," I said, looking down at the next
chapter as we walked. "I think if it's dualistic, it's only temporarily so. According to the Vesta, the Zoroastrian sacred writings, Ahriman lived in a
hellish underworld and would send his demons up to torment people on
the earth. When a man died, his soul would spend three days hovering
around the head of its corpse. Then it would be judged by the angel of
justice, Rashnu, along with another angel named Mithra."

"Just a minute," Neil said. "I thought Mithra was worshiped during the
Roman Empire. I think there was a Mithra cult even in the time of Christ."

"Yes, the Greeks adopted Mithra," I replied, "from Zoroastrianism.
It turns out that Zoroastrianism contributed a lot of ideas to a lot of

religions—Judaism and Christianity and also Greek religions, along with Hinduism and Buddhism, and of course, Islam too. I was surprised to realize that the 'seven deadly sins' of Catholicism originated there, for example. Anyway, if the soul is judged unworthy, it goes to the Zoroastrian version of hell, which is ruled by Yima, the first human to die. If the soul is judged good, it's escorted by a beautiful maiden to the House of Song, which is like heaven. The judgment process was all very mathematical— a kind of accounting audit of good deeds. If the soul did exactly the same number of good and evil deeds, it went to a middle zone called Hammistagan, which seemed a lot like the old Babylonian concept of the underworld. Anyway, it struck me earlier on the train, when you were talking about the mechanisms of justice above God, how much that sounds like this Zoroastrian view, because even if Ahriman wanted to forgive someone for his evil deeds, he couldn't: the justice of Rashnu and Mithra was final, and even Ahriman couldn't overturn it."

"And is the idea of hell eternal for Zoroastrians?" Neil asked.

"No. There will be a final cosmic battle between Good and Evil, and Evil will lose. A savior figure named Soshyans will go into hell and rescue and forgive everyone who is penitent, after they go through some kind of ordeal involving molten metal. Hell will then be destroyed, along with any unrepentant people left in it, I guess. All the souls of the just and the penitent who are forgiven will be reunited with bodies and will return to earth to live forever."

At this point, we had arrived at the Vietnam Veterans' Memorial. I'm always moved when I come here, the 58,235 names etched in polished black marble, my own face reflecting back to me over the names, the slow descent to the center of the memorial, and then the slow ascent to the far end. It seemed appropriate, somehow, to walk this path commemorating war as we were talking about death and hell. Then we walked over to the statue of four soldiers—so different from other war statues in the city. The soldiers are kids, boys, hardly old enough to shave. They don't appear brave and bold; this statue isn't about the glory of war. They look afraid and exhausted and worn; the statue is about the horror of war. We walked to the nearby statue depicting women soldiers too, equally full of ambivalent emotion—care for the wounded, fear for whatever might be incoming. We were the only people at this statue, and we stood there for some time, just staring, each absorbed in our own thoughts and feelings.

Our voices remained low, hushed, somber. "It's not just theory, is it, Daniel?" Neil said. "It's something we all live with . . . this awareness of death, this anxiety. It colors everything in our lives. It's part of what makes war so horrible, and sickness too, and old age . . . and it's what makes health and peace and youthfulness so good." We walked slowly around the women soldiers once more, studying them from all angles, and then headed toward the Lincoln Memorial.

Neil asked, "Well, you said there were four streams, and we've had three: Mesopotamian, Egyptian, and Zoroastrian. The fourth must be Greek?"

"Yes," I said, flipping open my book to the relevant chapter. "It's incredibly complex. You've got Odysseus visiting the land of the dead called Hades in Homer's *Odyssey* back in the eighth century B.C. It's more like the Mesopotamian view—the good and the bad are all there together, although for Homer, Hades does seem to segregate the dead. But their segregation is due to their social status in life rather than their moral status. One thing is for certain: when you're dead, that's it. There's no coming back, and there's nothing good to look forward to. It's very grim. The whole scenario gets developed by several other Greek writers too." I found the right page to refresh my memory: "There's Hesiod's *Theogony,* Aristophanes' *Frogs,* and then of course Plato's works. As with the Egyptians, Hades is situated somewhere far to the west because that's where the sun sets. It's also described as down below the earth, but I don't know how it can be both to the west and below. There's the River Styx running through it, and it seems to be organized like a city with gates and so on. Then there's another region, or maybe a sister city, called Tartarus, within or beside or below Hades—it's hard to tell, or else it varies in different accounts. There don't seem to be normal humans in Tartarus, though; it's populated with superhumans called Titans."

Neil asked me what Plato had to say about hell. As he remembered, Plato believed in reincarnation, which didn't match with belief in hell as far as he could see.

"Actually, with Plato you have it all: heaven, hell, reincarnation. Plato seems to have believed that the earth was like a sponge, full of holes and channels and caves. The souls of the dead are flushed through those chambers by rivers, and they are judged in four categories: the good and holy, the indeterminate, the curable evil, and the incurable evil. The incurables are punished forever—I think Plato is the first writer to claim eternal torment in any of the cultures. The curable are punished until they're purified. I'm not sure how reincarnation fits into all of this. Maybe the people in the middle categories have to keep being recycled until they become either good or incurable.

"But," I added, "it's hard to tell to what degree Plato really believed all this to be literally true and to what degree he thought it was simply useful to believe it for the sake of social order. Listen to this . . ." I needed a few seconds to find a quote I had underlined: "Here it is: Plato has Socrates say—right before his suicide—'If death were a release from everything, it would be a boon for the wicked, because by dying they would be released not only from the body but also from their own wickedness together with the soul.' I think he's saying, 'Look, it's important to believe in postmortem punishment; otherwise wicked people will feel that they can get away with wickedness. As long as they die before being brought to justice, crime pays—unless there's an afterlife with judgment.'"

I leafed through the book to find another quote: "But here it sounds like he really believes it's true: 'We must at all times give our unfeigned assent to the ancient and holy doctrines, which warn us that our souls are immortal, that they are judged, and that they suffer the severest punishments after our separation from the body. Hence we hold it better to be victims of great wrongs and crimes than to be doers of them.' He believes that justice requires the possibility of eternal punishment for those he calls the incorrigible. He envisions newly dead souls coming into Hades, seeing these incorrigible souls suffering, and being deterred from becoming incorrigible themselves."

We reached the bottom of the long stairway that rises to the Lincoln Memorial. Neil motioned for us to sit on a stair, halfway up, giving us a view of the Reflecting Pool, the Washington Monument, and beyond it, the Capitol. It was the same view made famous in the Forrest Gump film. Neil's thoughts were on more lofty things, and he commented on how similar the Lincoln Memorial was to ancient Greek temples and then asked, "So, Daniel, how is all this affecting you? You really do seem fascinated by it, morbid as it is."

"Well," I said, "I guess I'm kind of relieved. I used to believe that Jesus must have invented all the talk about hell, you know, since it isn't overtly found in the Old Testament. I think a lot of people feel that way: since Jesus is the first to talk about it in the Bible, he was revealing it. But now I realize hell has this long and . . . and fascinating history. Jesus isn't to blame for thinking it up."

"But," Neil said, "doesn't the fact that he uses the hell language imply an endorsement of it?" I was going to protest, but he continued. "Matthew actually has him use the Greek word *Hades* in that famous passage where he says, 'The gates of Hades will not prevail' against the church. Would that mean Jesus is endorsing all of Greek mythology? Or in the little book of Second Peter you can find a reference to Tartarus, straight from Greek mythology, where the angels seem to be identified with the Greek Titans. What do you do with that?"

"I haven't even begun to think about that yet," I said. "I've got enough to deal with just processing this history from outside the Bible. In the meantime, all this historical data causes me other problems, you know, with my whole view of Scripture. I still don't know how to put historical background together with any concept of divine revelation. But we've talked about that before."

I was hoping Neil would offer some insight to help me at this point, but instead, he just gazed out over the majestic view. Once more, sitting on the marble stairs with the columns of the Lincoln Memorial rising above us, he reviewed what he had heard me say about the Mesopotamian, Egyptian, Zoroastrian, and Greek concepts of life after death—for his benefit or for mine, I wasn't sure.

10

THE SCAPEGOAT FACTOR

He led me in among the secret things.

—*Inferno,* III.21

"OK," NEIL SAID, "so the concepts of heaven and hell seem to have been borrowed from other religions—Mesopotamian, Egyptian, Zoroastrian, and Greek—all in the intertestamental period, between the last Old Testament prophets and the coming of Jesus. The Jews have a lot of contact with these people of other cultures and religions during the Exile in Babylon and during the continuing occupation by the Persians, Greeks, and Romans, so it's natural that there would be some amount of syncretism or mixture between the very this-worldly Judaism of the pre-Exilic period and these other-worldly, speculative elements, especially with the Persian religion of Zoroaster. Does that sum it up?"

"Pretty much," I said. "But as you know, not all the Jews accepted these foreign ideas. This was really a shock for me, because I had always thought of the Pharisees of Jesus' day as the conservatives and the Sadducees as the liberals, but apparently this is a case of our reading our own contemporary definitions back into the Gospels. It turns out that the Sadducees were the more conservative Jews who resisted this mixing. They wouldn't accept Persian ideas such as hell, heaven, and angels. For them, a person dies and that's it, with no resurrection. The more liberal or progressive Jews were known as the Pharisees; according to my book here, *Pharisee* means Farsi, or Persian. The Pharisees integrated these Persian-Zoroastrian concepts into their belief system."

Neil cocked his head and turned to me with a slight frown. "Since the Jews felt themselves so different from their neighbors, Daniel, don't you wonder how this kind of Gentile thinking would make its way into the heart of the belief of the Pharisees?" Neil turned to me with a critical look: "I think some people might dispute that meaning of *Pharisee*; I've heard it comes from a Hebrew word meaning 'separated ones.' If your book's analysis is legitimate, it's very significant."

I flipped over to the last few pages I had read in the book and, after refreshing my memory, went on to recount how during the intertestamental period, various Jewish "freedom fighters" arose with Messianic dreams. They sought to throw off the oppressive power of the Roman Empire through violent revolutions. Without exception, these attempted revolutions were brutally crushed, leaving the Jews with a crisis of faith: Why didn't God give victory to these brave, heroic martyrs? Comfort came through a new belief: that the heroic martyrs would be resurrected when the final victory came, led by the Messiah, the Deliverer. On that day of victory, the Day of the Lord, these martyrs would be raised from the grave, not to ascend to heaven but to share in the new post-Roman era of liberation and joy. Eventually, they would presumably die again, this time forever.

"So," I repeated, "this belief in resurrection did not entail eternal life in heaven." I shook my head as my mind rehearsed the facts. It was not a matter of an immaterial soul leaving the body to be with God forever in a timeless "spiritual" state. It was far more earthy: it involved bodies coming back to life to share in the joy of glorious military victory on earth. Nor was it universal—at least not in its initial stages. Not everyone would be raised. Not even all good people would be raised. Only the heroic martyrs would be raised. Gradually, some Jewish thinkers expanded the resurrection to include all good people, so all would share the joy of the Messianic kingdom. And some extended the resurrection to all bad people as well; they would be raised not to joy but to condemnation and retribution for their evil.

"So," I said, "it all comes together in the intertestamental period when many Jews, to greater and lesser degrees, are attracted to a belief in life after death. Since they don't have resources for that in their own religion, they start weaving together elements from the first four foreign threads— the Mesopotamian, the Egyptian, the Zoroastrian or Persian, and the Greco-Roman—with their own key fifth thread: the Messianic. That's it. That's as far as I've gotten."

"I think you're missing something," Neil said. I raised my eyebrows to invite him to continue. "The scapegoat factor. I could probably never prove this, but I'll bet the scapegoat factor comes in here somewhere. It sure helps explain the prevalence of hellfire rhetoric at several other times in history."

"What do you mean by 'scapegoat factor'?" I asked.

Neil replied, "Hellfire language is most popular when people have an enemy they need to vilify, some feared individual or group they need to blame for whatever is wrong with the cosmic order. Anti-Semites have often used the Jews as a scapegoat. Whites have used blacks. Capitalists used Communists, and Communists returned the favor. Protestants and Catholics have used each other; so do the rich and the poor. I think something similar must have been at work in Jesus' day. When Jesus was born, the Jews faced this unanswered question: Why hadn't God given victory to the heroic freedom fighters who sought to overthrow the pagan Romans? Why hadn't the Messiah come to liberate God's people from Rome just as Moses had liberated them from Egypt centuries before? *Why hasn't God saved us, and who's to blame?*

"The Zealots, Herodians, and Essenes—those three parties at the time of Jesus—gave varying answers to these questions," Neil continued. "They chose varying scapegoats, varying 'others' to blame. For Zealots, the problem was cowardice: if enough Jews would just arise to confront the Romans, either the Messiah would suddenly appear to lead them to victory, or they would discover themselves to be the Messiah. Their scapegoats would have been the cowardly Herodians who chose to collaborate with the Evil Empire rather than fight to subvert it. Meanwhile, the Herodians themselves despised this revolutionary talk, knowing it was suicidal. Since the Romans were just too powerful to defy, the Herodians preferred the route of adjustment, adaptation: get along with the Romans, make do, and if you can't beat them, join them. For them, the Zealots would be the dangerous ones—the ones to blame and scapegoat.

"The Essenes were disgusted with both Herodians and Zealots: the whole situation was beyond remedy, so the only faithful path was to withdraw to the wilderness as a righteous elect, a faithful remnant. To hell with all of them!"

"Right," I interrupted, remembering a conversation with Neil about this subject from a few years earlier. "But then there's that fourth party— the Pharisees. 'The reason we are still under Roman domination,' they would have said, 'is that we have too much sin among us. There are too many prostitutes, drunks, and other sinners among us.'"

Neil was getting energized. "Yes! Precisely! And maybe that's the juncture at which these things all seem to come together. Your Mesopotamian and Egyptian and Zoroastrian and Greco-Roman threads supply the idea of an afterlife in hell, and the frustrated Messianic thread supplies the need to create scapegoats. At their convergence, the Pharisees offer this message: the reason we remain under oppression is the sinners among us. If we could simply get these sinners to stop sinning, God would send the Messiah to deliver us from Roman domination. To hell with all sinners!"

"No, Neil," I said, "I don't think they'd say 'to hell with all sinners'; I think they'd say, 'You sinners better repent, or else you'll go to hell.' Right? How else would the Pharisees motivate the sinners to stop sinning?"

"Good point," Neil replied. "First they would threaten sinners with hell. Second, they would extend the reward of resurrection from the heroic martyrs to all good people—*good* meaning those who fulfilled the Pharisees' ideal of good. Finally, they would use the language of hell to accomplish what they felt they needed to accomplish—to frighten sinners enough to repent and change their ways for the good of the nation."

I was troubled by something: "Are you saying that they didn't really believe what they were saying—that they were just using it, maybe the way parents try to use the Santa Claus story so their kids will be nice, not naughty? That doesn't sound . . ."

"Not at all," Neil replied. "I'm not saying that they were being intentionally dishonest, but I don't think parents are being intentionally dishonest either. I think they're trying to get their kids to behave; they're trying to reinforce good behavior and correct bad behavior using the cultural resources at their disposal. That's not dishonest. That's persuasive rhetoric. At least, that's what they'd tell themselves."

"Well, my book didn't get into all this, but it's an interesting theory. It sounds like a crime scene, and you've just given a motive for the crime. The Pharisees need a scapegoat—the tax collectors and prostitutes and such—and so the rhetoric of hell gives them a powerful stick with which to threaten the sinners into better behavior. Maybe it works kind of like the death penalty, as a deterrent."

Neil's gloved hand went up slightly to show disagreement: "Well, the death penalty doesn't actually work as a deterrent, but your point is still valid. So picture it. Into this scenario, Jesus came. He didn't create the beliefs about hell promoted by the Pharisees and embraced by many of the common people, and he didn't endorse them either. This is exactly what I tried to tell you a few years ago, Daniel, but I don't think you were ready to hear it. I didn't know all these details, but this is the basic line of thinking I've held for years."

I nodded. He was right. I had remembered his hinting at some of this in the past, but it never clicked. Now, at that moment, as I was beginning to shiver a bit on the frigid steps of the Lincoln Memorial, the epiphany hit me: "So whether or not Jesus endorses the idea of hell, when the Pharisees use hell to threaten sinners to fly right, Jesus takes it and kind of turns it back on them, doesn't he?"

Neil smiled and nodded: "He took their doctrine of hell and deconstructed it. He was like a practitioner of jiu jitsu—he turned the force of the argument back on the heads of the Pharisees. It's marvelous, Daniel! But let me ask you a question: What's his purpose? What does Jesus accomplish by doing this? What's his motive?"

I thought for a minute and then offered this: "Well, first, I guess he's trying to protect the scapegoats themselves. So he shows that they have dignity and value by eating with them, which is sure to make the Pharisees' blood boil! And just a minute—because I know there's more—yes, maybe he was trying to alter their definition of what goodness or righteousness is. For the Pharisees, *good* meant disdaining, stigmatizing, excluding, and avoiding sinners. For Jesus, *good* meant forgiving sinners and reconciling them to the community. For the Pharisees, *good* meant explaining why the poor and sick deserved to be poor and sick and blaming scapegoats for the bad status quo. For Jesus, *good* meant helping the poor and healing the sick and seeking through love to transform the status quo. So for Jesus, *good* is always compassionate and . . ."

Neil interrupted, "As soon as you say that, I think about Jesus' words in the Sermon on the Mount, where he quotes *Leviticus* and says, 'Be perfect as your Father in heaven is perfect.' Jesus has just told them to love their enemies, and he has said how God blesses the good and evil alike with rain. It's in that context that he says be perfect as your Father in heaven is perfect . . ."

Now I interrupted. "You mean, Jesus is saying, 'Your Father in heaven has a compassionate perfection. Mercy is part of God's justice. Kindness is part of God's righteousness. But the righteousness of you Pharisees is cold, exacting, heartless, merciless.' Wow. I think I'm getting it. So Jesus is telling them that their perfection isn't perfect and needs improvement? They have an imperfect perfection? Wow! He's saying their merciless righteousness is actually out of sync with the merciful righteousness of God. So he turns their concept of hell back on their own heads. Neil, that's stunning! That makes the whole Sermon on the Mount come together for me. But wait a minute . . ."

I was cold, so maybe I was just shivering, but I think it may have been a chill of excitement, or maybe dread, that came over me at that instant.

BETTER THAN WE REALIZED

Thee it behoves to take another road.

—*Inferno,* I.91

"NEIL, WE CHRISTIANS USE the whole doctrine of hell exactly as the Pharisees did! We're playing on the wrong side! Our concept of righteousness is like theirs—it's like we've missed Jesus' whole point!"

"Well, my friend," Neil said, turning to me, "I think you're finally getting it." Then he began fishing around in his waist-pack, and a mischievous smile formed on his face. "Actually, I think some congratulations are in order," he said with a wink and a wry smile. "I think you may be in danger of becoming a radical follower of Jesus." Then he pulled out two cigars. "Can we celebrate?"

I remembered a few years earlier, the first time Neil got me to drink a beer—appropriately named Pete's Wicked Ale. Now he was further corrupting me with a cigar. "This is really too good a cigar to share with someone who can't appreciate it," he said. "It's Cuban, hand-rolled . . . smell it!" I liked the smell but suspected that cigars would turn out like most coffee—their taste could never quite match the aroma. I let him light it and tried to puff as gingerly as possible, a little afraid I might get sick or else start choking and embarrass myself.

If the people of Potomac Community Church could have seen me sitting on the steps of the Lincoln Memorial holding a cigar in my mouth as Neil lit it, they would have been sure their worst suspicions about me were true. Just twenty-four hours earlier, they had gathered for their worship service in all dignity and sincerity, and here I was, smoking—or pretending to smoke, since I was completely inexperienced—a Cuban cigar with a big black Jamaican who couldn't stop laughing and slapping me on the back and telling me I was finally following Jesus into the deep end of the pool. He laughed all the harder when I did in fact start choking and coughing on the cigar smoke, but as soon as I got control of myself, I started laughing too. It was embarrassing and glorious, in a strange sort of way.

"Come on," Neil said, after he finished his cigar and gave up trying to relight mine. "Let's go in and see Abe. After all, it's Presidents' Day." We moved up the stairs, passed between the massive columns, and paused in front of the huge statue, feeling the grandeur and pain of Lincoln's life, captured so powerfully by the whole monument. After a few silent moments, we moved to our right, to the wall on which Lincoln's second inaugural address is inscribed. Neil leaned over and down and spoke to me quietly. "In the weeks leading up Lincoln's second inauguration, the weather was terrible. It rained and rained, and back then, Pennsylvania Avenue wasn't paved, so the street was all cold mud and icy puddles. Thousands of people gathered in the mud to hear Lincoln's speech—just behind us, in front of the Capitol. Of course, the whole scene is even more poignant when you realize that Lincoln would be dead in less than a month. Daniel, would you do the honors? The speech really must be read aloud."

So I read, softly at first, but soon a little circle of people moved closer to listen to me read, so I increased my volume:

> Fellow-Countrymen: At this second appearing to take the oath of the Presidential office there is less occasion for an extended address than there was at the first. Then a statement somewhat in detail of a course to be pursued seemed fitting and proper. Now, at the expiration of four years, during which public declarations have been constantly called forth on every point and phase of the great contest which still absorbs the attention and engrosses the energies of the nation, little that is new could be presented. The progress of our arms, upon which all else chiefly depends, is as well known to the public as to myself, and it is, I trust, reasonably satisfactory and encouraging to all. With high hope for the future, no prediction in regard to it is ventured.
>
> On the occasion corresponding to this four years ago all thoughts were anxiously directed to an impending civil war. All dreaded it, all sought to avert it. While the inaugural address was being delivered from this place, devoted altogether to saving the Union without war, urgent agents were in the city seeking to destroy it without war—seeking to

dissolve the Union and divide effects by negotiation. Both parties deprecated war, but one of them would make war rather than let the nation survive, and the other would accept war rather than let it perish, and the war came.

"That's striking, isn't it?" Neil interrupted. "Rather than demonizing the South, he portrays them as people who deprecated war. No scapegoating there. His goal is reconciliation, not revenge."

One-eighth of the whole population were colored slaves, not distributed generally over the Union, but localized in the southern part of it. These slaves constituted a peculiar and powerful interest. All knew that this interest was somehow the cause of the war. To strengthen, perpetuate, and extend this interest was the object for which the insurgents would rend the Union even by war, while the Government claimed no right to do more than to restrict the territorial enlargement of it. Neither party expected for the war the magnitude or the duration which it has already attained. Neither anticipated that the cause of the conflict might cease with or even before the conflict itself should cease. Each looked for an easier triumph, and a result less fundamental and astounding. Both read the same Bible and pray to the same God, and each invokes His aid against the other. It may seem strange that any men should dare to ask a just God's assistance in wringing their bread from the sweat of other men's faces, but let us judge not, that we be not judged. The prayers of both could not be answered. That of neither has been answered fully.

Neil interrupted again: "What a move! Lincoln does the very opposite of what we might expect. He takes the way of Christ, the way of reconciliation. He seeks to put the North and South on the same level. He even portrays slavery not as a moral outrage, which he knew it was, but as the extension of a financial interest, something Yankee businessmen could understand. He realizes that once slavery is defeated, the next enemy to the Union might be northern arrogance." When Neil nodded to me to continue reading, suddenly, unexpectedly, I felt somewhat overcome with emotion, and I asked Neil if he'd pick up instead. The little crowd—just seven or eight people—gathered in a little closer around us. Perhaps they took Neil and me for tour guides of some sort. He read with his beautiful accent in full force:

The Almighty has His own purposes. "Woe unto the world because of offenses; for it must needs be that offenses come, but woe to that man by whom the offense cometh." If we shall suppose that American slav-

ery is one of those offenses which, in the providence of God, must
needs come, but which, having continued through His appointed time,
He now wills to remove, and that He gives to both North and South
this terrible war as the woe due to those by whom the offense came,
shall we discern therein any departure from those divine attributes
which the believers in a living God always ascribe to Him? Fondly do
we hope, fervently do we pray, that this mighty scourge of war may
speedily pass away. Yet, if God wills that it continue until all the wealth
piled by the bondsman's two hundred and fifty years of unrequited toil
shall be sunk, and until every drop of blood drawn with the lash shall
be paid by another drawn with the sword, as was said three thousand
years ago, so still it must be said "the judgments of the Lord are true
and righteous altogether."

Neil looked across our little impromptu group. "This is what makes
Lincoln so brilliant to me. His ultimate concern is neither his presidency
nor the American national interest. His ultimate concern is . . . justice,
God's justice, which puts everyone on level ground. We could only wish
that all presidents—ah, well, I'll keep reading before I insult anyone . . ."
As a few more people drifted in to join our little group, Neil completed
the speech in a booming bass voice that turned the empty space of the
memorial into a resonating chamber.

With malice toward none, with charity for all, with firmness in the
right as God gives us to see the right, let us strive on to finish the work
we are in, to bind up the nation's wounds, to care for him who shall
have borne the battle and for his widow and his orphan, to do all which
may achieve and cherish a just and lasting peace among ourselves and
with all nations.

Our little circle spontaneously applauded, perhaps for Neil's reading
but surely more for Lincoln's "just and lasting peace among ourselves and
with all nations." Suddenly a guard rushed over and pointed to a sign that
said QUIET PLEASE, and our ephemeral community quickly dispersed after
a few handshakes and thank-you's. Most memorably, a small Japanese
man shook our hands and said to us, full of both accent and emotion,
"Thank you so many times for this eloquent oration. These few seconds
climb to the highest point of my visit to your country. Thank you. Thank
you for this priority. So much thank you's."

We left the memorial and walked down the grand steps, pausing once to
imagine the crowd gathered in the mud to hear Lincoln as we looked east
to the Capitol. As we continued walking, Neil added this: "Could God's

response to sinners be any less magnanimous than Lincoln's response to the South? Or will God say, at the end of all things, 'with malice toward many and charity to a few'?"

This is exactly the kind of thing that often bothered me about Neil: he had a tendency to push a point just a little too hard. Yet on this cold winter day, I couldn't quarrel with him. As we walked down the remaining marble stairway and crossed the road, a thought arose in my mind seemingly from nowhere, and the thought seized me so that for several minutes, I couldn't speak: *No thought of God that you can ever have is too good. Nothing about God is too good to be true. You are safe when your thoughts of God grow greater. Don't be afraid.*

"You're very pensive, Dan," Neil said as we walked toward the Holocaust Museum. "What's on your mind?" I hadn't planned to tell him about my late-night phone call from Jess, about my surprise at feeling of pride when she stood up against the very doctrine of hell that I had been taught and had in fact taught others—albeit as gently as I could—for all these years. But the story poured out.

"Jess plays theology just as she played soccer—with lots of spunk! She keeps the goal in mind and drives right for it." Neil said.

I replied, "But how will we put it all back together, Neil? If we've been confused—so confused, so many of us, for so long—how will we recover? You know how pastors are treated when they question the standard exclusivist position on hell."

Oddly, Neil now put into words almost the very thoughts that had come to me descending the steps of the Lincoln Memorial. "We have to tell people the good news," he said, "the good news that God is even better than we thought, that the gospel is better than we realized. That their thoughts of God have been too small, too unworthy . . . that the truly good news is bigger and better and more powerful than the conventional news they've been believing and preaching. And, " he added with a wink, "we've got to tell them that they were right to be worried about universalism."

"But just a minute," I replied. "I thought . . . I thought that's what you've been talking about. You've lost me."

"Daniel, I agree with you. Exclusivism isn't good enough. Inclusivism isn't good enough. But universalism isn't good enough either. It's too easy. The good news is even better than that!" I looked completely baffled, so he stopped in the middle of the sidewalk, and as others—tourists, government workers, a few homeless folk—passed us on either side, Neil finally gave me a straight answer to the hell question, or something like a straight answer.

SOMETHING LIKE A STRAIGHT ANSWER

And in this manner busied did we leave them.

—*Inferno,* XXII.151

I TURNED TO FACE NEIL, whose back was to the oncoming pedestrians. His girth made it necessary for them to walk onto the snow-covered grass on either side of the sidewalk as he talked. A few times, his broad gesticulations almost slapped a passerby in the face. It was hard for me to concentrate with people swerving by us to the left and right, with the sound of crunching ice and snow punctuating our conversation, but Neil was completely focused: "The problem with universalism is not just the answer it provides. True, its answer creates problems—but so do the alternative answers. The problem is the question it seeks to answer. The question assumes that the purpose of the gospel is to get individual souls into heaven after they die. No matter how good your answer is, it's not good enough if you're asking the wrong question."

"And the right question would be . . . ?" I countered.

"Not just how individual souls will be saved but instead how the world will be saved. When I say 'saved,' I mean not just from hell, and not just from God's wrath either. After all, God's wrath is a good thing, a saving thing. No, Daniel, the gospel is about how the world will be saved from human sin and all that goes with it—human greed, human lust, human pride, human oppression, human hypocrisy and dishonesty, human violence and racism, human chauvinism, human injustice. It's answering the question, How will humanity be saved from humanity? How will earth be saved from evil that springs from within human individuals and human groups?" Neil's arms were waving so wildly that I had to reach over and touch his shoulder so he wouldn't hit a woman who was walking up behind him, about to pass on his left.

"Hold on, hold on!" I interrupted. "You're going way too fast for me. What did you mean that God's wrath is a saving thing? A lot of people would say that God's wrath is what puts us in peril."

"Maybe that's because you're a white male, my friend," he said with something like irony, "and all that you represent is put in peril by God's wrath." Just then a tall white guy wrapped up in an expensive camel-hair overcoat walked by, heard what Neil said, and gave us both a strange look. Neil continued: "All of the oppressed people of the world are praying, 'God, how long? How long will you restrain your wrath? When will you intervene and cause the masters to let the slaves go free? When will you intervene and pour out your fury on the careless wealthy colonizers and dominators who profit'—how did Lincoln say it?—'by wringing their bread from the sweat of other men's faces?' You could say that God's wrath is the emotion that puts God into motion, intervening against oppressors and their injustice. God's wrath is God's justice in action. God's compassion is the counterpart—it's God's response to those who suffer from the abuses of power of the unjust. Only the oppressors fear God's justice. The oppressed pray for it to come. In fact, when they pray, 'Your kingdom come,' they are in part praying for God's just wrath to intervene and bring them liberation."

"No offense, Neil," I said, "but I don't think white male bashing is all that helpful in this whole thing."

"I don't mean to bash. As Lincoln said, quoting our Lord, we must not judge. I shouldn't have said it that way. But the coming of the wrath of God on those who are careless about injustice should prompt everyone to ask this question: Which side are we on? Are we on the side of God's justice, or are we on the side of human oppression and sin? Are we welcoming God's judgment, or are we seeking to avoid it?"

"Hold on again, Neil," I interrupted. "Let me see if I understand you. You're saying that God's wrath and God's judgment are God's feelings and response to human injustice and evil. So we should welcome God's justice when . . ."

"Remember what Jesus said?" Neil replied, cutting me off in midsentence. "Seek first God's kingdom and *righteousness*—which means God's justice. Don't seek to avoid it. Seek it! Want it to come! It's what we're praying when Jesus teaches us to pray—your kingdom come, your will be done on earth. We're praying for God's justice to break in. We're saying, 'God, don't just stand there feeling angry! Intervene! Express your anger by exposing the oppressor and the hypocrite! Like a mother seeing her child get teased or pushed around by the playground bully—lose your cool, God! Intervene! Enough is enough! Save your people from oppression!' That's what Jesus teaches us to pray!"

People continued to pass by. I didn't know what to say, but it seemed strange to just be standing there in silence, so I said, "I need some time to process this. Where does hell fit in then? Is there such a thing?"

Now Neil leaned down, his taller frame bending so that his eyes met mine. "Daniel!" He was almost shouting: "That's not the point! Can't you see? That's not the point. The point isn't hell: the point is justice! The point is God's will! Just as we've been saying, over and over—Jesus doesn't invent the idea of hell. It evolves—I know you hate that word, but it's the best word—it *evolves* over time; it's constructed, as all human ideas are, through the interaction of religions and cultures as we were talking about earlier. The point is not whether there is a hell: the point is God's justice! The point isn't whether Jesus—by using the language of the construction—confirms it. The point is, for what purpose does he use the language? What's his point in working with the construction?"

At this moment, an elderly black woman stopped as she walked by on my left, and seeing me being yelled at—or nearly yelled at—by a tall black man, she looked at me and said, "Are you OK, young man? Is everything OK here?"

Realizing how menacing he must have looked, Neil patted the woman on the shoulder and with a laugh said, "God bless you, sister. I'm just preaching to my friend here. I'm just trying to put the fear of God in him. I'm trying to help him repent."

A smile slowly appeared on her face, and she looked at me and said, "Are you OK with that?" And I smiled and said yes, that I was fine with it, that I needed a lot of repentance, and she said, "Well, then, boys, praise the Lord! But don't overdo it!" and she walked on.

"Neil," I said, "are you saying that Jesus was wrong—wrong about hell? I mean, even if you're saying he uses it to make a valid point, it still sounds pretty serious to say he was wrong, literally, I mean."

"Ah, the *literals* versus the *liberals*!" he replied, stretching out the syllables of both words. "Daniel, you know my last degree was in science. Can I use an analogy to science?" I nodded, and he continued: "Science is all about models. For example, we have the Bohr model of the atom, which pictures the atom as little billiard balls called protons and neutrons with little electrons circling them like marbles. We use those models—even though we know they aren't literally true."

"Not literally true?" I asked.

"I know it's what you were taught, but that was so twentieth-century!" he replied with a laugh. "Picturing protons, neutrons, and electrons as little solid balls is—we know this—literally false. Yet we use the model because it helps us understand and picture what's happening."

"But if you know the model is false, why don't you use a better model?"

"Well, we do. We use all kinds of mathematical models. But nobody fully understands the realities depicted by the models, even the people who use them." Now I was completely baffled, but Neil went on: "That's the purpose of a model. A model helps us work with a mystery. The fact is, we don't know what the true model is. In fact, there may not be one that human minds can understand. For example, we have a theory called string theory that tries to get beyond the billiard ball model. But it's just a model too—strings are just another metaphor, just another analogy, working with the metaphor of threads and fabrics rather than marbles and billiard balls. Even if we try to move beyond strings and talk about matter being patterns of distortion in the fabric of space and time, we're creating more visual images of waves moving in water or of wrinkles in a blanket—still more models that we know aren't *lit-er-al-ly* true."

"So basically," I said, "you're lying. Science is lying. And that makes it OK for Jesus to be lying." I was being provocative, but I hoped not in an unhelpful way. In fact, the thought struck me that this was exactly the sort of thing Neil himself might say to move a conversation along.

"No, Dan, we're not lying. We're telling the truth in the very best way that we can at this point. What more can anyone ask? We realize that a model can be valid—it can be the very best we have to offer, it can be truth-depicting and truth-conveying—even when it's not literally true. That insight is what a school of philosophy called *critical realism* is about: it's saying, look, we need to be critical and realize that language is about models, symbols, metaphors. We need to realize that there is some distance between the symbols and the realities they represent. But that doesn't mean we give up language, and it certainly doesn't mean we stop trying to describe reality or pursue truth. No, it means we acknowledge that all human beings, as Paul said it, 'know in part.' We even prophesy in part, he says—which means that even when God speaks directly to us and we speak boldly for God, we still see through a glass darkly; we aren't capable—not yet anyway—of knowing as God knows. In a sense, whether we're scientists speaking of atoms or theologians speaking of God and God's kingdom, we're using poetry—metaphors, models. We're speaking in parables. We're reaching the unknown through the known. What other option do we have?"

A large group of Asian students, all appearing to be about ten years old and wearing school uniforms under winter coats, streamed around us, their laughing and talking momentarily growing silent as they went by and then resuming a few paces later.

"Dan—I've been trying to help you see this for years. Are you getting it? Am I making any sense?"

I nodded. "Actually, a little, I think. Something you just said, even though you've said it several times before—that Jesus isn't necessarily endorsing the whole construction of hell by using the language but that he's using a truth-depicting model—that helps me. Obviously, if Jesus says the sun rises and sets, that doesn't mean he's endorsing the old Ptolemaic model of the universe." Neil interrupted to remind me that Ptolemy came after Christ but affirmed my point as valid anyway and asked me to continue. "OK, so if Jesus talks about the four corners of the earth, it doesn't mean he is endorsing a flat-earth geography. So if he uses the language of hell, it doesn't necessarily follow that he's endorsing the Zoroastrian model or the Egyptian or Mesopotamian or Greek model. But then the question is, just as you were saying, how does he use the language? What is his point? And you're saying . . . well, I'm still not completely sure what you're saying. I thought I had it a few minutes ago, but now its getting foggy. It's slipping through my fingers." Now over Neil's shoulder I saw another group of Asian students approaching, also in uniforms, also about ten years old. "Come on, let's get out of these people's way." I motioned to a coffee shop just down the street. "Why don't we go in and sit down? I'm pretty cold." My feet were completely numb, but worse, I felt tense all over—partly from our conversation, partly from the cold, and partly because I needed a restroom.

Neil nudged a finger between the cuff of his coat and the edge of his glove to see his watch. "I'm just worried that we won't have enough time in the museum if we stop. Let's make it fast, OK?"

"Sure," I said, "but we can't lose this train of thought. This is the core of what I need right now. How do you see Jesus working with hell? How do you see him using it to make a point about God's righteousness—or God's justice, or God's kingdom?"

13

END IN EMBRACE?

What I beheld seemed unto me a smile
Of the universe . . .

—*Paradiso*, XXVII.4–5

WE CAME TO THE COFFEE SHOP, entered, and found a seat near a heating vent. I went to the men's room, and when I returned, Neil was ordering two large vanilla lattes from a spunky server named Nick. "I feel better," I said, getting settled. "Let's pick up where we left off outside."

Neil leaned back in his chair. "Let me try to say it once as clearly as I can, but then let's get specific and think about concrete examples. OK?" I nodded and he took a deep breath and said, "OK. The Pharisees used hell to threaten sinners and other undesirables and mark them as the excluded out-group, hated by God. Their rhetorical use of hell made clear that God's righteousness was severe and merciless toward the undeserving. Jesus turned their rhetoric upside down and inside out and used hell to threaten those who excluded sinners and other undesirables, showing that God's righteousness was compassionate and merciful, that God's kingdom welcomed the undeserving, that for God, there was no out-group."

I nodding, assuming that he was finished, but then he added, "As you said back on the monument steps, a lot of Christians today use hell to threaten all non-Christians and put them in the excluded out-group, and you can decide which pattern that conforms to most."

"Gosh," I said, shaking my head. "I wish Jess were here to hear this. This is exactly what she needs."

"I thought you said this is what you needed. Why do you mention Jess?" my friend asked.

I thought for a few seconds. "Of course, I need to talk this through—but I feel I especially need it to help her. Look, Neil, I'm a Christian. It really shakes me to think that I could have been so misguided or uninformed about so much, but even so, my roots go pretty deep. But for Jess and for Kincaid, if they don't get this hell thing worked out, they're never even going to send down roots. They're going to become . . ."

Neil finished the sentence: " . . . like the millions of others, young and old, who have given up on Christianity because our way of talking about hell sounds absolutely wacky. 'God loves you and has a wonderful plan for your life,' we say, 'and he'll fry your butt in hell forever unless you do or believe the right thing.' 'God is a loving father,' we say, 'but he'll treat you with a cruelty that no human father has ever been guilty of—eternal conscious torture.' No wonder Christianity—or at least that version of it—is a dying religion in so many places in the world."

Nick arrived with our lattes. We both cupped our hands around the bright orange mugs. I took a small sip: "But Neil, isn't it that hellfire-and-brimstone version of Christianity that's growing so quickly in Africa and Latin America? Maybe hell causes problems for some people, but it seems to offer something of value to other people."

"Good point," Neil said. "What might that value be?"

"Security," I said. "Confidence that the universe has some moral order. Motivation to do good. Maybe a healthy sense of fear is good. I mean—the opposite, a lack of concern about consequences, certainly seems to be part of the insanity of our world. Maybe some people need the language of hell, and deconstructing it would actually weaken the Christian faith for them."

Neil thought for a minute before responding. "Ah, but here's the problem: if the message of Christianity really sinks in, if the vision of God that we get through Jesus takes root, it's only a matter of time until—until the deconstruction begins."

"You're saying that Jesus inevitably deconstructs hell? He uses the language, but the way he uses it sows the seeds for its own demise and replacement?" I asked.

"That's exactly what happened. By the end of the second century, Origen clearly believes that hell isn't the last word. Some friends of mine have found quotes from a lot of the early church fathers that say similar things—Clement, Gregory of Nazianzus, Gregory of Nyssa, even Jerome. Besides, isn't that what Jesus does with the Law of Moses? Doesn't he replace—or maybe *fulfill* is the better word—the Law of Moses with the New Commandment, the Great Commandment to love? I'm saying that Jesus similarly fulfills the language of hell—or at least he sows the seeds of its fulfillment."

Our conversation was temporarily silenced. I think we were both a bit overwhelmed.

Nick bounced by and asked if we needed anything. Neil ordered another latte, then turned back to me. "You're right to want to test what we're saying by Scripture, so let's get specific. But we're going to have to work from memory since we don't have a New Testament in front of us. How about this: why don't you bring up a place where Jesus talks about hell, and I'll do my best to explain it in the terms we're talking about."

"All right," I said. "What do you make of the passage where Jesus says that anyone who calls his brother a fool will be liable to the fires of hell?"

"Ah, from the Sermon on the Mount," Neil said, "one of the most misunderstood passages in the New Testament, the passage people think is trying to answer how to go to heaven when it's really trying to picture how Jesus' concept of earthly justice and righteousness differs from the Pharisees'. A perfect place to start!

"Jesus has just said that the justice of his kingdom surpasses the justice of the religious leaders of his day, and he launches into a series of examples, including this one. That's his point, Daniel: the Pharisees talk a lot about righteousness, but God's goal is true justice and peace, a state of reconciliation so profound that people won't call one another 'idiot' or 'blockhead' anymore, they'll stop judging one another, and they'll do for others as they would have done for them. 'Idiot' and 'blockhead' are exactly the sort of judgmental things the Pharisees might feel completely justified in saying about other people, so Jesus turns their language back on them. As I recall, he also uses the imagery of being called before the Sanhedrin in the same passage. It's hell in one instance and a human court in another. If you have to take hell absolutely literally, do you also believe people will one day be called before a reconstituted Sanhedrin? Isn't it clear that he's using both hell and the Sanhedrin to convey accountability?"

"Well, what about later in the Sermon on the Mount, when he says it's better to cut off your right hand or lose your right eye than be cast into hell?" I asked.

Neil winked. "Well, let me ask you this: If you want to take that verse completely literally, why do you still have two hands and two eyes? I'm guessing you've lusted a few times in your life; if you want to be so literal, why didn't you take out a steak knife and cut off your . . ."

"OK, OK," I said. "What about when Jesus says that the road to heaven is narrow and the road to hell is broad? Wouldn't that imply, not only that hell is real, but also that most people go there?"

Just then, Nick returned with Neil's second orange mug; I wasn't half finished with my first yet. Neil took a long sip: "That's so good, and just the right temperature. Where were we? Oh, the narrow road. As I recall, Jesus doesn't say the road to hell is broad: he says broad is the road to *destruction*. That's one of the things you'll have to be more careful about. I've noticed that a lot of people tend to take anything negative—destruction, condemnation, judgment—and assume it all means hell. And that reminds me: I don't think he says the road to heaven is narrow: it's the road to *life* he's talking about."

I looked confused, and Neil responded before I could form a question. "Daniel, Jesus is concerned about one central thing—the Kingdom of God. Matthew calls it the Kingdom of Heaven, but as we've discussed before, that doesn't mean 'heaven after you die.' It's another way of saying Kingdom of God. John decides that the language of kingdom will be problematic for his unique audience, so he uses the words *life* or *life to the full* to say the same thing. And from the look of things, when you consider how many people make a mess of their lives, Jesus was right: not many find that kind of life. Add to that the political dimension that's always there in the gospel but seldom recognized—you know, Jesus is warning the people that it's very easy to get into trouble with the Romans, which may be the destruction that the broad road leads to, and—" At that moment, our server passed behind Neil just as another customer pushed his chair back. Nick tripped, and his whole tray of food crashed to the floor. Neil got down on his knees and helped him pick up the broken glass. Another server rushed over with a mop and tray, and Neil came back to his seat.

I got us back on topic but wished later on that I had heard Neil out on the political angle he had been exploring. "Neil, you were talking about life meaning life to the full, not life after death in heaven, but doesn't Jesus say *eternal* life? Wouldn't that mean—"

"I think the phrase would better be translated *life of the ages*," Neil said. "I think that Jesus means life that's above the biological level of respiration, reproduction, circulation, digestion, elimination—above the mundane level of survival, self-interest, and short-term gratification. He means life that participates in the grand creative and healing work of God across the ages—which is the same thing as the Kingdom of God. And when the apostles talk about walking in the light or walking in love or walking in the Spirit, they're saying the same thing: living in this new way, living in this new reality, moving in the Kingdom of God step by step. If the scientists have to use models to talk about creation, as we were saying before, how much more when we speak of the Creator and spiritual realities? Again, we have no choice but to use images, metaphors, similes, models. But these different images—life to the full, kingdom, walking, light—are all ways of talking about the same realities, and for Jesus, it comes back again and again to the Kingdom of God. Now I think that all these images talk about a kind of life that doesn't end in death, so I'm not in any way denying life beyond death. I'm just trying to keep our focus on what I believe Jesus was focused on."

I didn't want to get diverted from our main train of thought, so I asked, "What about the places where Jesus talks about being thrown outside into darkness, where there is weeping and gnashing of teeth?"

Neil nodded. "He also speaks of being thrown into Gehenna, which was a garbage dump with a terrible reputation where carcasses were cremated along with garbage. In fact, one of the main words translated as *hell* in the New Testament is that word *Gehenna*. Does that mean that people will very literally be deposited in that trash dump outside Jerusalem? And he talks about a place where worms don't die—a place of perpetual decay, I guess you'd say. Do you believe in literal eternal worms? Why be literal in one place and not another? Besides, all these images can't be taken literally at the same time—I mean, you can't have literal fire and darkness, right? So don't they all suggest waste, decay, regret, and sorrow? Isn't that what anyone would feel if he spent his whole life on accumulating possessions or wealth or knowledge or power but missed out on life to the full in the Kingdom of God? He would have wasted his life! He would have failed to become the glorious person he could have become and instead become something crabby and cramped and ingrown and dark and shabby and selfish. Wouldn't that make you weep and gnash your teeth? Isn't a garbage dump the perfect imagery to use for that kind of waste? It sounds to me like hell is one image Jesus uses among many others."

"What about those parables Jesus tells where weeds or fruitless branches are thrown into the fire?" I asked.

Neil replied, "They're all telling us that deception and false appearances will go up in smoke. The truth will be told. That's what judgment means: before the just judge, the truth comes out. Hypocrisy and fraud are uncovered, burned away. So a weed will be shown for what it is. A fruitless branch will be shown for what it is. Everything that's worthless or fruitless will be exposed as worthless, and everything that's worthwhile and fruitful will be celebrated, rewarded, saved. The point of all this, I think, is that Jesus wants us not just to avoid being bad; more, he wants us to avoid being fruitless."

"But it all sounds so final. Fire, burning," I protested. "It sounds more serious than just being judged."

Neil reached over, grabbed my arm, and spoke in a kind of fierce whisper: "Do you hear what you're saying, man?" He seemed as intense as I'd ever seen him—I reared back, as though from the heat of a fire. "What could be more serious than standing in front of your Creator—the Creator of the universe—and finding out that you had wasted your life, squandered your inheritance, caused others pain and sorrow, worked against the good plans and desires of God? What could be more serious than that? To have to face the real, eternal, unavoidable, absolute, naked truth about yourself, what you've done, what you've become?"

Neil withdrew his hand, and we sat silently for a few moments after that until a story came to mind that I decided to share with Neil. "You make me think of something that happened to the twins when they were about eight years old. They were out in the woods behind their elementary school one afternoon when they came upon an old abandoned couch and a bunch of other stuff somebody had dumped at the end of a dirt road. They were picking through it, and Cory found a half-full can of lighter fluid. It turned out that Trent found an old cigarette lighter. They decided to see what would happen if they drenched the old couch in lighter fluid and then set it on fire."

"Oh, boy," Neil said. "I can see what's coming. A kind of hellfire, eh?"

"It hadn't rained for a while, so in an instant, the whole couch was ablaze. Then the fire spread to the dry leaves around the couch, and pretty soon, there was a major forest fire in the making. The boys were terrified. They ran to the school and told a janitor, who called 911. Then they ran home. I'll never forget when they got in the door."

"Did they confess everything?" he asked.

"No, they couldn't even talk. They were so exhausted from running and so upset about what they'd done, they just burst out crying. They both—literally—fell on the floor and wailed. Cory was pounding on the floor with his fists. It was so pathetic—now I can laugh about it, but at the moment, I thought they'd seen someone killed or something. It took me a few minutes to calm them down—I think Carol was out somewhere with Jess, so I'm glad I was home. Anyway, when they could talk, they told me what they'd done. I put them in the car and drove down the dirt road to where the fire was. The firemen had just gotten the fire under control. I made the boys tell the firemen what they'd done. Poor Trent was shaking like a leaf, so Cory did the talking."

Neil asked, "Did you punish them?"

I shook my head. "I couldn't. They felt so terrible that there was nothing I could do to make them feel worse. When we got home, I took them up in my bedroom and sat them on my bed. Then I just stood in front of them and stared at them for the longest time. I couldn't think of anything to say, so I just stood there, and they just sat there, but somehow I think everything that was supposed to happen happened in the silence. Finally, I asked them if they ever wanted something like this to happen again. Then they burst out crying again and jumped off the bed and hugged me."

"That was judgment par excellence," Neil said. "They saw the truth. They faced it. And it changed them forever. Imagine what it means for people to stand before God . . . in the presence of truth. Nothing could be more serious than that. Compared to that, fire and brimstone are . . ."

"Mere metaphors," I concluded. "Mere word pictures to help us imagine what it would feel like to come clean, to face the truth, to be found out, in the presence of God. All right. I see what you mean," I said. "Nothing could be more serious than that." Neil waved our server over and handed him a credit card.

Nick returned with the credit card slip, and Neil spoke as he signed it: "I guess the question is whether God's story can end in an embrace, like your story with your boys did." I didn't answer. We bundled up and made our way outside.

After about five minutes of brisk walking, Neil broke the silence. "You know, Daniel, I've been running through Jesus' parables in my mind as we've been walking. I think it's notable how many of them end with something other than hell or outer darkness or anything like that."

"Like what?" I asked.

"Sometimes the bad guys are simply destroyed—like the vineyard employees who killed the vineyard owner's son. Sometimes what the bad guys have is taken and given away to the good guys. Sometimes a bad person simply suffers the consequences of his bad decisions—like the man who built his house on sand. Sometimes the consequence is that Jesus is ashamed of the person. Sometimes the bad person is punished or has to pay back a debt. I remember one place where it specifically says that a bad servant will be cut into pieces, which I've never heard anyone take literally. Another time, people who snubbed an invitation to a big banquet simply missed the fun."

"What's your point?" I asked.

"Just that the language of hell isn't the only end to the stories. It's one option Jesus uses among many others to give his parables a shocking choice between consequences, which reinforces my point."

"Which is . . . ?" I asked, still not satisfied.

"Let me try one more time. My point is that hell itself isn't the point. The point is the purpose for which Jesus uses the language of hell, or whatever other imagery he uses to convey the negative consequences of rejecting God's way. The point is that we can let Jesus' strong language arrest us so that we repent—we rethink our current path and choose a better alternative. Or we can distrust Jesus and keep going on our merry way. That reminds me—have you ever heard of rhetorical hermeneutics?" Neil asked.

"Can't say that I have. What's that?"

"It's an approach to Scripture that among other things tells us that we normally pay too much attention to what the writers are *saying* and not enough to what they're *doing*. Rhetorical interpretation would ask, 'What is Jesus trying to do by using the language of hell, plus all these other negative outcomes—missing the party, having to repay a debt, being cut to pieces, being sent into the darkness outside, whatever?'"

We had reached the Holocaust Museum and were entering the front doors as I asked, "Well? What *is* he trying to do?"

There was a hush as we stood in the lobby, waiting to pass through the security screening station. Neil glanced at me as he emptied his pockets for the screening: "He's trying to get us to repent so that places like this will no longer need to be built."

14

PIANO LESSONS AND
LUMPY HANDS

Such pity is in my heart.

—*Inferno*, XIII.84

I HAD NEVER VISITED the Holocaust Museum before. I will probably never visit it again, although I urge everyone to visit it once. It truly is a once-in-a-lifetime experience. I entered with my head already spinning from my intense conversation with Neil.

We got our free tickets for the permanent exhibit from a short sixty-something lady named Shirley. "Your tickets will allow you to enter in forty-five minutes," she explained. "We use this ticket system to manage the crowds. We want people to get all they can from the exhibit without rushing and crowding, so we limit the number of people inside at any one time. There are some other exhibits here that you can enjoy—well, that's not quite the right word for it, but you know what I mean—until the entrance time printed here on your ticket." Neil suggested we begin with an exhibit on eugenics.

Four memories stay with me from the two hours we spent at the museum. First, in the eugenics exhibit, we came to a large display featuring this quote from Joseph Goebbels, Minister of Propaganda for the Nazis in 1938:

> Our starting point is not the individual, and we do not subscribe to
> the view that one should feed the hungry, give drink to the thirsty, or

clothe the naked. Our objectives are entirely different: we must have
a healthy people in order to prevail in the world.

The quote justified the intense studies—begun before the Nazis came
to power—of human genetics and racial differences. It was all about
measurements—calipers, tape measures, sizes of noses, distance between
eyes. But the "objective" measurements were tools in the larger task of creating a super-race that would "prevail in the world." And essential to that
project was taking people with "inferior" characteristics out of the gene
pool. During the Nazi period, two hundred thousand adults were judged
"incurable" or "feeble-minded" and gassed. Thousands of infants born
with birth defects were determined unfit and therefore unworthy to survive. Their lives were extinguished.

What struck me was the realization that most Germans were, in name
at least, either Lutheran or Catholic. How could people with a Christian
heritage endorse such a bald contradiction of the teachings of Jesus? I
pointed out the quote to Neil and told him what I was thinking.

"Daniel, this is why your quest for a proper understanding of hell is so
important. Somehow, modern Western Christianity found a way to neu-
tralize the teachings of Jesus so that people could bear the name *Christian*
and commit atrocities like these. Our conventional doctrine of hell could
possibly be part of the problem."

A few people came and stood next to us. I felt uncomfortable about
them hearing what we were discussing, so I whispered, "I would think
the opposite. Wouldn't people be afraid of going to hell for committing
atrocities?"

Neil leaned toward me and whispered back, "Well, if they're told they
don't need to fear hell because they're Christians, maybe not. And if
they see outsiders as hell-bound anyway, maybe their lives are easier to
dispose of now, since God will consider them disposable later."

"That's horrid," I whispered. "I hope you're wrong."

My second memory centers on another display in the same exhibit. It
was another quote, easy to miss, on a small panel in a corner. Karl Brandt,
Hitler's personal physician, had written:

> The Führer was of the opinion that killing the incurably ill would be
> easier and smoother to carry out in wartime, since the public resistance
> of the churches would not play such a prominent role amidst the events
> of wartime as it otherwise would.

Neil pointed out this quote to me. I read it in silence and restated it in my
own words: The Führer realized that his agenda of killing the weak rather

than caring for them was contrary to the ethos of the churches; wartime, he felt, would create an environment where the churches would be less likely to break ranks and speak prophetically to the state.

Neil turned to me, whispering again. "Could the same sort of thing be happening today? Could the so-called war on terrorism be keeping the churches here in America from speaking prophetically to the state?"

I nodded slightly to acknowledge I heard his question without signaling agreement because I didn't fully understand what he meant. Neil continued, "And could our preoccupation with individual salvation from hell after death distract us from speaking prophetically about injustice in our world today?" My mind was so jammed full that I nodded slightly again and said nothing.

My third memory comes from the permanent exhibit, where a huge pile of shoes is displayed. Jews, Jehovah's Witnesses, homosexuals, gypsies, psychiatric patients—all who were judged as inferior, outsiders, deserving to be banned from the gene pool of the future "prevailing" nation—were "processed" from their homes to ghettos to concentration camps to gas chambers. The residue of their lives? Huge piles of empty shoes, each telling a story, each bearing the imprint of the feet of a person who was burned away to ash.

As I stared at those shoes—men's shoes, women's, children's—I felt stabbed in my soul, stabbed with a sense of loss, grief, shock, sadness. Those were real lives, precious people, fathers, mothers, daughters, sons, brothers, sisters, friends. How could they have been judged expendable? The memory of those shoes will never leave me, and when it returns, it is generally accompanied by this haunting question: What would it mean for God's story to end with an even more horrible furnace?

One other memory stays no less vivid in my mind, but it was not part of any display. It was a conversation Neil had with Shirley as we left. She had moved from the ticket counter to the information desk, and Neil stopped by to chat with her, asking her how she had become a volunteer there. Shirley's father was a Holocaust survivor, she explained, and she felt she was honoring him and all he suffered by her service there.

"Tell me about your father," Neil asked.

Shirley leaned forward on the information desk and folded her hands, gazing first into Neil's face and then into mine. "My father was a concert pianist before the Nazis came to power," she said. "In the concentration camp, a Nazi soldier beat his hands with an iron rod. He never received medical treatment, and the bones healed all wrong, so he never could play again. He had X-rays done after the war, and the doctor told him he had six breaks in one hand and seventeen in the other. I remember holding his hand when we would cross a street, and they were all lumpy and deformed."

She shook her head and continued, "Whenever Papa heard piano music, he would bite his lip, and tears would stream down his face, and he would stare down at his deformed hands and rub them together like this." Shirley stiffly wove and unwove her fingers and then softened her voice: "Humans can do terrible things, but they can also do wonderful things. You know what my father did after the war?"

"Tell us," Neil said.

"He spent the rest of his life teaching piano lessons to children. And he always told them the story of his hands. He begged them to love music and play it from their heart, to do it for him, because he never could. He was a great man." Shirley smiled a gentle smile.

At that moment, I was overcome. Yes, judgment was needed—judgment on the injustice of Nazism and every deceptive, oppressive evil like it. But hell as I had always seen it didn't improve the equation: it made it worse. It minimized human injustice and instead focused all the attention on whether one believed in Jesus in a certain prescribed way. The black-and-white photographs of concentration camps and naked, emaciated men were flashing through my mind. The quotes. The piles of shoes. Barbed wire. Calipers. Boxcars full of people. Stars of David. Shirley's father's deformed hands. I felt sweat on my forehead, and my mouth filled with saliva.

"Excuse me," I said, and I rushed out the doors and turned right, slipping in some slush, and made it to the side of the building, where I bent over, gagged twice, and then vomited in the snow. Neil followed me a few seconds later and said nothing as I composed myself, hunched over, my hands on my knees, spitting and breathing heavily. He gently put his hand on my shoulder.

"Neil," I said, breathing hard. "How am I supposed to believe that after all Shirley's father suffered, he's going to burn in hell forever, eternally tortured, because he didn't believe in Jesus? What kind of God would add his own eternal torture to the obscenity of human torture her father suffered? I can't take any more, Neil. This is going to drive me crazy. This isn't just theory. I can't take any more."

"Try not to think of all that, now," my friend said. "Just try to let yourself calm down."

I coughed and then nearly shouted, "Neil, how can I calm down? If people's lives end in eternal torture, if every good thing they ever did is swept away into insignificance because they weren't one of the chosen or they weren't lucky enough to believe the right things, how can I be calm?" I began coughing again and couldn't go on speaking.

A few moments later, Shirley was there with us, bundled up in her coat, with a paper cup of water and some moistened paper towels. "Here, young man," she said, handing me the towel and cup. "This sort of thing happens every once in a while. Sensitive people, kind people like yourself, internalize what they see in the museum, and it makes them sick. I can't blame you. It makes me sick too. There, there." She was rubbing my back, as my mom did when I got sick as a kid. "There, there."

15

YOU HAVE A TOUGH JOB

Not only that my language I distrust,
But that my mind cannot return so far
Above itself, unless another guide it.

—*Paradiso*, XVIII.130–133

IT WAS ABOUT DINNERTIME when I dropped Neil off and pulled into my neighborhood. We had talked little on the Metro ride, during our walk across the parking lot to my car, or during the drive homeward. There wasn't much to say. He began to apologize as he got out of the car. "I hope that wasn't too much. I feel terrible that maybe . . ."

"No apologies needed, friend," I said. "This was an important day in my life. Painful but important. I'm OK."

When I reached my neighborhood, I was hoping for a quiet night to compose myself and reflect on the day. But as I turned down my street, I noticed Ky Lang's car parked in my driveway. When I walked into the house, he and Carol were in the living room. Ky was slumped on a chair looking miserable, perching a teacup on his knee, and Carol sat in the couch with a manila folder in her hand. "Bad news, darlin'," she said. "Real bad news."

I walked over, and she handed me the folder and said, "Ky just brought this by. This is the doctrinal statement Nancy Zeamer forgot to send you— you know, the one from the Biblical Evangelical Fellowship. It's—"

"It's a joke, that's what it is, Dan," Ky broke in. "Nancy gave it to me yesterday and asked me to bring it by. I thought I was doing you a favor with that plan I got the council to pass. But now I realize I made things worse. The whole thing is rigged. You'll never be able to sign the BEF doctrinal statement. Neither will I. The jig is up. I had no idea what the statement would be like. None of the council members ever saw this when they voted to join. We were just told that we'd get a free consultation from . . ."

"From someone named Chip," I said. I sat down in slow motion and began skimming through the stapled packet inside the folder. I was stunned. "This isn't . . . this isn't evangelical. This is pure fundamentalism. Look at this: six-day literal creation, eternal conscious torment, whoa—they're completely overt about exclusivism, literal fire and brimstone, even . . . three, four, five-point Calvinism. Wow. They've even got the timetable of the Last Days defined—everything but naming the Antichrist." I closed the folder and dropped it on the floor. "Well, I guess I won't have to write answers to their questions."

Carol started to cry. "Nancy was my friend," she said, her face in her hands. "A good friend. Some friend."

I moved over to comfort her, and Ky got up and touched my shoulder. "Call me later," he whispered. Then he took his teacup out to the kitchen sink and let himself out the front door.

It was a long, hard evening. I was still shaken and queasy from the Holocaust Museum and more than a little tired from an intense day of walking and talking with Neil, but Carol needed me. She was scared, wondering what we'd do for money mostly, wondering what I'd do for a living. And she was hurt—by Nancy, by the council, by how life seemed to be going.

I went outside and got some firewood and lit a fire in the hearth, something that Carol always finds soothing. Then for the longest time I just sat beside her, my arm around her shoulder, her head pressed into my chest, as I gently stroked her hair and her hands, something else that soothes her. Then suddenly, as if she were waking up from a dream, she sat up straight and said, "I'm going to call her. I'm going to call Nancy. And I'd rather you not listen to what I'm going to say."

She shot up and headed to my home office in the attic, not looking back or pausing for a comment from me. At that moment, Trent burst into the room, frantic, saying he needed some posterboard for a history project that was due the next day and if he didn't get the project done, his history grade was *screwed*—not a word I liked my kids to use, but there it was. I looked at my watch: 7:40, and the stores would probably close at 8:00 on Presidents' Day evening, if they hadn't already closed at 5:00. I told Trent to ask Cory if he needed anything, and I called down to Casey, who was running on the treadmill in the basement, to see if she needed anything. "Could you bring me some Gatorade?" she said. "I'm aiming for five miles."

In a few minutes, Cory, Trent, and I were rushing out to the drugstore before it closed. But the drugstore didn't have posterboard, so we rushed over to a department store a bit farther away and got what the boys needed just before the store closed. I picked up some Gatorade for Casey and a box of chocolates for Carol—something else that I hoped would make her feel better.

The boys hadn't eaten dinner, so I pulled into a Wendy's so they could get something; I waited in the car, still feeling queasy. I stared out at the empty parking lot as the boys went inside, feeling numb, alone, overwhelmed, exhausted, and afraid. "Help me, please" was all the prayer I could muster as the boys climbed back in the car, Wendy's bags in hand.

When I pulled into the driveway for the second time that evening, another car was there, one I didn't recognize. It had a University of Maryland sticker on the back window.

I was shocked when I came through the front door to see Nancy Zeamer hunched over on the couch between Carol and Casey. Carol was rubbing Nancy's back, and Casey's hand rested on Nancy's knee. "What's going on here?" I asked.

Nancy raised her head. She looked terrible—red eyes, mascara smeared down her cheeks. She jumped off the couch and threw her arms around me. "Oh, Dan," she said. "I'm so sorry. I can't believe . . . I can't believe what I've done. I can't ask you to forgive me." Then she sobbed, and I tried to help her sit down again.

"What's going on?" I asked again. It took a few minutes for Nancy to be able to speak.

"Dan, from the very beginning of this whole ordeal, I've been having misgivings. I have never really been for this heresy trial at all. It's my husband. Gil hasn't been your biggest fan for a while, and I guess I let him pressure me into taking action. I'm the one who kept voting to postpone any kind of formal meeting with you because I've just been sick about this whole thing. I'm really sorry. My daddy was a pastor, and I know how hard your life can be. But you know how Gil can be, and I'm in a difficult spot—but that's no excuse for what I've let happen here. I'm just sick about this. Sick. Brokenhearted. I'm switching sides, Dan. I'm going to stand up to Gil and bring this thing to an end."

Nancy looked at me directly and said, "Dan, I love this church. And I love you and Carol. I don't want you to go. Gil has always been so strict, and he's so set in his ways, and he's got this anger problem. Sometimes I let him frighten me. When he puts his anger together with the Bible, I just get . . . intimidated."

Carol spoke up, "Bless his heart, Nancy. It's OK. It means a lot to us that you'd come over. Does he—"

"Does he know I'm here?" Nancy finished the question. "Heavens no. He'd—well, that's his problem. It's not right that I've been letting Gil push me around. The people of PCC didn't elect him to the council. They elected me. But I've been letting him speak through me, and I'm not proud of that." Then she couldn't speak again. She didn't cry, but she squeezed her eyes shut and held her breath and pressed her fist into her forehead. After several seconds she relaxed and began to speak again.

"Gil preached yesterday at church. It just made me crazy. He's been such a bear around the house, so grouchy, so selfish. Then he gets up there and pontificates. Dan, I sometimes think this whole episode is about his jealousy, his wish that he could be up there preaching instead of you. You know, he was in campus ministry for several years, and if it weren't for his inability to raise financial support, I think he still would be in full-time ministry of some sort. I was just sick listening to him yesterday morning. I've been somewhere between depressed and furious since the service yesterday, and then, Carol, when you called . . .

"Dan, I keep remembering your sermon last year at the candlelight service. You talked about how Jesus came with vulnerability. You talked about how God's kingdom comes gently, the way Jesus came. It doesn't come with politics and power and pushing, but that's exactly what's been going on at PCC these last few months. When I looked around yesterday and saw the empty pew where your family always sits, and I heard Gil up there preaching, I felt heartsick to think I'm part of this . . . this plot against you. I asked myself, *What's happening to us? This isn't the way of Christ.* I was so relieved when Carol called me. Oh, Carol . . ."

Carol asked, "What are you going to tell Gil? Will he be mad at you?"

"That's not your problem," Nancy said. "It's not my problem either. Way too many people have been letting Gil push them around for way too long. It's about time. Dan, what do you think we should do? We've got to stop this thing. It's totally out of control. I never even read that doctrinal statement until yesterday. I know you can't sign it. I'm not sure I can either. It was Gil's idea. Everything's Gil's idea."

Then we just sat for a minute or two, looking down, nobody moving, until we heard Casey's beads tinkling as she nodded her head and spoke up. "I think we should pray," she said. Then she just bowed her head and began. She didn't just pray with her mouth and voice; she prayed with her whole body. Her beads made their music as she swayed, and then she would slap her hands on her knees as if to tell the Lord she was really serious. Then she'd shake a finger in the air, as if she were preaching, and then slap her knees again. It felt like her heart was breaking out of her chest as she prayed.

"Lord, we don't know what to do. Each of us in this room loves Potomac Community Church, Lord. Even me, even though I'm not a member there. Nancy loves it enough to stand up to her husband for it. Carol has sacrificed so much and been hurt so deeply and has forgiven so often. And you know . . ."—at this point, her voice cracked, and she seemed to lose her breath—"you know how Pastor Dan's heart has been carrying this concern. We're your children, Lord! We're calling out in faith to our Father in heaven! So here we are, and we care, but we don't know what to do. This is a mess, Lord! We need wisdom, Lord! Please help us, Lord! We want to wait in silence now and keep our hearts and minds open to listen to your Spirit. We want to receive wisdom, Jesus, so we'll know what to do. We're waiting on you."

And then we sat in silence. At the sound of a slight crinkling of paper, I realized that Cory and Trent were still standing in the foyer, and they couldn't even put their bags of school supplies down because they didn't want to distract anyone, so they just stood there, frozen, and watched and listened. It was a kind of holy silence that I can't begin to explain. There was the fire crackling and hissing in the fireplace. There were the sounds of our breathing and occasionally Casey's beads. I remember thinking what an amazing thing prayer is, a kind of everyday miracle that we just take for granted, but to think that human souls can actually open up to God and just wait, just wait to receive something, or just wait in quiet trust.

After maybe three minutes of silence, I cleared my throat and said, "Well, does anyone have any ideas?"

Then Trent spoke up. I'm sure he wasn't planning to say anything. But something, he later told me, just jumped into his mind, and before he could stop himself, there he was, spilling it out.

"Dad, I don't understand everything that's been going on, but I have something to say. It's like Mrs. Zeamer said: the way of Christ is vulnerability. So you have to be gentle, and you have to go through"—he nodded toward the fireplace—"the fire. You can't fight for yourself. You can't fight fire with fire. That's the only way you'll have peace on the other side. I know I'm just a kid and all, but I am thirteen, and I think you should listen to me." I winked at him and smiled and nodded, and I noticed that Cory took a step closer to his brother and actually looked proud of him.

Then Carol spoke up. "Trent, I think you're wise beyond your years, dear. As we were praying, I just kept hearing the phrase 'speaking the truth in love.' I'm not sure what that means, but that's what I have to offer."

"That's what I need to hear," Nancy said. "I need to go home and tell Gil the truth. I'm angry at him, because I feel he's been manipulating me. But I need to be loving. Gil comes on so strong, but inside, I know he's scared. He's like a frightened kid whenever he thinks things are out of his control. Well, I'm just going to tell him the truth, in love—that if he wants this church to be an FBE or BFE or BEF or whatever it is, then his wife won't be able to be part of that church. If you go, Dan, I go too. And Dan, first thing tomorrow, I'm calling all the council members. I'm going to re-sign. I've let everyone down."

Casey shifted in her seat: "No, Nancy. I don't think you should resign. I think you should be the kind of leader you wish you would have been. I think you should be strong and do what's right. I hope you don't mind me saying this, but if you resign, you're staying weak—not weak in the vulnerable way but in the victimized way, and that's just another invita-tion for Gil to manipulate you. You know?"

Cory and Trent came in and sat on the carpet, cross-legged, and a plan began to emerge. As soon as our little meeting ended, the boys microwaved their half-eaten fries and hamburgers and sat at the kitchen table with Casey, who offered me a Gatorade, but I still didn't feel like eating or drinking anything. Instead I called Ky on his cell phone and shared the plan with him. It felt right to him, and so we began to implement it imme-diately.

When Nancy got home, Gil was in the living room, reading. "Where have you been, dear?"

"I've been out talking to some friends from church." She hung up her coat and went to the bathroom. Gil got up and stood outside the closed door.

"About what?" Gil called through the door. "Who were you talking with?"

Nancy didn't answer. She let him wait to hear the toilet flush, the faucet run, and the towel holder squeak as she pulled off the towel to dry her hands and then squeak again as she replaced the towel. When she opened the door, his brow was furrowed. "What's going on?" He wasn't used to her going out without telling him beforehand, and he was even less ac-customed to her being vague. "Are you upset about something?"

"No, " she said, smiling and giving him a kiss on the cheek. "I actual-ly feel better than I've felt in a long time." Then she went into the kitchen to boil some water for tea.

He followed her, obviously curious and off balance somehow. "What were you talking about and with whom?"

"It was church business, Gil. Remember, I'm the church council chair, and some business is confidential." She just let the silence last as she got out a teacup, a tea bag, and a container of honey.

Gil was standing in the kitchen doorway, arms folded, not moving a muscle. Finally, he couldn't contain himself. "What are you talking about?" his voice was rising, and it got a little shaky as he continued. "What's going on? You always tell me everything. What's . . . I demand to know!"

Nancy smiled. "I'm sorry, dear. I'll be glad to tell you what we were doing." Gil's whole posture relaxed, and he leaned against the refrigerator. Nancy took her time to pour the hot water into her teacup. She positioned herself across the island counter from Gil, leaned over, put her elbows on the counter, and smiled again. "We were working on a plan, Gil. A confidential plan. You'll just have to wait and see what happens. Now I hope you don't mind, but I need a little privacy. I'd like to take a few minutes to drink my tea and be alone."

"Is this about—is this about Poole? You aren't getting cold feet, are you? You know what needs to be done," Gil said, following her into the living room, where Nancy sat down and began stirring her tea. He stood there for less than a minute and then stomped up the stairs to bed.

That was easier than I thought, Nancy said to herself, sipping her tea, smiling.

Back at my house, I wish things had gone as well. As Carol and I prepared for bed, Carol asked me how my day had been and specifically what Neil and I had talked about. I began to explain, but Carol looked upset. "What's wrong?" I asked.

"Dan, I've been really patient; I really have. But sometimes even I think you've gone too far. Look, if so many Christians have been so wrong about hell, how can they be right about anything? I mean, hell is pretty central to the whole—"

"No," I interrupted, "that's the point. It's not really that central. I mean, we've made it central for a long time, but anti-Semitism was pretty pervasive in Christianity for a long time, and we came to the point where we realized we'd been wrong about that. The early church believed that God was impassible—incapable of feeling or experiencing or suffering sadness or pain. Now we see God's empathy and compassion as part of the beauty of God's character. That's what it means to be part of a living tradition. You can admit you've been—"

"I don't think you understand me," Carol said. "Daniel, I'm not like you. I take things as they're given to me. I'm that kind of person. For me, a person can't just go rethinking things all the time. I'm not against change. I'm not like Gil; you know that. But for me, things have always been black and white. That's just the kind of person . . ." She didn't finish her sentence. "I mean, Daniel, aren't you ever afraid—afraid that you're just plain wrong, that you're compromising, that you're just plain old *going astray*?" She sat down on the bed.

I came over and sat beside her. "Look, Carol, even if I'm wrong in my new thinking about hell, I'm sure about one thing. I was wrong in my old thinking too. I used my old understanding of hell to minimize the importance of justice on earth. And you've done it too, Carol. Remember that time a couple of years ago when Jess was bugging us to start recycling and you told her we didn't need to recycle because we were in the end times and the earth was going to end soon anyway, so we might as well use up all the resources while we can?"

"I said no such thing," Carol snapped back, slapping the mattress. "Well, maybe I told her not to get fanatical about all that environmental stuff, but I didn't say it like that. Besides, you don't recycle that much yourself."

It had been such a long day, and so emotional, that neither of us could handle an argument, which we were getting close to, and we both knew it. So we backed off from the conversation, got ready for bed in silence, and were lying next to each other, looking up at the ceiling in the dark, when Carol finally spoke. "It's kind of strange," she said, almost whispering, "to think that what might help our daughter's faith could actually hurt mine and that what helps my faith—having everything clearly defined and at the core at least, not changing—could actually hurt our daughter's faith."

"Yes. Strange," I said.

"I don't envy you, Dan. You have a tough job."

"Yes. Tough," I said. We were both so drained that we were asleep within a few minutes.

ALL OVER THE MAP

As God may let thee, Reader, gather fruit
From this thy reading, think now for thyself . . .

—*Inferno,* XX.19–20

BY 9:00 THE NEXT MORNING, Nancy had sent an e-mail to the church council, calling an emergency meeting for Wednesday night. She asked for a reply to confirm that each member could be present. Surprisingly for our group, everyone said yes, even with just one day's notice.

I was at the kitchen table on Tuesday morning when Casey came up with a stapled document in her hand. "Here, Pastor Dan," she said. "I've been reading through the books and articles I photocopied for you. I took these notes. I hope they'll help you. I worked on this most of the night. It seemed like things were coming to a head, you know, so I figured I could help you with your research."

"Notes?" I asked, looking them over. "Oh, about hell. Wow. Thanks, Casey. This looks fascinating. Really helpful."

"They're not organized or anything," she said. "I just typed up anything that looked interesting. It's a fast gleaning, I guess you could say. Pretty random. But they give you an idea of how differently different Christians address the issue. I mean, they're all over the map."

"No, this is great," I said, "just what I needed." I sat down and read through the single-spaced document while she fixed herself some breakfast.

NOTES AND QUOTES ON HELL

1. "It is impossible to be a biblical Christian and a universalist simultaneously." (John Stott, *Authentic Christianity: From the Writings of John Stott,* chosen and introduced by Timothy Dudley Smith, Nottingham, England: Inter-Varsity Press, 1996)

2. "We may, and I think we should, preserve a certain reverent and humble agnosticism about the precise nature of hell, as about the precise nature of heaven. Both are beyond our understanding. But clear and definite we must be that hell is an awful, eternal reality." (Stott, 1996, p. 395)

3. "I have always derived much comfort from the statement of Revelation 7:9 that the company of the redeemed in heaven will be 'a great multitude which no man could number.' I do not profess to know how this can be, since Christians have always seemed to be a rather small minority. . . . A biblical Christian can—even must—assert that the redeemed will somehow be an international throng so immense as to be countless. For God's promise is going to be fulfilled, and Abraham's seed is going to be as innumerable as the dust of the earth, the stars of the sky, and the sand on the seashore." (Stott, 1996, p. 404)

"Hmm," I said. "These first couple of quotes from John Stott are especially interesting. He seems to be softening his position over time."

"Yeah," Casey said, turning toward me from the counter. "I think I have another quote from him later on." I continued reading silently.

4. "We are not referring to earthworms or earthly fires but unending misery over willed sin." (Gregory of Nyssa)

5. "The reader of the Word cannot select out comfortable passages and ignore those that make us uneasy. . . . Yes, I know a chill comes over you on hearing these things. But what am I to do? . . . Ordained as we are to the ministry of the word, we must cause our hearers discomfort when it is necessary for them to hear. We do this not arbitrarily but under command." (Chrysostom)

6. "Hell is not merely a rhetorical hyperbole." (Basil)

7. "Those who finally reject salvation suffer eternally in both body and soul." (Augustine)

8. "New Testament teaching about hell is meant to appall us and strike us dumb with horror, assuring us that, as heaven will be better than we could dream, so hell will be worse than we can conceive. Such are the issues of eternity, which need now to be

realistically faced." (J. I. Packer, *Concise Theology: A Guide to Historic Christian Beliefs*, Carol Stream, Ill.: Tyndale House, 1993, p. 261)

9. "Rather than a place, hell indicates the state of those who freely and definitively separate themselves from God. . . . [The Bible] uses a symbolical language [that] figuratively portrays in a 'pool of fire' those who exclude themselves from the book of life, thus meeting with a 'second death.'" (Pope John Paul II, *U.S. News and World Report*, 31 Jan. 2000, p. 44)

10. "Scripture clearly speaks of hell as a physical place of fiery torment and warns us we should fear." (R. Albert Mohler, president of Southern Baptist Seminary, Louisville)

11. "How can Christians possibly project a deity of such cruelty and vindictiveness [as to inflict] everlasting torture upon his creatures, however sinful they have been? [Such a deity] is more nearly like Satan than God." (Clark Pinnock, in *Criswell Theological Review*)

12. "If there is no God, no heaven, no hell, there simply is no persuasive reason to be moral." (Jerry Walls, Asbury Seminary)

13. "Most of the passages in the New Testament which have been thought by the Church to refer to people going into eternal punishment after they die don't in fact refer to any such thing. The great majority of them have to do with the way God acts *within* the world and history. Most of them look back to language and ideas in the Old Testament, which work in quite a different way from that which is normally imagined." (N. T. Wright, *Following Jesus: Biblical Reflections on Discipleship*, Grand Rapids, Mich.: Eerdmans, 1995, pp. 92–93)

14. "There cannot be a kind of curtain which comes down at death, dividing humanity irreversibly into the companies of the saved and of the damned. God's loving offer of mercy cannot be for the term of our earthly life alone. . . . Every turning away from God will make the return journey that much the harder. . . . If these ideas are correct, they illustrate the claim that theology can make to be a discipline concerned with the progressive exploration of truth, not held for ever in thrall to past understanding alone. . . . Eternal punishment was a source of moral scandal which helped to alienate many thoughtful and sensitive people from contemporary Christianity. Charles Darwin called it a 'damnable doctrine' and said he could not 'see how anyone ought to wish Christianity to be true.' . . . [The rethinking of the doctrine of hell] has come about, not through surrender to a secular sentimentality, but through the

realization of its incompatibility with the mercy of a loving God, who cannot be conceived to exact infinite punishment for finite wrong. Theology has proved itself to be open to correction." (John Polkinghorne, *The Faith of a Physicist: Reflections of a Bottom-Up Thinker,* Princeton, N.J.: Princeton University Press, 1994, pp. 170–171)

15. "One day we too shall be resurrected and placed before the awful white throne. . . . All [camouflage, trenches, arms] will fall away, vanish under the penetrating ray of the Judge. We ourselves shall wonder whether we still really exist. No place will be found for our poor being. The same Power that created us will weigh us to see how much of us actually *is,* for genuine existence is possible only through truth and justice, faith and love; our existence, then will be appallingly questionable. We shall feel ourselves being undermined by nothingness, sucked down toward the void. Only our naked conscience will stand before God's gaze. May his mercy sustain us in that hour! . . . In the final act every sentiment, every thought, every action will be drenched in light. Above all, man's most secret intentions will be disclosed: his fundamental attitude toward Revelation and God's will. If, ultimately, he believed, was receptive, loved good, he will be reckoned to the 'men of good will' (Luke 2:14), and Christ himself will cause the full, sweet being to ripen round this sound kernel. Nothing will be lost; everything fulfilled— from this central point. With that which constituted the decisive characteristics of his earthly self, he will be perfected and established in his eternal form to live forever in the sight of God. If, on the other hand, he closed himself fundamentally to God, refused faith, rejected obedience, then whatever he did and experienced will be determined from this core of rejection. In all eternity he will remain a part-reality, a spiritual fragment living the non-life of 'the second death.'" (Romano Guardini, *The Lord,* South Bend, In.: Gateway Editions, 1978, pp. 521–522)

16. "Aquinas argued that unbaptized infants went to limbo (not to hell, as Augustine had supposed). . . . Hell, of course, has been lavishly described by thousands of theologians, preachers and poets, notably again Dante. The New Testament, interestingly, doesn't have nearly as much to say about it, though there are plenty of warnings of judgment to come, couched in the apocalyptic language which first-century Jews would have found easier to decode than later Greek and Latin theologians. . . . The New Testament is full of sober and serious warnings of the real possibility of final loss, and I do not

think they are merely rhetorical devices to frighten us ahead of time into a salvation which will in fact come to all sooner or later. . . . Stress again, in leaving this topic, that it is not up to us to say who's in and who's out. . . ." (N. T. Wright, *For All the Saints? Remembering the Christian Departed,* London: Society for Promoting Christian Knowledge, 2003)

17. "Like the Kingdom of God, the subject of Hell is treated differently among the gospels and other NT writings. In the synoptics, the primary command of Christ seems to be to follow and do the will of God. In John, and in Paul's writings, the prime directive is more often to believe in Jesus, or the gospel. Evangelicals tend to conflate the former into the latter, so that believing in some way seems to negate the need to follow and do the will of God. Meanwhile, even in Paul's writings, judgment is consistently associated with the phrase 'according to their deeds,' not 'according to their beliefs' (Rom. 2:6; 1 Thess. 4:6). Also, while the synoptics frequently use similar language regarding hell, John uses a different kind of language. So, it seems to me that we are left with an embarrassing failure to take all of Scripture seriously, and we are left with a difficult challenge: how (or whether?) to integrate the various approaches to hell found in Scripture." (Maundet, p. 76)

18. "We tend to try to turn the rich and varied biblical lexicon into a limited range of synonymous technical terms. For example, judgment for us equals hell or condemnation. Condemnation equals hell, etc. We should be more careful than this in assuming words are synonyms, because the Bible is horribly disappointing as a modern-style technical textbook, even of theology. The Biblical lexicon of judgment includes sheol, hades, tartarus, gehenna, the abyss, death, darkness, fire, lake of fire, unquenchable fire, where the worm does not die, the Day, the Day of the Lord, etc." (Maundet, p. 84)

19. "Much of what we think we know about hell from Scripture (as with the devil and with heaven) actually comes from other sources, such as Dante, Milton, Greek mythology, etc. . . . Biblical writers themselves seem to use hell-language figuratively (i.e., not in a theological sense), as in James 3:6 or Matthew 23:15." (Maundet, p. 90)

Casey had made and finished her breakfast while I was deep in concentration. I hadn't even noticed that she had been sitting across the table from me until she interrupted my reading. "Well, what do you make of it?" she asked.

"Fascinating. What do *you* make of it?" I asked back.

DECONSTRUCTING HELL

To hell I thought we were returning.

—*Inferno*, XXXIV.81

"IT'S FUNNY, PASTOR DAN, but I think I come at this different, as a woman of color, from the way you'd come at it. It seems like most white folks like to read the Bible as a kind of textbook, and they're always looking for abstract, universal information. You know, it's kind of an Easter egg hunt for propositions. But in the African American church, we don't read the Bible that way, or rather, we didn't used to. (Lately, I think a lot of black preachers have been getting paler, if you know what I mean.) Anyway, we've always read the Bible to *preach* it, to *feel* it, not so much just to study it and theologize on it. You know, sometimes we say, "That'll preach," which is like a saying my daddy used to have, being from the country and all: "That dog will hunt," he'd say. When my daddy said that, he meant that whatever we were talking about would *work*. It would make a difference. It would achieve the goal, like a dog would find a raccoon or possum or whatever. I read the Bible more that way.

"So, when it comes to hell, I just use my common sense. Look, Jesus said God is good, like a caring father. Caring fathers don't torture their children, even though they sometimes need to take them out to the woodshed or make them stand in the corner or take a timeout or go on restriction or whatever—it's always for their own good. All that talk about God preselecting some people to be hell fuel—you know, all that predestination stuff—that seems wacky to me. It's the kind of thing a lot of black folks wouldn't have time for. Whatever God does, we know God's doing it for our own good, and there's no cruelty to it at all. Maybe this isn't making much sense, but for me, I just hear Jesus talking about hell and think, well, he's trying to scare the hell out of us. It takes strong language to do that, you know? It makes you think: *Am I really pleasing God, or am I getting off track?* I think we need that kind of unsettling from time to time."

"It strikes me," I said, "speaking as a thoroughly white guy, how messed up our approach is. Because when we talk about hell, it's generally not to unsettle ourselves. It's generally the opposite—to reassure ourselves, so we think, *Aren't we glad we're insiders with God and going to heaven? Isn't it a shame those other people are so bad and wrong and going to hell?* It's part of a system that reinforces us-them thinking, I guess—to strengthen the 'us' identity. Sometimes I guess we might use hell to motivate people to try to evangelize others: 'They're going to hell, so don't you want to reach out to them?'"

"Oh, give me a break on that," Casey said. "That just makes the evangelizer look down on the evangelizee. It brings in pity and condemnation and all that patronizing junk. I think that's generally counterproductive because people can sense that a mile away. Although I guess God can use anything to get through to people. I guess—to use my dad's words—that dog will hunt, but it might come back and bite you from time to time too, you know? Of course, you know I'm Episcopalian, and our denomination has as strong an aversion to evangelism as Baptists have to whisky. So we probably need a dose of something to get us off our butts."

We both laughed, and then I started looking over Casey's notes again, engrossed in my own thoughts. I didn't realize she was staring at me until she said, "Pastor Dan, you really feel the need to work this thing out, don't you? Like, you really need to get to the bottom of it."

"I guess so, Casey."

"I'm not sure about all the details, but here's something I'm pretty sure of. Hell might have a place, but it can't get the last word. I mean, if hell seems to have the last word, there's got to be a word after that."

"What would that be, Casey?" I asked.

"Grace," she said. "I think the last word is always grace."

"Where sin abounds . . . ," I said, quoting Paul in Romans.

"Grace abounds all the more," Casey said, finishing the sentence. "I have a lot of unanswered questions, but that's all I really need to know. I can live with that." Then she told me she had a meeting with a new Episcopal youth minister in Baltimore and needed to leave. "Shoot," she said, doing a little drumroll with her hands on the kitchen table, "maybe I can convince this guy to do some evangelizing—for heaven's sake, if not for hell's!" Then with a wink and that sliding handshake she always gave me, she was gone. I finished reading her notes, some of which were new to me, but most of which I had come across in my own reading.

20. "Gehenna (Matt. 5:22, 18:19) was the name of a valley outside Jerusalem. It was a place where child sacrifices were offered (2 Chron. 23:3, 33:6). It was also known as a dump where dead bodies and garbage were burned. It came to be used as a name or image for hell, the most common term in the Synoptics (unused by John). In postbiblical Jewish literature, two groups of people would be spared the tortures of Gehenna: those who were righteous in this life and those who were especially unfortunate in this life.

   "Tartarus (2 Pet. 2:4) was the place in Greek thought below Hades, also a place of divine punishment. The fact that this term is used may only show a linguistic borrowing, but it suggests the influence of Greek mythology on early Christian (via Jewish) thought." (Maundet, pp. 104–105)

21. "*Sheol* can mean grave, or it can mean the place where both the good and evil dead remain (Gen. 37:35; Num. 16:30; Ps. 30:3; 9; 31:17; Prov. 7:27; Eccles. 9:10). While for some writers Sheol is inescapable (Job 7:9–10; Isa. 38:10, 18), some OT literature has some hope of escape from Sheol (Hosea 13:14; Ps. 16:10, 49:15; Job 14:13; 1 Sam. 2:6). . . . In the four Gospels, Hades occurs four times and Gehenna eleven times." (Maundet, p. 110)

22. "For some Christians, the horror of hell is assuaged by realizing that it is chosen; in other words, if people end up there, their fate is purely their own fault. Other Christians seem to imply that the condemned are in hell to some degree by God's choice, whether directly (because God actually predestines them for hell) or indirectly (because God chooses not to predestine them for heaven). Even if the damned are damned through their own free choice (and not God's), some theologians wonder if the gift of this kind of freedom of choice is a good and perfect gift after all—might it be like giving a six-year-old a gun? The Bible itself seems to convey some degree of ambivalence on these matters. For example, Jesus said, "Father, forgive them, for they don't know what they are doing," which seems to imply some mitigation of their responsibility (they don't know what they are doing) along with some level of responsibility (otherwise, why would they need to be forgiven?)." (Berton and Chase, p. 22)

23. "The horror of hell has elicited three Christian responses: (a) accept it and preach it as the terrible but unavoidable truth, (b) understand

it as temporary and leading to annihilation (called 'conditionalism' or 'conditional immortality,' a view espoused by Seventh-Day Adventists and embraced late in life by John Stott, along with Clark Pinnock and John Wenham), or (c) understand it as purgative and effective at bringing all to repentance and ultimate salvation. (The view of Origen, who lived from 185 to 254, rejected at the Second Ecumenical Council of Constantinople in 553 is sometimes called 'ultimate reconciliation.')

"The relation of hell to the victory of Christ has likewise elicited three Christian responses: (a) exclusivism (Christ's death and resurrection may not have been intended for the whole world but only for the elect; in any case, the gospel is only effective for those who believe or follow), (b) universalism (the work of Christ will ultimately redeem all and result in the complete unmitigated triumph of God), and (c) inclusivism (the work of Christ can extend beyond those who have heard of Christ but not necessarily to all)." (Berton and Chase, pp. 43–45)

24. "Lesslie Newbigin proposes a unique understanding of election (to service, not privilege; to mission, not just salvation; to be agents of the salvation of the whole world, not receivers of salvation denied to the masses) that leaves the issue open. In fact, he suggests that it is improper and disobedient to try to speculate on the eternal destiny of others. Our approach, he implies, should be predicamental: we should focus on ourselves—believing, following, doing the will of God, joining God in his mission, coming to the light, etc." (Berton and Chase, p. 51) NOTE TO PASTOR DAN: I know Neil sees it like Newbigin, and actually, so do I.

25. "Universalism is not as bankrupt of biblical support as some suggest (John 12:32; Acts 3:19–21; Rom. 5:12–21; 1 Cor. 15:20–26; 2 Cor. 5:19; Phil. 2:9–11; Eph. 1:10; Col. 1:16–23; 1 Tim. 2:4, 4:10; Titus 2:11; Heb. 2:9; 2 Pet. 3:9; 1 John 2:2). Any case for exclusivism must do justice to these and similar passages." (Berton and Chase, p. 72)

26. "One wonders if our talk about individual salvation and damnation is too narrow; would it be more biblical to talk about the restoration of all things, the salvation of the world—including human and nonhuman creation? There are biblical passages (Rom. 8, Eph. 1, Col. 1) that suggest God's frame of reference for salvation is broader than our categories. Perhaps narrowing his broad frame of reference to a strictly human and individual one guarantees that we will

miss the point (just as Jewish nationalism guaranteed that
they missed the point when Jesus came)?" (Berton and Chase, p. 71)

27. "When Jesus is speaking in parables (Luke 16:19–31; Matt.
25:41–46), we may err gravely in trying to turn that genre into a di-
dactic description on eschatological realities. Parables tend to make
one point sparklingly well . . . but we often want them to make
many points with a kind of wooden, unsparkling didacticism. We
may also err gravely in failing to place Jesus' teachings in their dramatic and narrative context. For example, how did Jesus' teaching
on hell relate to the Pharisees' teaching? How might this dynamic
compare with other dynamics in the Gospels? (see Matt. 5:22,
23:15, 33)." (Berton and Chase, p. 98)

28. According to George Barna's research, 76 percent of Americans believe in heaven, and 71 percent believe in hell. Only 32 percent
believe that hell is "an actual place of torment and suffering,"
and 40 percent believe it is "a state of eternal separation from
God's presence." Sixty-four percent believe that they will go to
heaven, and only 0.005 percent believe that they will be sent to
the flames.

   According to *U.S. News and World Report* (31 Jan. 2000), 64
percent of Americans think there is a hell; 25 percent don't; and
9 percent don't know. (More believed in hell in 2000 than did in
1990 or in the 1950s.)

30. More people in 2000 than in 1997 see hell as "an anguished state
of existence eternally separated from God" (53 percent versus 46
percent), more don't know what to think (11 percent versus 4 percent), and fewer see hell as "a real place where people suffer eternal
fiery torments" 34 percent versus 48 percent).

31. All major religions have a conception of hell. Among Jews, only Orthodox Jews retain the concept. In the Koran, there are seven layers
of hell, into which departed wicked and infidel people fall (body
and soul) as they try to cross a narrow bridge to paradise. In Hinduism, there are twenty-one hells that souls must pass through during reincarnation to burn away bad karma. After passing through
those twenty-one hells (where they may be cooked in jars or eaten
by ravens), they begin their assent through animate and human life.
In classical Buddhism, there are seven hot hells, which include torture chambers, a fiery pit, and a swamp of quicksand. In Tibetan
Buddhism (think of the geography), there are eight cold hells, along
with lesser hells for people who have committed lesser sins. Most

African and Asian tribal religions also have some conception of a hell; among Native American religions, however, this belief is notably absent.

32. "At a primitive level of development—with children, for example—punishment and reward can elicit good moral choices, observes [Rev. Thomas] Reese. 'The threat of hell basically appeals to people at that level.' With teenagers and mature adults, however, says Reese, it is seldom effective. Nonetheless, he says, 'there are times when we fall back into primitive behavior, when we want to kill somebody. If hell keeps us from doing it, I say, "bless hell."'" (*U.S. News and World Report*, 31 Jan. 2000, p. 144)

When I finished reading Casey's notes, I felt a strange mixture of emotions. "It's so complicated," I thought. "And so much is at stake." I couldn't get Carol's words out of my mind: what might help our daughter's faith would actually undermine Carol's, and what might help Carol would hurt Jess. Is there any way that both could get the help they need—reassurance for Carol, breathing room for Jess? My head sank into my hands, and I felt overwhelmed.

My cell phone jolted me out of my melancholy thoughts. It was Casey. "Pastor Dan, I'm stuck in traffic on 270. Do you have a minute?"

"Sure," I said, adding an attempt at humor: "My official mandate is to do anything but fulfill my official job description, so I've got a lot of minutes. What's up?"

"Have you ever heard of deconstruction?" she asked.

"Yes, Neil uses the term sometimes. But I'm not exactly clear on what it means," I answered.

"It's hard to explain," she said, "but I've been thinking about our talk a few minutes ago, and I realized that that's what you're doing to hell. You're trying to deconstruct it."

"OK. Can you define the term for me?" I asked.

"You're trying to show that hell is a human construction. Human beings constructed the idea by taking elements from lots of other cultures. You're trying to go back and show how those elements were used to construct the idea so that you can see what's left when you deconstruct it. If it's an idea that arises in human history, then it's constructed by humans, and if humans constructed it, then humans can deconstruct it," she said, ending rather decisively, as if that would somehow solve a problem for me.

But it didn't: "So, Casey, how exactly does this help me?"

"In seminary, we read a lot about deconstruction, and I remember this one author saying that deconstruction was about hope. In fact, this French dude named Derrida said that deconstruction was preparing the way for the Messianic. It's like taking apart a cheesy billboard that somebody built along the highway so that people can see the beautiful view the billboard was hiding. I remember a couple of examples we talked about back in seminary. If you deconstruct a theory, you're doing it in the hope that a better theory can be imagined. If you deconstruct a social system, you're doing it in hope that a better system can emerge. And if you deconstruct laws, you're doing it in the hope that a greater understanding of justice can come. That's what I think you're doing, Pastor Dan. You're deconstructing our popular Christian conception of hell—not so that you'll say 'anything goes' or whatever but so that you can get to an even better understanding of God's justice."

"Ah," I said. "And God's grace."

"Yeah, right," Casey said. "Well, my cell phone battery's almost dead. Just wanted to encourage . . ." With that, the signal faded and I lost contact. Her battery must have gone dead.

PROPOSAL, PLAN, IMPLEMENTATION

And the true fruit shall follow on the flower.

—*Paradiso*, XXVII.148

THE PLAN WE HAD WORKED OUT the previous night gave each of us some homework. Nancy had hers, Ky had his, and I had mine. I needed to prepare a short proposal for the council's Wednesday night meeting. I spent all of Tuesday and Wednesday working and reworking the proposal. It was going to be one of the most important documents I had ever prepared.

When we arrived at Ky and Leticia's townhouse—the first time we had ever met in a council member's home instead of room 316 at church—Leticia had refreshments set out for us: fruit, brownies, chips, and crab dip, the last a Maryland tradition but a luxury in winter. We were all a little tense, largely because several council members hadn't seen me in quite a while, nor I them. Ky had some unusual music playing in the background—"minimalist," he called it—and it set a kind of oddly soothing mood. Gradually we settled down for our meeting.

After a few minutes, Ky gathered us around the antique dining room table, each of us with our little plate of refreshments and a drink. Nancy opened with a prayer, and then she asked us to spend five minutes in silence, each of us quieting our heart before God by slowly repeating the phrase, "Your will be done here as in heaven." We had never done anything like this before, and five minutes can seem like a very long time, but I think the exercise had a positive effect. Then Nancy began to speak.

"Thanks for coming to this emergency meeting on such short notice. I need to begin with an apology. I have misled this council since I became chair. I choose the word *misled* intentionally, for two reasons. First, I have not led the council well. I've allowed us to make decisions that were not thoroughly thought through. This represents poor leadership on my part. Second, and even more serious, I have misled in the sense of deceiving. I have led you to believe that I was chairing this council, but in fact, I was not. My husband was really leading through me. I allowed myself to be manipulated by Gil, and the results have not been good. The church didn't elect Gil to the council, and the council didn't elect Gil to be chair, but because of my lack of backbone and character, Gil has effectively been functioning as the chair of our council, and I've been his puppet.

"I can't blame anyone for this but myself. My first instinct upon acknowledging my failure was to resign, but upon further reflection, I would like instead to make this formal apology to the council, and I would like to ask the council to allow me to continue to serve as chair, this time, though, without compromising my leadership. I've done wrong; I would like the chance to make it right. I misled us into this swamp; I'd like to responsibly lead us through it to some firm ground on the other side." She cleared her throat, and her eyes filled with tears; she reached into her pocket to find a tissue.

Stan Corder spoke up. "I'd like to thank you, Nancy, for your honesty. I had wondered on a few occasions if this might be the case. I should have spoken up and raised some concerns, but I thought I was the only one. For my part, your apology is accepted, on the condition that it be joined by my apology for not speaking up. And I want to say that you have my fullest confidence and support and my promise to speak up in the future if I have concerns."

Heads were nodding around the table. Ky spoke up next, agreeing with Stan, and then the two Terrys (the male Terry Fink and the female Terry Torrance), then Frank Roberts, and finally, Patricia Jurgen, the secretary, who added, "I'll note this as Stan's motion, with Ky's second, and a unanimous *yea*."

"But we haven't heard from Dan yet," Nancy added. "I'm not sure if he's allowed to vote, given his current status, but I think it's important that we hear from him." Everyone turned toward me—at the opposite end of the table from Nancy, but Nancy wasn't finished speaking: "Beyond my general apology, I need to make a special apology to Dan, which is why I asked you to be here tonight. Dan, under my misleading leadership, this church council placed you on administrative leave. Perhaps this could have been legitimate, but it wasn't, because from the beginning, this whole process has been . . . disingenuous."

Heads were turning back and forth from Nancy to me, from me to Nancy. She continued, "Gil had convinced me that unless we maneuvered you into resigning, the church would split, but the split wouldn't have been your fault, Dan. It would have been Gil's. I owe you a deep apology, for what we've already put you and Carol through and for what we were about to put you through. Will you . . . will you forgive me?"

I wish I could say that feelings of mercy and forgiveness flooded me at that moment. The fact is, I again felt sick to my stomach. A familiar acidic taste filled my mouth, and I wondered if I would have to leave the room. I wanted to say, "Yes, I'll forgive you," but a pool of grief and pain, and way in the background, a muddy reservoir of anger, seemed to be released in me, and instead of feeling warm, I felt cold. Ky later told me I turned pale, like I was about to faint; all I remember is looking down at my hands, which I unfolded and placed flat on the table, and said, "No problem, Nancy. I accept your apology. Let's move on. Let's figure out where to go from here. I don't hold anything against you. I appreciate your honesty. Your forthrightness . . . that helps a lot." I meant what I said, but I realized that the word *forgive* was nowhere to be found in my response.

Then, her voice low and unsteady, Nancy explained to the group that she had asked me to prepare a proposal on what I felt we should do to get beyond our current impasse. I took out from a manila folder a one-page single-spaced plan and read it to the council:

> As the council has recognized, I have been going through some changes in my theology in recent years. These changes have found expression in my preaching and teaching. I cannot in any way blame the council for raising concerns about these changes in my thinking. You have every right to raise questions and concerns; in fact, you have a responsibility to do so. However, the decision to join the BEF strikes me as an unwise and dangerous overreaction. If my new thinking would lead us into one sort of new territory, the BEF would lead us into other territory less in keeping with our mainstream evangelical heritage and more in keeping with fundamentalism. Here is my counterproposal:
>
> 1. We schedule a special congregational meeting to choose between three options.
>   a. To continue affiliating with the BEF, which would require us to release me and seek a new pastor more in line with the BEF doctrinal statement.

    b. To retain me as our pastor and discontinue association with the BEF.

    c. To break ties with the BEF and also to release me as pastor.

2. If the congregation chooses option a, I would resign immediately.

3. If the congregation chooses option b, I would continue to preach and teach what I'm learning on my journey. Each year for the next three years, the church council would take a vote of confidence; if at least two-thirds do not approve my continuing ministry here, I would immediately leave, no questions asked. That way, if the council feels I've gone too far or gotten off track, there can be an easy way of having me go.

4. If the congregation chooses option c, I would either leave immediately, or at the council's request, I would be willing to stay long enough to find a successor.

After I finished my presentation, Stan spoke up. "Nancy, I wonder if we could read the doctrinal statement from the BEF before we discuss Dan's proposal. I'm embarrassed that we didn't read it when we voted to affiliate." Nancy took out a few copies of the statement, and we passed them around the room. For a few minutes, as the council members read the statement, there was silence punctuated by the sound of turning pages, a few sighs, and two or three audible *mmmm*'s from Stan. Stan was the first to speak up: "I'd have to say, for myself, that I'd be unwilling to accept option a. I don't think we should be affiliated with the BEF. That's a step backward. No offense to Gil or to you, Nancy, but I think this was a terrible direction for us to go—straight back into the 1920s."

"Or the 1620s," Terry Fink said. "I agree."

Then Stan spoke up again: "Dan, I wonder if we could still get answers to the questions we sent you. Just as we were unwise to affiliate with the BEF without reading their doctrinal statement, I think we'd be unwise to present option b to the congregation without knowing in whatever detail we can exactly where you are in your thinking."

I reached into my folder and took out copies of my answers. "Stan, I was just going to hand these out. I think you're absolutely right." I read through my answers aloud:

1. What is your doctrine of Scripture? Please include specific affirmations or denials of the inerrancy of the Word of God.

I believe that the Bible is inspired by God and is profitable for teaching, reproof, correction, and training in right living, so that the people of God may be adequately equipped for every good work. I believe that God has spoken to us through the ages at various times and in various ways, and I believe that God spoke most decisively and fully in his Son, Jesus, who is the Word of God and who fully images God with the living radiance of God's glory. I believe that the Scriptures do not simply tell people what to think; rather, by wrestling with the difficulties and counterpoints of Scripture, we are challenged to think, and in this process, we become wiser than we would have been any other way. Wisdom gained in this way will save us from many errors and confusions.

Words like *inerrancy, infallibility,* and *authority* are related to a philosophical approach to belief systems that I used to hold but no longer do. I believe that the Word of God is inerrant, but I do not believe that the Bible is absolutely equivalent to the phrase "the Word of God" as used in the Bible. Although I do not find the term *inerrancy* useful, I want to affirm that my regard for Scripture is higher than ever. I would prefer to use the term *inherency* to describe my view of Scripture: God's *inerrant* Word is *inherent* in the Bible, which makes it an irreplaceable, essential treasure for the church, deserving our wholehearted study and respect, so we can be equipped to do God's work.

2. What is your understanding of the gospel and salvation?

I believe the gospel of Jesus is that the Kingdom of God is at hand and is open to all. I believe that God loved the world so much that God sent Jesus, God's unique Son, so that all who have confidence in Jesus will not perish but will have life in God's kingdom forever, beginning now. I believe that God did not send Jesus into the world to condemn the world, but to save the world.

Salvation has many dimensions. There are many images that help convey these many dimensions. For example, there is a medical image. God sent Jesus to save the world by bringing healing to the world and by training and sending apprentices to become agents of healing. There is a caretaking or shepherding image. God sent Jesus as a shepherd to find lost sheep and bring them back to the flock. There is a harvesting image. God sent Jesus to harvest a field of wheat, so the wheat isn't wasted. There is an educational image. God sent Jesus to teach so that people wouldn't live in ignorance. There is a legal image. God sent Jesus to show what is truly good and what isn't and to offer forgiveness to all who repent. There is an economic and political image. God sent Jesus to buy back people who had sold themselves into slavery so that they could live in freedom and dignity.

I believe that salvation is elucidated through all these images and more.

3. What is your position on heaven and hell? Explain your position in reference to universalism, inclusivism, exclusivism, and conditionalism. What is your position on homosexuality?

As for the first question, the only way I can answer it is as follows:

Re exclusivism: I believe that God in justice wants to exclude from creation all that is evil and wrong, including the irreligious sins of the irreligious and the religious sins of the religious.

Re inclusivism: I believe that God wants to include everyone and everything redeemable by mercy and grace.

Re universalism: I believe that God's love is universal, that God has goodwill toward all, universally, and that God looks on all with mercy and justice, universally. I also believe that Jesus is the universal Savior, meaning that he brings good news and hope to all people.

Re conditionalism: I believe that God's love is unconditional and that God's truth is also unconditional. In other words, God shows no favorites. All will have to stand before God's merciful and just gaze and will be judged by justice and mercy. In this context, all evil will be judged and excluded, all good saved and included, universally.

I respect and will continue to respect those who feel or think differently on all of these questions.

Regarding homosexuality, I wish I had a clear opinion. As it is, any position I imagine taking, including the conservative position I have held all my life, has so many downsides and problems associated with it that my most honest answer is, "I don't know." I do know that we need to treat homosexuals with respect; as we treat "the least of these," so we treat Christ. Until recently, I never knew a homosexual personally, much less a confessing Christian who is homosexual. Recently I began getting to know an intersexual person living as a lesbian. I can never speak of homosexuality in the abstract again. I have to keep my new friend's face in mind and seek to treat this person as I would treat our Lord, in the guise of "the least of these." I do not believe that homosexuality is among the most pressing moral issues of our time; for example, I believe that heterosexual marital infidelity is a far more serious and pervasive problem. Similarly, I believe that the stresses put on people sexually by advertising and entertainment interests are also more serious and pervasive than the effects of homosexuality, suggesting that the love of money, not sex, is at the root of our problems, as Paul said in I Timothy.

On that last point, Terry Torrance shocked us all by telling us that both her own adult daughter and her older sister had come out as lesbians, and she felt as I did. A lively dialogue followed. Several clarifying questions were raised about my answers, but to my surprise, no one expressed strong disagreement, and the tone was gentle, not tense. I felt that I was being shown respect, whether or not the council members agreed with me. Even though Gil had never been physically present at our meetings, the absence of his influence at this meeting was almost palpable. Fear was gone. There was freedom in the air. So we modified my proposal slightly to reflect our conversation, and it passed unanimously. In May, we held a series of congregational meetings at which members could ask questions of the council and of me. Nancy was articulate, frank, and discrete in her description of what had been going on for the previous seven months. Although she never mentioned Gil's name, his absence from church services and these meetings confirmed what people had probably suspected; they were kind enough not to probe too deeply. We brought in a church consultant—not from the BEF this time—to guide us in the process, and her professional insight helped us a great deal. In mid-June, we held our congregational vote, and I was welcomed back to our pulpit with a nearly unanimous vote. My first Sunday back—June 20—was followed by a church picnic, and it truly felt like a new beginning, both for PCC and for me.

Gil never returned to the church after that council meeting at Ky and Leticia's. He had staked everything on joining the BEF, and I think he was too angry, or ashamed, to show up after his plan had failed. Along with him, seven or eight people left PCC as well.

Sadly, after coming to services alone for a few months, by summer's end Nancy felt she could no longer come either, in the interest of her marriage. "Gil feels betrayed," she said on her last Sunday with us, "betrayed by me, by you, even by the BEF. He was hoping the BEF would come in and assert itself, but Chip refused. He said the BEF existed to help churches, not interfere where they weren't wanted. I think we'll end up at Dr. Road's church. There's a lot Gil doesn't like there, but at least he thinks the preaching is, as he says, 'sound.'"

Nancy and Carol stayed in touch. In fact, they became closer friends than ever. Whenever Nancy visited our home, she treated me with warmth as a friend, and we were genuinely glad to see each other. Through her smiles, I saw a hidden pain in her face, but we didn't talk about it.

I understood, and she understood that I understood, and neither of us could think of anything good that would come from talking about how hard it must have been to live with Gil.

HOMEWORK ASSIGNMENT

Here, Reader, fix thine eyes well on the truth,
For now indeed so subtile is the veil,
Surely to penetrate within is easy.

—*Purgatorio*, VII.19–21

I RECEIVED AN E-MAIL from Neil a few weeks after our trip to the Holocaust Museum.

Dan:
I know you're still trying to work out this confusing issue of hell, and I still feel bad that perhaps our day in D.C. was too much too fast. You have a sensitive soul, more sensitive than mine. Please let me apologize once more. I had an idea I wanted to suggest that might help you in grappling with the Scriptures on hell.

The real issue is Matthew's gospel. Mark talks much less about hell, and Luke actually softens many of Matthew's statements. John, of course, never uses the word. So here's what I'd suggest. Make a table with four columns, headed "Passage," "Behavior," "Consequence," and "Point." Read through Matthew, and note each passage that deals with the subject of judgment (not just passages that explicitly mention hell or Gehenna or Hades). Then note the behavior that will be judged, along with the consequence that follows that behavior. Then try to identify the point: what is the rhetorical purpose of the passage?

Here's what I think you'll find.

1. Our contemporary modern Western conservative Protestant gospel would say this:

> Behavior: Not accepting Jesus Christ as personal savior, not being saved or born again, not asking Jesus into your heart so your sins can be forgiven, etc.
>
> Consequence: Being sent to hell.
>
> Point: Accept Jesus as your personal Savior.

2. Not one passage from the Gospels says anything remotely like this.

Let me know what you think.

Neil

P.S. Can you and Carol do a double date with my new lady friend and me sometime soon? We heard about a great Ethiopian restaurant in Adams Morgan, and we want to check it out with some friends. Maybe we can talk hell over dinner.

I chuckled when I read the e-mail late one night. Carol happened to be passing by the stairway to my attic office and called up to me, "What's so funny, darlin'?"

"Neil just gave me a homework assignment," I said. "Can you believe that guy?"

"You'd better do it," she said. "Jess always did her homework from Dr. Oliver, and look where it got her!"

Over the next few weeks, I completed the survey of Matthew as Neil suggested. I picked a red-letter Bible, so it was easy to skim to Jesus' own words. I was so intrigued that I also skimmed Mark and Luke and noted places that differed from Matthew. It was just as Neil said: there, Jesus spoke less often and less strongly about judgment and hell than in Matthew's gospel. Then I followed the theme through John as well. I filled up most of a yellow legal pad with my scribblings and then copied them into a table on my computer.

Passage	Behavior	Consequence	Point
Matthew			
3:5, 12—John the Baptist	Trees bear no fruit.	Ax cuts trees and burns them. Chaff burned.	Repent! Be fruitful!
5:13	Salt has no taste.	Will be thrown out, trampled underfoot.	Have taste: be what you should be. Live your identity.

Passage	Behavior	Consequence	Point
5:19	Breaks least commandment.	Called least in kingdom.	Don't reduce standards; raise them.
5:21–26	Angry at brother, call fool.	Judgment, danger of hellfire, imprisoned, pay last penny.	Reconcile!
5:27–30 (repeated in 18:8)	Failure to amputate offending part of body.	Thrown into hell.	Don't be complacent! Take drastic measures to avoid sin!
6:5–18	Praying, fasting to be noticed.	No further reward beyond being noticed.	Be sincere, genuine, nonhypocritical.
6:19–34	Storing treasures on earth.	Moths, rust, thieves will waste investment.	Invest in heaven with God; be rich toward God; treat others kindly.
7:1–5	Judging.	You will be judged as you judge.	Treat others kindly, not harshly.
7:13–14	Going through wide gate and on broad road.	Destruction.	Choose life by following the difficult path.
7:15–20	Tree bears bad fruit.	Will be cut down and burned.	Bear good fruit!
7:21–23	People say "Lord, Lord," but don't do Father's will.	Will hear, "Away from me! I never knew you!"	Do the Father's will! Don't just say the right words.
8:10–12	Insiders (Jews) have less faith than a Gentile (centurion).	Thrown out into outer darkness, weeping and gnashing teeth.	Have faith in the authority of Jesus.
9:12–13	Not caring for sinners, thinking of self as healthy.	Not healed.	Learn this: "I desire mercy, not sacrifice."
10:11 ff.	People reject disciples, message.	Better for Sodom and Gomorrah on day of judgment.	Don't be afraid of rejection.
10:28	Fearing rejection, persecution, martyrdom.	God can destroy body and soul in hell (does not say he will do so).	Don't be afraid of mere humans. (Note: Does this verse imply that

			the soul is not inherently immortal?)
10:33	Being ashamed of Jesus.	Will be disowned before the Father.	Don't fear persecution.
10:37	Seeking to save your own life.	You will lose it.	Don't worry about self-preservation.
11:20–24	Cities refuse to repent.	Gentile cities will be better off in judgment, go down to depths.	Repent when the message comes to you!
12:30	Speaking against the Holy Spirit.	Will not be forgiven.	Don't reject the Holy Spirit!
12:36	Uttering careless words.	Give account, be condemned.	Don't misjudge Jesus.
12:39 ff.	Not repenting.	Nineveh and other Gentiles will rise to condemn.	Repent when you hear the message!
13:1 ff.	Not receiving message with a good heart.	No fruit.	Hear and receive the message, bear fruit!
13:24 ff.	Being weeds, no fruit, no harvest; everything that causes sin, all who do evil.	Burned, weeping and gnashing of teeth.	Bear fruit. Hear and respond to message.
13:47	Being bad fish caught in net with good.	Sorted out, thrown out, burned in fiery furnace, weepingand gnashing of teeth.	Rightly understand the message!
15:13	Pharisees offended at Jesus' message.	Pulled up by roots, fall into a ditch.	Don't be like the Pharisees.
16:24 ff.	Deeds.	Rewarded according to deeds.	Do good.
18:5–8 ff.	Causing a child to stumble or sin.	Better to be drowned in sea. Thrown into hell.	Be gentle to children, the weak, value as lost sheep.
18:21	Unmerciful servant received but didn't show mercy.	Given to jailers, tortured until paid back.	Be merciful! Forgive! Don't seek revenge.
21:43	Don't produce fruit.	Kingdom taken away and given to others. Rebels broken, crushed.	Produce fruit.

Passage	Behavior	Consequence	Point
22:1–14	a. Refused invitation to banquet.	a. Destroyed by army.	a. Respond to invitation to kingdom.
	b. No wedding clothes.	b. Tied, thrown out into darkness, weeping and gnashing of teeth.	b. Have wedding clothes (?).
23:13	Shut others out of kingdom.	Won't enter it.	Welcome others into kingdom; don't be like Pharisees.
23:15	Pharisees win converts.	Turn into twice sons of hell they are.	Don't be like Pharisees.
23:33	Woe to Pharisees! Snakes!	How will you escape being sent to hell? Righteous blood on you.	Don't be hypocrites like Pharisees.
24:45 ff.	Servant in charge mistreats other servants.	Cut to pieces, put with hypocrites, weeping and gnashing of teeth.	Take care of fellow servants, don't mistreat.
25:14 ff.	Parable of talents, used money entrusted to them, one hid talent.	Called wicked and lazy.	Don't waste what you've been entrusted with. (Bear fruit again.)
25:31 ff.	Sheep and goats, didn't care for those in need.	Told to depart, cursed, sent to eternal fire prepared for devil and angels.	Show kindness to least of these.
26:24	Judas betrays Jesus.	Better if not born.	Be loyal to Jesus, don't betray.
28:18–20			Is making disciples the way the disciples should be fruitful?

Mark

Passage	Behavior	Consequence	Point
3:24	Blasphemy against Holy Spirit.	Never forgiven.	Don't say Jesus is from the devil.
9:42 ff.	Causing children to sin, failing to cut off hand if it causes you to sin.	Cast into hell where worm never dies. (Isaiah 66:24—dead bodies, not	Don't cause children (weak and vulnerable?) to stumble, take sin

		disembodied souls; worm never dies, not people.)	seriously.
12:9	Tenants reject messengers, kill son.	Kill them, give vineyard to others.	Respect messengers!
12:38–40	Teachers of law want to be respected, devour widows' homes, show off prayers.	Punished most severely.	Don't be like Pharisees.

Luke

1:46 ff., Mary's prayer	Proud, rulers.	Scattered, brought down.	Humble are blessed, reversal of status quo.
6:35	Ungrateful and wicked.	God is kind to them.	Imitate God's mercy.
6:46	Hearing but not doing.	House falls.	Hear and do.
9:23	Save life.	Lose life.	Don't be ashamed of Son of Man.
12:4–7	Fearing persecution.	God can kill you and send you to hell (doesn't say he will, just that he can— but he cares for sparrows).	Don't fear people; serve God.
12:47 ff.	Knows God's will, doesn't do; doesn't know and does wrong.	Beaten with many blows; beaten with few blows.	Be alert, wake up, know times.
12:54 ff.	Doesn't reconcile.	Thrown into prison, pay last cent.	Reconcile now.
13:6 ff.	No fruit.	Given second chance, then cut down.	Bear fruit.
13:1 ff., 22 ff.	Those who don't strive, those who consider themselves first.	Banished away from God, weeping and gnashing of teeth again.	Don't speculate about others; pay attention to yourself.
14:15, gentler version of Matt. 22	Don't accept banquet invitation.	Miss banquet.	Respond to God's invitation.

Passage	Behavior	Consequence	Point
15:11	Lost son story—older brother stays outside.	Misses party.	Welcome sinners.
16:19 ff., rich man and Lazarus	Living in luxury, careless toward poor neighbor, receiving good things in this life. Brothers won't listen to law and prophets.	Sent to Hades.	Be compassionate to needy now; don't hoard good things.
19:11, like Matt. 25 but gentler	Failed to return on investment.	Take away mina from unfaithful servant. Kill those who rejected king.	Be faithful and fruitful.

John

Passage	Behavior	Consequence	Point
3:17, 18	Avoiding light to avoid exposing evil deeds.	Jesus doesn't condemn. They are condemned already.	Don't avoid light; come to light, face evil deeds, believe in Jesus.
5:28	Do evil.	Condemned. (Note: All raised to receive reward for deeds.)	Jesus doesn't condemn; he judges, that is, tells truth about our actions.
6	Don't believe in Jesus, don't receive living bread from heaven.	Do not live; die.	Believe, receive living bread.
8:21–24		Die in your sins.	Repent.
12:47 ff.	Do not keep Jesus' words.	Jesus doesn't judge, but his words judge them at the last day.	Keep Jesus' words.
15:6	No fruit.	Fruitless branches burned.	Bear fruit, especially love.

My homework assignment did me a lot of good. I was more confident than ever that our modern Western use of hell was far different from Jesus' use of it, and I was beginning to be convinced—not just because Neil told me but because I was seeing it myself—that Jesus wasn't endorsing the Pharisees' view of hell: he was turning it on its head to make a point about what really matters to God. I shared this conclusion with Neil when we were driving down to the Ethiopian restaurant with him and Ashara, the woman he had been spending so much time with. She and Carol were in the front seat, so Neil and I could talk in the back.

"What's the point that Jesus is trying to make?" he asked.

I thought for a minute and replied, "One thing it definitely wasn't, just as you predicted. It wasn't 'hold the right beliefs,' 'affirm the right doctrines,' or anything like that. Instead, Jesus was clearly interested in action, in what we do, in how we treat others especially, and in whether we trust him enough to follow his teaching even if it means difficulty and persecution. It was clear that Jesus wasn't just saying that anything goes, everything's OK. He was telling people that they would be held accountable, that how they live now would count forever."

"So," Neil said, "according to Jesus, everyone will face judgment, even his followers."

"Yes, but he emphasizes this so that we'll not be hypocritical or complacent now. The strongest theme was clear," I said. "Bear fruit now—don't just talk or say the right things, but live out the teaching of the Kingdom of God, especially in the area of compassion for the weak and needy and vulnerable. Have confidence in Jesus so that you will actually do what he says."

At that point, Carol interrupted and told us we needed to stop talking theology. "For heaven's sake," she said, "can't we have a nice dinner without you two talking about eternal perdition? Especially with this lovely lady in the car!" We laughed and took her advice.

BOOK TWO

THE WORD
AFTER THAT

20

HOW CAN I HURT HIM?

Where there are people in a like dispute;
. . . a base wish it is to wish to hear it.

—*Inferno,* XXX.147–148

IT WAS APRIL 2004. A year had passed, a good year in the life of PCC, maybe our best year ever. The council did a good and thorough job of communicating what had transpired, and the fact that the congregation had a say in the outcome contributed greatly to the smoothness of my transition back into leadership. Gil's disappearance had no small role either. I don't mean to portray Gil as a spiritual arsonist, but without him there, sparks of contention never seemed to catch fire as they had before.

It was a good year for the Poole family too. Cory and Trent were thriving in school, in youth group, in sports—Corey in track and field, Trent in lacrosse. Sure, they occasionally had meltdowns typical of adolescent boys, but they were good guys, doing well. Of special joy, Jess and Kincaid had gotten engaged at Christmas and planned to get married in the fall of 2005, after Kincaid graduated in the second summer session. I had never seen Jess happier, which predisposes a dad to be positive about the man in her life. Carol was recovering from our ordeal with PCC, maybe more slowly than me, but she was thrilled about Jess's engagement and was already dreaming of being a grandmother—the sooner the better, she said, always eliciting a groan from her daughter. "The last few years were full of hard days," Carol said, "but I reckon we outlasted them, and better days have come."

I was doing well too, happy again in my ministry, feeling more solidarity than ever with our church council, preaching as well as I ever had. Carol and I started a fellowship group in our home to which we invited a number of our neighbors and friends, some from PCC, others not. We invited Pat and soon she and Chloe became regulars. We would read a passage from the Bible out loud together each week and then discuss it, with no opinions censored and with a lot of humor every week. Chloe, it turned out, was a stand-up comic incognito, and sometimes she'd get us laughing, and then she would start laughing uncontrollably herself, which would get us laughing all the more. There was something about seeing her large, frail frame jiggling with laughter that seemed so good, so right. Quite often Pat would read us an original poem she had written in response to the previous week's discussion. "About half of her poems I get," Carol told me one night after our guests left. "The other half don't make much sense to me. I reckon it's like a friend who always brings you cookies—you're grateful for the burned ones just as much as the good ones, since it's an act of kindness either way." I agreed.

Occasionally, like an old injury, a surge of resentment would flare up about Gil. The last flare-up occurred on a Saturday morning in April. I had made a quick trip to the local Home Depot for some supplies for a garden Carol wanted to put in. As I pushed my shopping cart to my car and began unloading some flats of flowers and bags of fertilizer into the trunk, I noticed out of the corner of my eye that a man about my size had pushed his cart to the car beside mine and that he, too, was unloading flats of flowers and bags of fertilizer into his trunk. I glanced to my right, and immediately a shiver ran through me, a kind of shock: it was Gil, not fifteen feet away from me. What would I do?

I thought of speaking to him. But what would I say? I thought of pretending I didn't see him and getting into my car until he left. But what if he had seen me glance over at him—wouldn't my avoidance of him be taken as an insult? And then, for a delicious, shameful second, another thought blossomed in my mind: *an insult—now is my chance, so . . . what can I do to hurt him?* Maybe the insult of ignoring him would be just fine, or maybe there would be a single sentence I could utter that would be even more effective.

In a flash, I felt the old resentment burning hot again, just for a second, as if a brushfire had suddenly flared in my heart. But then just as quickly, I realized that I hated how the hatred felt. In fact, I hated the hatred more than I hated the man who had caused me, my wife, and his own wife such pain.

So somehow, bending over, lowering a flat of marigolds into my trunk, in an instant, I just let it go: I let that flash of revenge pass, dropped the thought of it like a hot piece of metal. In its place came this thought: *What could I do to reconcile with him?* So I turned toward him, having no idea what I would say, took one hesitant step in his direction, held out my hand, and said, "Gil. Gil Zeamer."

He straightened up and for some reason didn't look the slightest bit shocked or uncomfortable seeing me. Maybe he had recognized me already, or maybe I was somehow unworthy of registering any emotion on his face. He pursed his lips, folded his arms, nodded slightly, looking grim, but didn't say anything. Then came a long awkward moment when I didn't know what to say, so I pointed to Gil's cart with my outstretched hand and said the first thing that came to mind: "Can I return your cart for you?" And he stared at me for a second, pressed the trunk closed, and then stepped away from the cart, without a word, and got into the car. As I pushed his shopping cart and pulled mine back to the line of carts at the front of the store, I heard his engine crank, start, reverse, shift gears, and drive away, not fast, not slow. He didn't look back.

From that moment, neither the boiling hatred nor the simmering resentment ever returned. In its place came a sadness, a sadness I still feel when I think of Gil even now. The next day during worship, as I preached on the story of Palm Sunday, the words of the gospel struck me: "If only you knew what makes for peace . . . I wanted to gather you as a mother hen gathers her chicks, but you would not." I almost wept—for Gil, for Nancy, for myself, for us all.

Shortly after Easter, we received some major news, good news, news of another engagement at our future son-in-law's house. Kincaid's housemate, Neil, was engaged too—to Dr. Ashara Nandorvir, the thirty-something oncologist he'd begun dating in 2003. Ashara had treated our mutual friend Kerry Ellison, Kincaid's mother, during her final days at the National Institutes of Health. A few months after Kerry's death, a nurse was cleaning a room in the cancer ward. There in the back of an otherwise empty bedside drawer she found an unfinished note to someone named Neil. The nurse read it, remembered Kerry, and touched by its contents, shared it with Dr. N (as the nurses called her), knowing that Dr. N had also grown very close to Kerry. Ashara decided to present the card to Neil herself, so she did the necessary detective work, and when they met, a friendship began that gradually became a romance.

Neil was like a new man, even more enthusiastic, jovial, and passionate than ever. Ashara, Indian ethnically, had been born and raised in Trinidad, so she was "an island person, like me," Neil said. When the two of them talked, the dueling accents were absolutely delightful, and although Ashara was a bit more shy, she loved to laugh even more than Neil: "When you work in oncology, you have to celebrate all the good you can," she'd say. As their romance grew, I saw less of Neil than I would have otherwise, since the two of them were always together, building a bank of shared experiences—museums, art galleries, mountain hikes, beach trips, restaurants, and cooking, cooking, cooking—Ashara's passion, which Neil enjoyed as well, evidenced by his gain in weight over the year.

In late April, they invited Carol and me to a dinner they prepared one Sunday evening, a mix of Indian and Caribbean flavors, with the best fruit salad I ever tasted for dessert. I can still taste sharp and sweet on my tongue now as I write. That was the happy night they announced their engagement to us. Upon hearing the news, Carol cried and I clapped and hooted as if I were at a sports event.

Then I hugged Ashara, and then Carol hugged them both, and then we stood together in a circle between the dining room table and the living room couch. Neil asked me to pray a prayer of blessing over them, which I did, after which we took our drinks and desserts into the living room and sat down. Even though I was overjoyed, I was careful to turn down the celebratory cigar Neil offered me. Ashara scolded him for smoking, and told us he promised to quit before the wedding.

21

NICE WALLEYE FISHING CHARTERS

Thus I beheld the glorious wheel move round,
And render voice to voice, in modulation
And sweetness that can not be comprehended . . .

—*Paradiso*, X.144–145

SINCE THE BEGINNING of the year, Neil had been planning a reunion with a group of four special friends for the week after the school year ended. Through the years, Neil had accumulated a handful of mentors and friends who shared his unconventional views to one degree or another, and they had a kind of pact to meet together regularly, once a year if possible. For the previous few years, their rhythm had been interrupted, which made this year's gathering all the more significant. "Truth be told," he said to me one afternoon that June, "these are the people I know with."

"'Know with'?" I asked.

"Haven't you noticed how learning and knowing are ultimately communal experiences, social experiences?" he asked in reply.

"I can see how learning is communal—like learning in a class or small group," I replied. "But knowing?"

"Think of the word *consciousness,* whose components mean *know with.* I've found I can only know so much until I find a community that shares my knowing. If I begin growing very far beyond my what my community allows me to know, I need to persuade my community to think with me or else find or form a new community. These people I'll be meeting with are the group that I've been knowing with for many years," Neil replied. Then he cocked his head and added, "Daniel, would you like to join us? I'd need to check with the group, but I think we could add another person or two."

I had regretted saying no to one of Neil's invitations in the past, so I gave my most affirmative reply possible: "Let me check with Carol." She OK'd the trip, so I was in from our end. Later that evening, Neil contacted his former pastor, Father Scott Clark, a retired Episcopal priest now living in Minnesota. Scott would be hosting the gathering at his lakefront cottage in northern Minnesota. Neil also arranged for another friend to join us—our housemate, Casey Curtis. And so the second week of June came and went, and Neil, Casey, and I boarded a plane for Minneapolis. Father Scott met us curbside in a van.

Father Scott was the senior member of our little group. Wiry, tanned, his wrinkled face always smiling under an old red Farm-All cap, Scott looked like he had spent his life climbing down from tractors, not pulpits. When he spoke, his Minnesota roots came through in his habit of starting or ending nearly every other sentence with *here, then, now, well,* or *there*— or sometimes two of the five. "Well now, this is a beautiful day we've been blessed with here," he said as we loaded into the van. "Now that's quite a hairdo you've got there, Casey. Pretty sound along with pretty looks. Well then, looks like we're all loaded in here. So what do you say we hit the road now?" Bathed in Father Scott's kindness, we drove to another airport nearby, where we picked up three more of Neil's friends.

Dr. Ruth Mitchell was a theology professor and was highly respected by Father Scott: "Now that woman can really write about the gospel and justice. There's a real scholar for you." She was known both as a feminist theologian and a black theologian. She had an elegant southern accent reflecting her roots in Mississippi, where she had worked alongside Dr. Martin Luther King Jr. when she was in seminary in the 1960s. She was plump, her hair more salt and less pepper than Neil's, and she wore baggy brown pants and an African dashiki in a kind of burnt orange with black markings that contrasted beautifully with her dark coffee skin and copious silver jewelry. *Colorful* was my first impression of her, and it proved true. She now taught theology and religion at a secular university in southern California, though I never learned which one. She arrived on the same connecting flight from Chicago with another woman, also a former student of hers, a Latina pastor from New Jersey, Milagros Torres.

"Millie's the real thing," Neil had told me on the flight into Minneapolis. "She and I went to seminary together. After seminary, she planted an urban church called The Little Flower. They bought an old warehouse in a rundown neighborhood in Camden and use it as a community center. Only God knows how many lives they've touched there—tutoring, choirs, recreation, summer camps, plus there's a studio where kids make music and poetry and art. Of all the churches I've ever visited, The Little Flower is my favorite—no offense to PCC, of course! But her work is so hard. There are so many discouragements, so many things to overcome."

Millie couldn't have looked more different from Ruth as they met us at baggage claim: thirty-something, tall, thin, with a diamond stud in her nose, a row of silver rings in her ears, another piercing in her eyebrow, and blue-green tattoos like vines on her arms, her hair bleached reddish-brown with blond streaks, her glasses having the same kind of thick black plastic rims that Ky Lang wore. She had a violin slung over her shoulder. She was the last person in the airport I would have identified as a pastor. Only one thing identified her: a certain sadness in the eyes, not just fatigue, but that special fatigue that comes from seeing so much suffering at such close range.

We waited half an hour or so for the arrival of our final guest, another black man, in his late fifties, I guessed. He had a deeply creased face and a patch of gray beard on his chin, his wiry gray hair combed back, longer than I'd expect in a man his age. Markus Park wore a black T-shirt under a black suit jacket, black jeans, and white tennis shoes—a combination Carol never would have let me leave the house wearing. He and Neil embraced warmly, and I heard Neil say, "Together again, my friend," and he replied with the same words. Then Ruth, Scott, and Millie similarly embraced and exchanged exactly the same greeting. Then Neil introduced Markus to Casey and me. "I've heard so much about you both," he said, and embraced us warmly. As he stepped away, I saw that his black T-shirt had writing on it: "I'm not *THAT* kind of Baptist!"

The seven of us loaded into the van and drove north for about three hours. We passed small town after smaller town, lake after lake, signs that said "NICE WALLEYE FISHING CHARTERS" and "FREE KITTENS" and "AGED FIREWOOD." We survived a major argument about where to stop for a late lunch, with Ruth and Millie insulting the meat eaters in every way they could think of, all in good fun. After lunch and on the road again, Neil asked each of us to share a five-minute autobiography, and then the others could ask questions. Millie and Casey were hilarious, and between their stories and their comments on the rest of our stories, they had us laughing for most of the trip. Neil went last, and it became clear to me that everyone there knew even more about his story than I did. Clearly, this circle, minus Casey and me, was already a tight-knit group. "How did the five of you get to know each other?" I asked.

"It's Markus's fault," Ruth said with a gentle laugh. "Markus was my colleague in seminary back East. One semester he told me he had found an extraordinarily bright black student in one of his classes, a middle-aged gentleman, perhaps the most impressive student he had ever had. I told him I also had an extraordinary student, a young Latina. He suggested we meet with them together for coffee every week, to do some more personal mentoring. 'The classroom is only a beginning,' Markus would always say. The four of us became close friends, and when Neo and Millie graduated, we made a deal—*covenant* would be a more religious term—that we would be friends no matter what. Our goal was to meet for at least three days each year for the rest of our lives. We've missed a few years, but by and large we've remained true to our covenant."

Markus added, "Later, when Neo got to know Scott, he joined our little community, our token Anglo."

Casey, in the rear seat, asked what they did when they met. Millie, sitting in the front seat next to Father Scott, turned around in her seat and answered, "I guess you could say we're church for each other. Or maybe we're more like an informal religious order. Or maybe we're just a group of friends who try to get together for a few days once a year. By being together, we find some strength to foster church for others the rest of the year. That's how we know about you two, Dan and Casey. Neo has been telling us about you two for years, and we're so glad now to be able to meet the both of you and welcome you into our little conspiracy." I wasn't sure what that last word meant, but the conversation quickly moved on to Ashara. Neil's three friends wanted to know what Casey and I thought of her and whether we approved of their marriage. There was a lot of joking and poking fun at Neil, some of it slightly off-color. "Let me assure you," he said in retaliation, "when you meet her, your only question will be why a fine woman like Ashara would be willing to marry a person with such humdrum friends as yourselves." His reply set off more rounds of banter that continued through the rest of our trip.

We arrived in the late afternoon and settled into Scott's spacious cabin. Each of the women had her own room, and the men shared a bunkhouse attached to the cabin.

After dropping off my suitcase in the bunkhouse, I walked down a steep gravelly path to the dock and watched the sun setting across the lake in the southwest. I couldn't remember the last time I'd seen a sunset. Actually, I couldn't remember the last time I had sat still for very long at all. I took off my shoes and dangled my feet off the dock. The water was cold but refreshing. What struck me first—a suburban guy from the East Coast—was the quiet. No white noise of traffic in the background, just the haunting sound of strange birds, then some laughter from the cabin, and the gentle sound of water splashing as my feet swirled ankle-deep.

My thoughts went back to the previous few years, my conversations with Neil about hell, my readings, and the table I had made as "homework." Why couldn't I shake the subject of hell? Other people didn't seem as obsessed as I was. I breathed a prayer: "Help me, God. Help me get beyond this."

I was about to return to the cabin in the fading light when I heard the sound of shoes on gravel. I turned but couldn't see anyone for a few seconds. Then Markus emerged from the shadows, walking unsteadily down the steep path, reaching from tree to tree to keep his balance. The dock squeaked as he walked out toward me, and he groaned a bit as he first knelt and then sat beside me on the dock, rolled up his pant legs, removed his running shoes and white socks, and dipped his feet in the cold water alongside mine. He let out a long sigh. "A good place you found, young man," he said in his gravelly voice, and patted me on the shoulder. I've always liked it when I was called "young man," ever since I actually was one.

"You're in an ideal place for some deep thinking. Cool feet warm up the mind, you know. What are you thinking about?"

"I'm thinking about hell, Markus," I said. "It's been my obsession for a couple years now."

22

WOLVES IN LAWYERS' TUXEDOS

Infinite Goodness hath such ample arms,
That it receives whatever turns to it.

—*Purgatorio*, III.121–123

"AH, HELL," MARKUS SAID. "Neo told me about that. He asked me to be sure to bring up the subject if you didn't, but you saved me the trouble. Hell is the frequent preoccupation of recovering fundamentalists."

If Neil had said that, it would have had a bit of a bite to it, but from Markus, it sounded harmless, even affectionate. "I guess the shoe fits, Markus. Can you help me recover?"

"Well, there's a lot of good that comes from being a fundamentalist. You generally learn the Bible better than anyone, at least you used to. But the problem isn't just fundamentalism. The problem goes back to dear old Aurelius Augustine, and maybe before," he said, swinging his feet in the water like a boy. "The church latched on to that old doctrine of original sin like a dog to a stick, and before you knew it, the whole gospel got twisted around it. Instead of being God's big message of saving love for the whole world, the gospel became a little bit of secret information on how to solve the pesky legal problem of original sin. That raised a bunch of other questions—like about why some people believe the information and others don't. And soon you had God selecting some for eternal perdition and others for eternal blessing. That theory satisfied some people, but for others it made God seem like a tyrant. So they emphasized human free will instead of God's selection, but either way, the central question the gospel answered was how to solve the original sin problem."

"You sound like Neil, I mean Neo," I said.

Markus laughed. "No, he sounds like me! I taught him most of what he knows!"

I felt that I was being given a rare chance to be mentored by Neil's mentor, so I seized the moment. "Recently, back home, Neil and I have been talking politics. He said something that's been troubling me. He said—or maybe he just implied it—that my conservative politics and my conservative doctrine of hell are related. I haven't felt comfortable asking him about it because . . ."

"Because he'll get too fired up about it, right?" Markus said with another laugh. "Yes, when it comes to this election, the man's got a bee in his bonnet, as my mother used to say. Could I try to interpret Neo for you?" I nodded. "It's as I was just saying. I'm not denying the old doctrine of original sin, but it can be abused in a way that shifts the focus away from human injustice, oppression, and suffering on Planet Earth. It shifts the focus to getting your hindquarters into heaven after you leave Planet Earth. So it makes you worry less about how *bad* humanity is and more about how *mad* the deity is." I smiled, noting that Neil had used nearly the same language as his mentor . . . and also noting that the teacher was less obscure, more direct, and calmer than the student.

He continued, "Now that might be fine for the folks in power, which generally wasn't us black folks. The folks in power could afford to shift the focus away from injustice on earth. In fact, there were many distinct advantages to doing so, since they were perpetrators of a lot of it. If they talked about sin, it tended to be sexual sins, or drunkenness, that sort of thing—all personal or individual sins that they, being middle-class and living in nice suburban homes, found it easier to avoid and condemn or at least hide than some of us. They stayed pretty far away from systemic and social sins like racism and greed. If it wasn't related to the individual and his precious little soul, it pretty much disappeared from view for them.

"But for my people, that other-worldly focus had the smell of something rotten—an evasion of responsibility, a kind of denial. So . . ."—he began fumbling with something in his pocket and pulled out a pipe and loaded it and lit it. Soon, a soothing, sweet aroma filled the air—definitely not "the smell of something rotten."

"So, Dan, that's why black theology and feminist theology have been suspicious of the traditional approach to hell: because it distracts people from justice on earth. It kind of pacifies people so they'll let injustice continue."

"I guess I've heard that before. I mean—that's an idea from Marx, right—religion is the opiate of the masses?" I asked.

"Yes, indeed. But it doesn't just pacify the rage of the masses so they'll keep working for an unfair wage in the plantations or factories or whatever. It also pacifies the shame of the elite, those in power. It makes their injustice a side issue, so they can live with it and keep perpetuating it. After all, life is so short anyway, and history is about to be wrapped up, and then we'll all be in heaven. On judgment day, all God will care about is opening up our skulls and checking in our brains . . ." Here in the dusky light, I could see Markus pretending to unscrew the cap off a person's skull, as if it were a peanut butter jar and then miming as if he were looking for something inside the brains, as he continued, "to see if we had the right notion of salvation by grace through faith in there somewhere. God just wants to see if there's some residue in there of having said the sinner's prayer—which, I might add, as a Baptist boy I myself said at least a hundred times before I was twelve. Hell, I didn't want to go to hell!" Then he laughed, and I chuckled along. "That reminds me," he said. "Did you ever see that *Seinfeld* episode when Elaine's boyfriend tells her she's going to hell, and they go to see a priest?" Then he laughed again.

"Sorry," I said, "I've heard of the show, but I never watched it." Markus looked a little surprised. Ever serious, I continued, "I follow what you're saying, but isn't there a lot of fire-and-brimstone preaching in black churches?"

"Ah, perceptive comment," the old teacher said. "But that generally happens either when the black church is imitating the white church or when it's dealing with internal matters—you know, sin in the camp, that sort of thing. It also might happen when a black preacher feels that his power is a bit threatened. You know, when the deacons are breathing down his neck, he might pull out that kind of talk. There's no more effective power language than the language of hell and the devil."

"I don't mean to sound like the devil's advocate—that's not the best choice of words, I know—but would that mean Jesus was guilty of using power language then, since he talked about hell so much?" I asked.

"Ah, another perceptive response. Neo was right about you," Markus said, puffing on his pipe. "That's the thing about Jesus. He uses the power language of hell to disempower the injustice of the powerful and to empower the disempowered to seek justice." He paused for a moment and then continued, "The Pharisees used hell language in one way. Jesus turned it around and used it in the opposite way. They threatened marginal people with hell unless they submitted to their religious dominance. Jesus threatened the religious establishment with hell unless they showed compassion for the marginal people. Hell has been used and abused, back and forth, ever since. The whole affair is pretty obvious once you realize that a lot of what we call Christianity is actually Phariseeism, you know, wolves in lawyers' tuxedos."

Maybe Neil had been trying to tell me this all along, but Markus seemed clearer, more direct. I tried to summarize: "So if my politics makes me want to marginalize the poor, for example, I'll be tempted to adopt a view of hell that also marginalizes the poor by shifting the focus from their poverty on earth to their destination in heaven. Or maybe I'll say that the reason they're poor on earth is because they're going to hell anyway; it's all their own fault, either way, so I shouldn't intervene. Either way, if I'd like to avoid seeking justice on earth, I'll twist my own understanding of the gospel so that my earthly plans won't be too inconvenienced. Is that what you're saying?"

"Nailed it," Markus said, holding his pipe and scratching his chin hair with his thumb. "Not that I think individuals are all that clever or scurrilous, acting alone, rotten as we can be. I think the worst twisting comes on a systemic level, on the level of what Paul called 'principalities and powers.' Besides, people can find plenty of other excuses to forget or exploit the poor. Shoot, old Josephus said that the Sadducees who didn't believe in afterlife at all were a lot meaner than the Pharisees. Now maybe that was because Josephus was a Pharisee himself, but it may be because if you don't believe in an afterlife, you have even fewer reasons to be good. You know—this is it, so do what you want!"

"Wow. What you're saying makes me see how much is at stake in the way we understand all this. And it makes me respect Jesus a lot. A whole lot."

Markus chuckled, "Of course, even if you buy all that, you're still left with the question of what hell is. Is it real, or is it just a rhetorical device?"

"Yes. That's my question. How would you answer that?"

"Here's what I'd say. Judgment is real. Accountability to God is real. A good, just, reconciling, loving, living God is in everybody's future. The danger of wasting your life and ruining other people's lives is real. Whatever road you take, you'll end up facing God, and that means you'll face the truth about your life—what you've done, who you have become, who you truly are. That's good news—unless you're a bad dude, you know, unjust, hateful, unmerciful, ungenerous, selfish, lustful, greedy, hard-hearted toward God and your neighbor. You know, if God judges, forgives, and eliminates all the bad stuff, there might not be much left of you—maybe not enough to enjoy heaven, maybe not enough to feel too much in hell either."

He paused and then added, "Now I'm a recovering fundamentalist myself, so I know what you're thinking. Go ahead."

I said, "Gosh, I'm thinking two things at once. First, I'm wondering if you think it's possible for people to refuse redemption, you know, eternally. I mean, if God's love is always there, waiting, would they be able to hold out longer than God?" Markus seemed to freeze for a few seconds. I wasn't sure he even heard me. "Markus?" I asked.

"That is not a question that should inspire curiosity to seek an answer. That is a question that should warn a person to seek God, to seek God's kingdom, to seek God's justice. Look, if you need to nail it down, here's one way to see it. Maybe God's plan is an opt-out plan, not an opt-in one. If you want to stay out of the party, you can. Nobody will force you to enjoy it. But it's hard for me to imagine somebody being more stubbornly ornery than God is gracious." I expected more, but he stopped there. Then he turned a bit toward me: "You said there were two things."

"Well, what you said a minute ago sounds like salvation by works. Good people are saved, and bad people are not—at least not yet. But justification by grace through faith, isn't that at the heart of the gospel?"

He replied, "Well, it certainly is at the heart of the modern Western gospel. But at the heart of Jesus' gospel was the Kingdom of God, which certainly includes justification by grace and all the rest. So I'm not denying salvation by grace, no, no, not at all. It's all by grace. I'm just advocating judgment by works."

I literally snapped my head in his direction. "What?"

"Salvation by grace, judgment by works. There's nothing in the Bible clearer than those two realities. Of course, you have to define salvation in Jesus' way, not just modern Western Christianity's."

"But I thought . . ."

"You thought that if you are saved, you're not judged, right? Yep, I used to think that too. I didn't realize that being judged isn't the same as being condemned and that being saved means a lot more than not being judged. For a lot of folk, salvation still means little more than escaping from the legal consequences of having original sin on your passport. For them, until you have your passport changed, which is what being saved means, you can't get through customs in heaven and you're stuck going to hell. But remember—conventional Western Christianity is the religion of empire. It developed at a time when the church and the empire were joined at the hip, if not the heart. A lot of us didn't get too good a deal from Imperial Christianity. I guess you could say that some of us have seceded from Imperial Christianity, the theology of the empire. When you secede from the theology of empire, your understandings of salvation and judgment can change for the better. So young man, you have an alternative if you want it, if you don't mind getting on the bus with us black folk and poor folk."

He banged out his pipe on the dock, refilled and relit it, and continued speaking. "Try this, Dan. Try reading through your New Testament and looking for the word *judged* or *judgment*. You'll see it clear as day: we're judged by our works. But that's not in contradiction to being saved by grace—if you define salvation in a broader way. But I must be confusing you."

I was about to tell him about my homework assignment from Neil, but right at that moment, Casey whistled from the cabin and then called out, "Dinnertime! Come and get it!" We got our socks and shoes on—not easy when your feet are wet—and I helped Markus stand and then scramble up the gravelly trail to the cabin.

23

UP TOWARD THE STARS

I beheld through a round aperture
Some of the beauteous things that Heaven doth bear
Thence we came forth to rebehold the stars.

—*Inferno,* XXXIV.136–138

FATHER SCOTT HAD HEATED UP some vegetable soup that he had cooked
and brought with him. He also heated up some fresh-from-the-bakery
bread, which he served with real butter—something I hadn't tasted in
years. Each of us had at least seconds on the soup, and eventually we completely emptied the pot. Everyone but me had a glass or two of wine; I
stuck to ice water. After dinner, Ruth and I did the dishes while Father
Scott worked on a fire in the fireplace. Ruth put a pot of water on the
stovetop for tea and then leaned back against the counter with the dry-
ing towel in hand as I scraped Father Scott's soup pot, which had some
noodles burned to the bottom.

"I was intrigued by what Millie said in the van," I said, also leaning
back against the counter, the pot under my left arm, my right arm scrub-
bing with a scouring pad. "She said you were like a church to each other."

"Yes, dear," Ruth replied, "that's a peculiar little belief of ours. We call
it 'deep ecclesiology,' which is an expression one of my former students
coined. There are so many wild ideas associated with the word *church*.
It's like barnacles stuck on the hull of a boat, or maybe like those noodles
burned on the bottom of your pot there. For some people, church is an in-
stitution of a modern society, right alongside government and the media
and art and science and business and education, servicing the public or a

segment of the public. For others, it's a vendor of religious goods and services, servicing the needs and wants of customers."

I finished rinsing out the pot, which I then handed to Ruth. She continued speaking as she dried the pot, inside and out: "Deep ecclesiology for us means that we honor the church in all its forms, from the most historic and hierarchical forms of church—Roman Catholic and Eastern Orthodox—through the middle range of more congregational or local Protestant churches to the low range of storefront churches and house churches and even below that."

"Below that?" I asked, pouring myself a cup of hot water, adding a tea bag, and sitting at the table.

Ruth put the dry pot on the counter and turned back toward me. "Some forms of church don't last centuries or decades or even years. There are very ephemeral forms of church. Such as you and me, here at this table, as Jesus said: 'wherever two or three are gathered in my name.' According to deep ecclesiology, we're churching right now."

"So for you, this is church," I said.

"I don't mean that in an exclusive, Protestant sense. You see, our little circle here is post-Protestant. Protestants argued and argued about who had the right form of church. We're not doing that—we're not saying that the only valid form is the completely unstructured, ephemeral, spontaneous church, any more than I'd say the Presbyterian form that I love is the only legitimate form. Not at all, dear. That would just be more Protestant pride at finally getting it right. That would be a lateral conversion, from one form of fundamentalism to another. I think Neo calls it the 'church of the last detail.' That's not it at all. We're each very involved in a very conventional congregation, and there are things the conventional congregation can do that really need doing. So as I said, we value the church in all its forms—historic churches, congregational churches, megachurches, minichurches, microchurches, liquid churches, quantum churches, virtual churches, and everything in between. They all have their job to do. Lord knows, the problems our world faces are big enough that no single form of church can address them all."

Ruth added, "Not that the only purpose for the church is to address the problems of the world. I think we'd all say that the purpose of the church—at least, of the post-Protestant church in our way of thinking—is to spiritually form people to love God and others and themselves so that they can live life to the full in God's kingdom, in the way of Jesus. We want to change the world, but that requires people who learn to *be* the revolution they want to *see* in the world."

I was still stuck on the word *post-Protestant*. I simply repeated the word, inviting Ruth to comment more. But she wasn't finished on the subject of spiritual formation.

"Yes, post-Protestant churches see everything as spiritual formation—everything worth doing, that is. Public worship is an exercise in group spiritual formation through rituals like the Eucharist and preaching. Fellowship is exercise in the spiritual practices of community. The success of a church isn't measured by the numbers who attend but by the formation of people as agents of the kingdom of God, and . . ."

I interrupted because I could hardly concentrate on what she was saying: "Ruth, I'm intrigued by that term *post-Protestant*. What do you mean by it?"

"Part of it is that we're done protesting, saying the bad guys over there have it wrong and we here in our little circle have it right. That rhetoric distracts us from spiritual formation, and besides that, it protects injustice."

There was that word again. "Injustice?" I asked.

"Whenever we locate evil 'over there' with 'them,' we render ourselves innocent and proud. *They* are of the devil; *we* are of God. No one is more likely to commit injustice than those who think themselves incapable of doing so, those who are certain that God is on their side and vice versa." Then she shifted her position and turned more toward me. "My, you're attentive. Neo told us you were a thinker. He was right."

"It's a curse sometimes," I said. Just then, Father Scott came in the kitchen area and urged us to come out on the deck, where Neil was smoking a cigar, Markus was puffing on his pipe, and Casey and Millie were leaning over the deck rail in serious conversation—meaning that they only laughed about twenty percent of the time instead of eighty.

"We'll be out in just a minute, Scott," Ruth said. Then Ruth surprised me. "Let's pray before we go out there," she said. She came and stood behind me, placed her hands on my shoulders, and after a brief pause, began to pray. "Gracious Creator, who loves us as a father, who cherishes us as a mother, we are your little children, and we don't know how to go out or come in. We come to you seeking wisdom that transforms, Lord. My new friend Dan and I seek truth. Use these days together in this beautiful natural place to give us wisdom. The questions we have and the problems we face defy unaided human understanding. Grant us saving insight, Lord, by your Spirit of truth, and make us a blessing to one another, for the sake of your Son Jesus." Then she stood in silence for a moment and something happened.

It's hard to say what it was. Deep inside, I felt something fall away or break or evaporate. I say "felt," but it wasn't an emotion or a sensation; it was closer to a thought, a kind of mental experience. *Yes*, I said to myself, *it feels as though my thinking just shed its skin. I feel mentally sensitive, tender, fresh*. Then Ruth said, "Amen."

There was nothing extraordinary about the words of her prayer. But there was a kind of power there that I had rarely experienced. "Where did you learn to pray like that?" I asked.

"That wasn't *me* praying, Dan. It was *us,* praying together. It's just as Jesus said: 'when two or three agree' . . . This is something we've been learning: when we don't just say our prayers, and when we don't simply pray as individuals, but when we learn to pray as one, we experience things. It's the Kingdom of God, the dream of God coming true when people harmonize their wills with God's will. That was your prayer as much as mine; I was just finding words for both of us. Come on. Let's rejoin the others."

Like the words of Ruth's prayer, there was nothing extraordinary about the next few hours we spent in the cool night air on Father Scott's deck, chatting, joking, various groups of two or three forming and reforming, mingling and remingling. I felt, and later Casey told me she felt it too, that I had entered an alien place, something that appeared so natural and normal, and yet was so unprecedented in my experience. At one point, we persuaded Millie to get her violin, and she played several pieces for us, a few classical songs, then an Irish jig that had us all clapping to the rhythm, and then a slow, slow piece that brought tears to my eyes. It was an old Scottish melody, she said, one of the oldest melodies we know of. It rang out its quivering call, out across the lake, out over the treetops, up toward the stars. She followed it with a Mexican folk song, no less beautiful but less familiar to me.

Before we turned in for the night, Markus and I found ourselves standing together at the same place on the deck where Casey and Millie had stood earlier, leaning against the deck rail on our forearms, overlooking the dark woods and facing the lake below, a silver-gray pool, faintly shimmering, barely visible in the hazy moonlight. "I have a suggestion for you, Dan," he said. "As a recovering fundamentalist myself, here's what I've found. You can't leave a sinking ship until you begin to construct a seaworthy one. Hell is one of the leaks in your sinking ship. You're trying to patch the hole. During your days here, I'd recommend you try to imagine a new ship, a seaworthy one. Put your energy there. You may find that the hell problem sinks with the old ship, then, and you won't solve it, but you'll leave it behind."

I let his words settle in for a minute. "It's funny, Markus," I said, reflectively. "A couple of hours ago, Ruth prayed with me for wisdom, and I think you were just part of the answer to her prayer."

"That's a good thing. Well, it's been a long day. Let's prepare for to-morrow." He shook my hand, and I followed him back to the bunkhouse.

Just before we entered the building, Markus turned to me and said, "In the morning, let's sit together at breakfast. I'd like to share with you a theory I've been working on."

"A theory about what?" I asked.

"About how we got into the mess we're in, how the boat started sinking," he said. "And I have a quote I want to give you too, a little quote that might help you imagine a better boat."

"Great. I'll see you in the morning," I replied. "Thanks for everything, Markus."

Once in bed, I took out my flashlight and prepared to write a few lines in my journal, but when I opened it, an envelope fell out. Then I remembered: a few days before I left, Carol had handed me a letter from our friend Pat that I had stuffed into my briefcase to read later. It must have slid into my journal, and I forgot about it. By flashlight, I opened the letter and read these handwritten lines.

> Dan—I was in church last Sunday with my nephew. You probably didn't see me because I was hiding out in the back row. Your sermon inspired me, so when I got home, I wrote this poem and song lyric. I hope you enjoy them. Glad to see how well things are going at PCC. You survived your time of testing with grace. Chloe has been enjoying the fellowship group. She says she might start coming to church with me if that's OK with you. I assured her it would be. Your friend—Pat

RESONATING

Spirit of Creation, you
Fill all space as sound waves do.
Your music makes a chamber
Of my soul, resonating,
An organ-filled cathedral.
Bass pipes thunder; trebles sing.
When old spaces shrivel up,
Shrunk wineskins, crushed paper cup,
You seek new vessels to fill.
So, reverberating now,
New spaces blossom; you will
Rush in, wide wind, holy fire.
Filling, not consuming us,

With thankful joy, high desire.
Come Holy Spirit.

ALL WE KNOW

All we know is but a spark,
Rising from the blaze of mystery,
A falling star in the dark,
Descending from a height we cannot see.
In mists that rise from woodland streams,
The way that we could fly in childhood dreams,
Truth comes in on winds that blow
From beyond the rim of all we know.
I have my doubts about certainty.
It's not all that it's made out to be.
I trust in things I cannot see,
And reach out for the love that's reaching me,
In mists that rise from woodland streams,
The way that we could fly in childhood dreams.
Truth comes in on winds that blow
From beyond the rim of all we know.
The secret things remain concealed,
But this good news has been revealed
(And that's a gift): the rift is healed.
And there's a treasure hidden in this field,
In mists that rise from woodland streams,
And the way that we could fly in childhood dreams.
Truth comes in on winds that blow
From beyond the rim of all we know.

I didn't write anything in my journal after reading this. I just pushed Pat's note back between two pages into the spine my journal, clicked off my flashlight, lay back, and fell asleep, a calm joy bubbling in my heart. God was near.

24

A COLORFUL BREAKFAST

. . . then my mind there smote
A flash of lightning.

—*Paradiso*, XXXIII.140–141

EACH PART OF THE COUNTRY, I think, has its most glorious season. For northern Minnesota, many would say it's September, with its crisp days and vivid autumn colors. But since our time at Father Scott's cabin, I would choose mid-June. The warm sun, the long days, the deep blue skies, the bright clouds like a fleet of ships cruising across the sky, the light green of freshly open leaves, the water cool but still refreshing for swimming—even though I'm not much of an outdoors person, Minnesota in June captured my heart. At home, I always sleep with the windows closed, so I seldom hear birds. Here they began singing at dawn with such volume and exuberance that I lay awake listening to them for maybe half an hour. They set my mood for the day.

That first morning, I was the second one to get up. Father Scott was already brewing coffee—not in an electric drip machine but in one of those old-fashioned metal percolators with a little basket for grounds inside and a glass bulb on top into which the boiling water bubbled as it rose through a metal tube. He poured me a cup, and I think it was the best I'd ever tasted. "Well, now, it's not Starbucks, but our water out here is real pure," Scott said. "Fresh from the spring up on the hill there. And these fresh-ground Kenyan beans here don't hurt either!"

Casey was up next. Scott insisted that he had breakfast well in hand, so Casey and I walked together down the steep path to the little beach next to the dock where Markus and I had talked the night before. Each cradling a mug of Scott's coffee in chilly hands, we perched ourselves on a couple of large boulders strewn irregularly on the gravelly beach, over-looking the glassy lake where mist was rising into the cool morning air. I had my jacket on, and Casey had a black-and-red plaid wool blanket draped over her shoulders.

Casey said, "It's wild being here, Pastor Dan. I feel like the little boy who accidentally walked into the ladies' room. He knew he didn't exactly belong, but he figured if he stayed, he'd learn something." I laughed, and said, "I know how you feel."

Casey replied, "Now we know where Neil gets his stuff, you know, his fresh ideas. It's like he said: these people think together. It's like their minds are linked up in some kind of system circuitry. I guess this is what those business gurus mean by a learning community. But it's not just their minds. Last night, Millie prayed for me, and I've been prayed for before, but not like last night. There's some powerful spirituality brewing here."

"I know what you mean," I said, but didn't elaborate on my experience with Ruth.

"Did you hear us laughing last night? You know what we were doing?" she asked, and I didn't know whether to answer her first question yes or her second one no. She continued, "We weren't telling jokes or anything, Pastor Dan. We were praying. I've never laughed while praying before, but as we prayed, it felt like heaven was opening up, and this kind of joy seemed to pour into both our souls. It must have happened at almost the same moment. We just kind of erupted, laughing. I felt almost like, like I was going to split in two, like the joy was bigger than my capacity to contain it. I'll never forget that. Millie didn't seem surprised, like that sort of thing has happened to her before. It was totally wild."

"That sounds beautiful," I said. "The joy of the Lord."

"Yeah, it was something," Casey said, and then continued, "Pastor Dan, you and I have both been to seminary, but I feel like these next couple of days are really going to be seminary or maybe more like a monastery. It's like, we're going to learn a whole new thing here. And you know what's a little scary?"

"What's that?"

"I think the reason we're here is that they're asking us to . . . to join them, to be part of this thing. You know?" she asked. "It's like we're on a date, and they're planning to ask us for a commitment."

That thought hadn't really struck me until that moment. "You're right. That is a little scary. I'm not sure . . ."

"I'm not sure I'm ready for this," Casey said, finishing my sentence exactly as I would have.

"I'm not sure I'm . . . worthy, either," I said. "I still feel so stuck in old ways of thinking. I'm not where they are, at least not yet."

"Well, maybe we should pray about that," Casey said. "After praying with Millie last night, I think I'm ready to pray every chance I get." Then she looked down into her coffee mug and said thoughtfully, "I'm not like you, Dan. I don't have all that conservative baggage you have. But I have a lot of my own stuff, mostly about, I don't know, I guess you'd call it maturity, or character. I lack a lot of what you'd call patience."

Then Casey looked out across the water: "I never could have put up with all you've swallowed, Pastor Dan. I mean, you've got your conservative baggage, but you've gained a lot of character through dealing with it. Sometimes I feel lucky because I'm in a freer setting, but sometimes I think you're the lucky one. I wonder if it's even possible to develop the kind of character you have without going through the kind of . . . I don't know, maybe *persecution* is the right word for it, or maybe *hassle* is a better word. Either way, sometimes I think my life is just too easy, like I don't have enough opposition to become the kind of person you are. I've noticed that conservative backgrounds like yours produce some of the best people. Anyway, I have my own unworthiness to deal with." She got up off the boulder she was sitting on and came over and sat on the smaller rock closest to me and said, "So I'll pray for you to be loosened up, and you can pray for me to develop some character. Shoot, I make us sound like the Tin Man and the Cowardly Lion or something."

So we both leaned forward, elbows on knees, and we prayed. I'm a pastor. I pray all the time. But just as that morning's coffee was something special even though I drink coffee every day, that prayer time was unforgettable. The same power I had felt praying with Ruth was here again, surrounding us, inviting us deeper into itself. We didn't break out laughing, but there was a joy that pierced us, like the coolness of the morning. It was God's presence, I knew: as real to us as the mist rising from the lake.

When we heard voices coming down from the cabin through the fog, we both said, "Amen." "Well, I'm ready for anything now," Casey said, "beginning with Father Scott's breakfast. I'll race you up the hill, old man!" She flew up the hill, her plaid blanket like a cape around her shoulders, her beads swaying, gravel crunching beneath her feet. Of course she beat me to the top, but it felt good just to run, win or lose. It had been too long since I had been out of breath like that.

Markus was waiting for me at the table. He was pouring ketchup and Tabasco sauce on his scrambled eggs. "Colorful breakfast you've got there," I said, catching my breath.

"Tasty too," he replied. "Want some?"

I'm not a spicy food guy, so I said I'd pass. As soon as I sat down, Markus jumped right in with the theory he wanted to tell me about the night before: "Basically, it's a conspiracy theory about Paul and John ganging up against Matthew, Mark, and Luke—well, not really them, but people who interpret them."

Father Scott brought me a heaping plate, and I began eating slowly as Markus spoke: "When Matthew, Mark, and Luke talk about the Kingdom of God, it's always closely related to social justice. It's not just personal and eternal, as the conservatives say, and it's not only social and historic, as the liberals tend to say. The Kingdom of God integrates both sides—personal and social, private and public, secret and visible, spiritual and political, historic and eternal, earth and beyond. It's about character and love, which are personal and individual and hidden, and it's about justice and peace, which are public and social and visible. But once we get hung up on fixing the passport—as we were saying last night, solving the individual, legal original sin problem, we begin to lose the integration. We find that Matthew, Mark, and Luke's approach to the Kingdom of God becomes a problem for us. Their gospel of the kingdom is about God's will being done on earth for everybody, but we're interested in getting away from earth entirely as individuals, and into heaven instead.

"So here's what I think we do. We shift our focus to the Book of Romans. We make it the Rosetta Stone for the Bible. That's a questionable strategy to begin with, but to make matters worse, we grossly misinterpret Romans. We assume that Romans is Paul's attempt to explain the gospel. It's not that at all, of course, but . . ."

"Wait a minute," I said. "Paul begins Romans by saying he isn't ashamed of the gospel because it's the power of God to salvation. Doesn't that sound like his thesis statement? That's what I've always been taught and taught to others, that Romans defines the gospel."

"Ah," Markus said, pointing his finger at me with some enthusiasm, "that's what everybody says, but they don't quote the rest of the sentence. Remember what it is?"

"Let's see . . . he says the gospel is the power of salvation—to the Jew first, and also to the Greek," I replied.

He pointed his finger at me again: "Exactly. That's what Romans is really about. It's not answering the question 'What is the gospel?' That question has already been answered by Jesus. The gospel is 'Repent, for the Kingdom of God is available to everyone'—which is what *at hand* means. Paul doesn't need to answer that question. He's answering the question 'How do we bring Jews and Gentiles together in the Kingdom of God?' Justification by grace through faith—his theme in Romans—isn't the gospel: it's the means by which Jews and Gentiles are put on common ground in the gospel of the kingdom."

My head was already spinning, but he was shoveling scrambled eggs into his mouth and talking as fast as he could between mouthfuls, every once in a while shaking some extra Tabasco sauce on a forkful: "So we misinterpret Paul and focus on his word *faith*. In our misinterpretation, faith isn't what brings Jews and Gentiles together on equal footing, equally justified, in God's kingdom here and now; faith is what gets us into heaven after we die. Then, with that in our minds, we go to the gospel of John. We sync up John's use of the word *believe* with Paul's use of the word *faith,* and then we misinterpret what John means by the phrase *eternal life.*"

I nodded, recalling having heard something similar from Neil on several occasions.

"We act as if *eternal life* means *life in heaven after you die.* So now, according to both Paul and John, the gospel is all about getting into heaven after you die by believing. And the enemy of believing, we say, is doing good works. So we've now created a system by which we see good works as bad—or if not bad, at least a dangerous distraction from faith. And now the gospel focuses not on the Kingdom of God being available to everyone on earth but instead on the people who believe right escaping the earth to go to heaven after they die to enjoy something called eternal life. What matters now isn't good works but right beliefs. I know that's an overstatement, but . . ."

A NEW KIND OF CHRISTIANITY

. . . now was turning my desire and will,
Even as a wheel that equally is moved,
The Love which moves the sun and the other stars.

—*Paradiso*, XXXIII.142–145

MARKUS DOWNED A GLASS of orange juice in three gulps and smiled, "Anyway, Jesus himself defines the term *eternal life* later in John 17, in his prayer. Remember? 'This is eternal life,' Jesus says, 'to know you, the only true God, and Jesus Christ whom you have sent.' Now the word *know* doesn't just mean 'meet'; it means 'be in an interactive relationship with.' Not like 'I know Tiger Woods,' about whom I know a lot but with whom I've never even spoken, but like 'I know you' because we're developing an interactive relationship right here, right now. Well, what is the Kingdom of God if it's not an interactive relationship with God, the King, along with the other citizens of the kingdom? That's what a kingdom is: a web of relationships that all intersect with the same king. It's *a life,* a life that includes but also transcends day-to-day living. It's a life that interacts with the eternal dimension of the Spirit, so *eternal life* is a good way of naming it.

"But most of us don't get that. So we start with a misunderstanding of Paul, and then we win John over to our misreading of Paul. Then we go from there to the other three gospels, and every time *Kingdom of God* or *Kingdom of Heaven* is mentioned, we assume it means 'heaven after you die,' so it conforms to our misreading of Paul and John. Plus, we do some really outrageous things, like saying the purpose of the Sermon on the

Mount is to make us feel hopeless about pleasing God. You know, we say Moses' law was tough, but Jesus' law is downright impossible. This prepares us to need our misreading of Romans, you know, the believe-right-and-go-to-heaven version. At that point, the conspiracy is complete. *Voilà!* Now we've got Paul, John, Matthew, Mark, and Luke all signed up in the same gang, and from there, they can take over the whole Bible. Which is what we've done. Which creates the unjust and ineffective religious system we've created. Which is the mess we're in."

I said something nondescript, like "Wow. That's interesting. Neil has talked to me about some of this before, but you've made it very clear." Then Markus pulled out a folded piece of tattered notebook paper from his shirt pocket and unfolded it. He placed it on the table and smoothed it out with his hands. "I told you I had a quote for you. It's something I copied out of a book a couple of years ago. I keep it in my journal and reread it from time to time. This might help you imagine a better way of thinking about God's relation to the world."

He slid the paper over to me, and I read it aloud:

> To believe in God is to believe in the salvation of the world. The paradox of our time is that those who believe in God do not believe in the salvation of the world, and those who believe in the future of the world do not believe in God.
>
> Christians believe in "the end of the world," they expect the final catastrophe, the punishment of others.
>
> Atheists in their turn . . . refuse to believe in God because Christians believe in him and take no interest in the world . . .
>
> Which is the more culpable ignorance?
>
> . . . I often say to myself that, in our religion, God must feel very much alone: for is there anyone besides God who believes in the salvation of the world? God seeks among us sons and daughters who resemble him enough, who love the world enough so that he could send them into the world to save it.
>
> —Louis Evely, *In the Christian Spirit* (Image, 1975)

"Your conspiracy theory was interesting, but that's . . . that's breathtaking," I said. I pushed the paper back across the table to him. "No," he said, pushing it back, "you keep it. I've had it long enough; I think I've got the message. It's yours. But here . . ." Then he took the paper back and wrote these words on the bottom: "From Markus to Dan—here's to a new kind of Christianity," and refolded it and handed it to me. "Don't lose it, OK?"

"I won't, Markus. I won't," I said, tucking it into my shirt pocket. At that moment, Casey and Ruth came and joined us, and Casey started asking Ruth about her experience with Dr. King. I realized that to me, King had been primarily a political figure, and there was little connection between his political action and the gospel, but for them, the politics were interwoven with theology, and it dawned on me, listening to them, that Markus might be right about his little conspiracy theory. My inherited theological system really did marginalize concerns for justice and good works, and it really did represent a "believe-right" approach, as Markus had said. Dr. King's faith was about saving the world, not escaping it; it was about seeking justice and welcoming justice, not evading it so we can go to heaven.

After breakfast, we sat on the deck and spent the morning hearing the five friends take turns answering five questions that they asked every year when they gathered. "The five queries," they called them: How is your soul? How have you seen God at work in and through your life since we last met? What are you struggling with? What are you grateful for? What God-given dream are you nurturing?

Millie's sharing was most touching to me. As to the condition of her soul, she was exhausted, she said. As Neil had explained, she had formed a little community called The Little Flower to live out the gospel in one of the worst neighborhoods of Camden, her hometown. Their neighborhood was surrounded by toxic waste sites and factories that spewed pollution; as a result, almost everyone there suffered from asthma, she said. The neighborhood was infested with drugs, crime, trash, disease, and despair. Unemployment was high, and racial tensions—between blacks, Asians, and Hispanics—were high; white folks were excluded from the equation only because they were almost never seen. She felt so overwhelmed by the problems, she said through tears, yet she felt that God had called her there. Then she spoke of the Catholic parish they were part of. The priest there was the most hopeful man she had ever seen, and she was most grateful for his bright example in the midst of the darkness.

I was confused: "Millie, I understood that The Little Flower was a church, but now you're talking about being part of a Catholic parish." Ruth answered for her: "Dan, this is a perfect case of post-Protestant deep ecclesiology we were talking about last night in the kitchen. Milagros did plant a church. But in deep ecclesiology, churches aren't mutually exclusive. So the members of The Little Flower Faith Community are also active participants in Saint Claire's."

"Does that mean you all became Catholic?" I asked.

Millie replied, "Father Dominic is so glad to have some people who share his love for the community, he never asks any questions. If we wanted to convert, he'd be glad to welcome us, but he'd never push it. He knows I'm Pentecostal, and several members of The Little Flower are Baptist and Presbyterian, but down in the 'hood, all that's pretty irrelevant. If you love the city with all its problems, you're blood," she said. "'City lovers' is all the denominational identity you need, you know?"

I thought of the problems I had faced in my suburban church: petty squabbles, theological arguments, power struggles, church politics. I compared them with the problems Milagros faced every day as she told stories of gangs, drugs, shootings, rape, arson, robbery, beatings—which were the consequences of corruption, apathy, racism, greed, unemployment, abandonment, and more. Which of us was more involved in the real work of God's kingdom? It hardly seemed possible that we lived on the same planet, not to mention that we were ministers of the same religion. My heart ached for her, not with pity but with admiration. *If I've ever met a saint, it's Millie,* I said to myself. For a brief moment, Gil Zeamer came to mind: *All Gil would be saying, if he were here, is that Millie shouldn't be a pastor because she's a woman. And he'd have a fit about the Catholic thing. Oh well, that's his problem.* I came back to the present moment; Millie was crying.

She was a saint, but a drained and weary and discouraged one. She told us about her prayer time with Casey the night before, saying that it was the first time she'd felt full of joy in a long, long time. She spoke of her fatigue and wondered aloud how long it would last. She couldn't answer the last of the five queries because she felt that all her dreams had gradually been ground to dust by the depressing realities of life in the city. "I guess my dream is just to survive, you know?" Her lip quivered.

There was silence among us for a moment, but inside of me, something began to shout: *She can't quit! What she's doing is too important!* It was like a fire started glowing in my back and worked its way up my spine: it was a calling, a calling from God, directed at me. I couldn't contain myself: "I don't know how, Milagros. I don't know how, but I will do anything I can to help you. I'll do anything I can to enlist the people of my church to support you and help you. I don't know what we can do, but we will offer our friendship, and we'll see where God leads us." Then I went over to Millie and bent over and embraced her, and I returned to my seat feeling so overwhelmed with emotion that my hands were trembling.

It was clear that the others were choked up too, and Casey ran to the bathroom and came back with a roll of toilet paper. "Couldn't find any tissues," she said, "but this will do." We all laughed as we handed the roll around the room and dried our eyes.

I still felt I had more that I needed to say: "Milagros, my wife, Carol, is the most hospitable person on the planet. Anytime you need to get out of the city and have a place to go, we'll have a room waiting for you." Casey piped in: "Since I rent a room from them, I know that what Pastor Dan is saying is the straight-up truth. So if you visit, they'll show you hospitality, girl, and I'll show you some fun!" And with that we all laughed again.

That afternoon we relaxed. Neil and Markus went for a canoe ride on the lake, which was a panic to watch because Markus was completely un-coordinated with the paddle and Neil was a bit too heavy for the front seat of the canoe, so the vessel looked like it was about to submerge or capsize at any moment as it rocked and rolled and zigzagged across the lake and back. Ruth, Millie, and Casey took a walk along the gravel road that led out to the highway. Father Scott put on some binoculars to go birdwatching—a hobby that I was more likely to make a joke about than take interest in, but not wanting to be left alone, I joined him anyway.

We walked along the lakefront, pausing from time to time for Father Scott to train his binoculars on some branch or patch of weeds. He asked about my impressions of the group, which I expressed freely. Father Scott said he had experienced similar feelings at his first gathering. "Even though this is very relaxed, and we're just a handful of people, and Lord knows we're not highly agenda-driven," he said, "we take what we're doing very seriously here. We're part of something that's happening quietly, behind the scenes, around the world."

"What is it?" I asked. "What is it that's happening?"

"It's the emergence of catholic, missional, monastic faith communities," he replied, his binoculars aimed at a group of ducks paddling between cat-tail stands. Then he explained what each of those words meant. *Catholic*—with a lowercase *c*—meant "ecumenical," a post-Protestant celebration of the church in all its forms, as Ruth had said. "Instead of *protesting* what we're against, we're *pro-testifying*: telling the story of what we're for," he said.

Missional meant "focused on the good of the world." "We're exploring the territory beyond both Imperial Christianity and consumerist Chris-tianity," he said, "beyond the Christianity that seeks the good of one na-tion or the Christianity that exists to satisfy customers. We're pursuing a faith that seeks the good of God's whole world. Our mission is to join God in God's saving love for all creation. That's why Milagros talked so much about loving the city. For her, and for all of us, the church doesn't exist for itself; it exists to be a blessing to the world." This, of course, resonated with the quote Markus had given me, which I unconsciously reached up to touch in my shirt pocket.

Again, I was realizing how much of Neil's language was a shared lan-guage of this community. Father Scott then explained that *monastic* sug-gested an order or community of practice. "An order is different from a denomination, which is a group defined by structure and doctrine. An order is defined by practice. I suppose there's a lot of doctrine hidden in each practice, but we're more and more convinced that the best way to get to good doctrine is through good practice, instead of the other way around."

"What are your practices?" I asked.

"Really, all authentic Christian spiritual practices are practices of one thing: love. Love for God. Love for the other—the neighbor, the enemy, the last, the least, the lost. So our basic practice is to love each other. We do that by agreeing to meet every year that we possibly can and by asking our five queries when we meet. It's pretty simple, really, and not difficult. Actually, it's a joy. So our five queries help us focus on that one monastic practice of love. When we ask how it goes with our soul, we're asking how our soul is faring in love. When we ask where God has been at work since we last met, we're looking for movements of love toward God and the other. When we ask what we're grateful for, we're focusing on our receptivity to God's grace, which flows to us in a thousand ways, even when we're suffering. When we ask what we're struggling with, our struggles always deal with obstacles in our pursuit of love. When we ask about God-given dreams, they're always dreams of loving God and others."

"What about yourselves?" I asked. "Don't you have any dreams for yourselves as individuals?"

"Of course!" Father Scott said. "You're sleeping in one of my dreams, right here! It was just six years ago when I shared with the circle of five my dream to retire and return to my home state and purchase this cabin, which my relatives were about to sell after it had been in my family for three generations. But this wasn't just a selfish dream now. In my knowing of God, I know that God loved me and wanted to bless me in this way, so I simply had to receive God's blessing. And here, I get to share it with my friends, and just think . . . if the six of you are encouraged, you'll bring blessing to people wherever you live."

After *catholic, missional,* and *monastic,* Father Scott went on to explain how the term *faith community* helped them get around the baggage associated with the word *church*. I was a bit baffled. "Is this wrapped up with your deep ecclesiology that Ruth was telling me about?" I asked. "Are you saying that Potomac Community Church could be a church without being a faith community? And the seven of us could be a faith community without being a church?"

Father Scott had focused his binoculars on what he told me were some loons, which had just flown in: "Well, no, no. Here now, think of it like this. It's all church. All of it. Wherever Jesus is at work, church is there." He dropped his binoculars so that they hung on his chest and turned toward me. "That doesn't exclude the institutions, but it doesn't privilege them either. It's very all-encompassing, a deeper approach to ecclesiology. The issue that might be a challenge for churches like yours, and the ones I served during my career, would be the *catholic* and *missional* parts, because our institutions aren't very accustomed to being either catholic or missional, don't you think? But thank the Lord, they can learn. They can learn. Yes, indeed. There's so much hope. It may take some time, but I'm a convinced optimist, or perhaps I should say that I have contracted a chronic case of hope from Jesus. I mean, look at you. You're here. Think of how far you've come! And in so short a time!"

"So short a time?" I said. "This feels like it's taking forever, Father Scott. I feel like I'm in one of those dreams where you run in slow motion, like you're moving in molasses. It's killing me. I so much want to catch up and run with you and the others, but I feel I'm so far behind you."

"Daniel, you're wrong. You're wrong!" Father Scott moved toward me and put his hands on my shoulders. "Your heart is already far, far along. It's just taking a while for your mind to catch up. Your mind is important, and you can't rush it. It will catch up in time. You're going to be fine, Daniel. Just fine."

"Father Scott," I said, "I want to believe you." And at that moment, I did.

That week, the circle of five became the circle of seven. Casey and I came as guests and left as members of a catholic, missional, monastic faith community. Actually, I prefer to simply call it a friendship—a friendship in the spirit of Jesus, who said, "No longer do I call you servants . . . but I have called you friends." When we see ourselves primarily as servants, we're stressed, self-conscious, pressured, maybe even competitive. But when we accept our identity as friends, everything changes. We're friends with Jesus, friends in Jesus, friends for Jesus, who are hoping, praying, and working passionately for the salvation of the world.

SECOND THOUGHTS

*The Poet well perceived that I was wholly
Bewildered.*

—Purgatorio, IV.58–59

IT WAS A GORGEOUS fall day in early October 2004. I was in my office early when the phone rang.

"Hello, this is Chip Griffin. May I speak with Reverend Dan Poole?" the unfamiliar voice on the phone asked. It was a deep voice, with a kind of confidence or authority to it, but I couldn't place it. The name was vaguely familiar.

"Yes, good morning, Chip," I said, leaning forward on my desk at the church office. "This is Dan. What can I do for you on this beautiful Monday morning?"

"I feel a bit uncomfortable calling. I'm not sure if you remember me," he said. "We've never actually met, but I'm the regional director of the Biblical Evangelical Fellowship, and two years ago, I was assigned as a conflict interventionist for PCC until you pulled out of the association."

I immediately tensed up. Was the conflict that began all that time ago somehow resurfacing? "Sure, I remember now. Yes, I guess we never did meet."

"That's why I'm calling," he said. "I'd like to meet you. Actually, I need to, if you'd be willing."

I was still a bit concerned, but Chip's word *need* seemed to reduce my alarm. He didn't offer to explain what he needed or why, and I decided not to ask. We set up a meeting for early Thursday morning that same week.

My office at PCC is large and comfortable. Tall built-in bookshelves surround my desk; part of my library fills those shelves. The rest of my books overflow into the adjacent sitting area, where more books are shelved and stacked and still overflow to piles on tables and in corners. The sitting area is spacious, carpeted, with couches and a coffee table, neat except for the piles of books, the walls covered with photographs and other memorabilia from my years in ministry, with one large window that ushers in the morning light from the east. I was sitting on one of the couches when Chip knocked on the door. "I hope you don't mind—I let myself in," he said.

I offered to make a pot of coffee, and he said he would like that. We got a bit better acquainted as the coffee brewed, sharing where we were from originally, our seminaries, a bit about our families, and our feelings about the presidential election that was just weeks away. Then Chip said, "I'm grateful you would meet with me. The reason I'm here is, well, I don't think there is anyone else I can talk to about my situation.

"You know where we're coming from in the Biblical Evangelical Fellowship. We're unashamedly conservative. We stand for biblical values, biblical absolutes, the biblical worldview, and we also are strong supporters of pro-life causes, states' rights, and free markets. Lately we're working very hard to oppose genetic engineering and to reduce the size and power of the federal government. And we're really trying to push for a constitutional amendment to protect the family from, you know, immoral forces."

I couldn't help but notice that the BEF was against a stronger federal government yet wanted the federal government to be strong enough to "protect the family," but I didn't want to point out that irony. Chip continued, "So we're a conservative organization. And I'm actually one of the cofounders of the BEF, so it's more than a little ironic that I'm here talking to you now, especially because of the purpose of my visit."

"Which is . . . ?" I asked.

Chip leaned forward, his elbows on his knees, his coffee mug cradled in both hands: "As you know, a couple of years ago, I was contacted by Gil Zeamer to see if I would be willing to oversee a heresy trial so you could be removed from your pastorate. We called it a 'conflict resolution consultation,' but we both knew what it really was. But now I'm here to ask for your help, which makes me feel a bit like a heretic myself."

Chip's voice was deep and strong, a natural preacher's voice. Everything about him radiated confidence, and yet here he was, boldly vulnerable. "Tell me what's going on, Chip," I said.

He leaned back, rubbed his free hand over his crew-cut hair, and let out a long breath. "I left the pastorate ten years ago," he said, "back when I was forty-five. The BEF was my dream, and I wanted to make it a reality. I think you've seen the doctrinal statement that we wrote—I was the architect of that and used to be very proud of it. Our goal with the Biblical Evangelical Fellowship was to bring everyone who uses the name *Evangelical* under that banner. The name meant a lot to us, and frankly, we were bothered that charismatics, Pentecostals, Arminians, open theists, and others were being tolerated in our ranks. So our whole network was formed to force people like you who were already in our ranks to either get back in line or leave and to put the fear of God in everyone else so they'd know there were consequences for wobbling about the orthodox faith we were seeking to protect."

"Keep talking," I said as I went over to get the coffeepot to refill his mug.

"But lately, for the last six months or so, really, I've been having—"

"Doubts?" I asked as I returned to my seat.

"Second thoughts," Chip said. "Second thoughts about the whole thing. For the first time since seminary, I've got questions I don't have answers for. I haven't told anyone this, but I actually began seeing a counselor. I've been worried that I might, you know, crack up or something. I can tell you a couple of stories that I think make it clear."

"Sure. I want to hear all about it," I said.

"You know the *Left in Flames* series of books, right?" he asked.

I replied, "I've heard of them, but I never read any of them. I know they try to dramatize a dispensationalist eschatology: the rapture of the church, seven-year tribulation period, two-stage second coming of Christ, that sort of thing, right?" Chip nodded, and I added, "I was brought up dispensationalist, but I left that a long time ago. So I've never really had any interest in the books. Besides, I'm not a fan of fiction anyway. I haven't read a novel in years, especially a theological one. I'm strictly a nonfiction guy."

"Well, for better or worse, I've read them all," Chip said. "Last summer at the beach, I read the most recent one. It was called *The Glorious Unveiling*. There's a scene when the earth splits open and starts swallowing sinners, and that leads to a vivid description of non-Christians being cut into pieces, their bodies being strewn across the landscape. Drivers on the highway have to be careful to avoid all the body parts littering the road, that sort of thing. Gosh, it sounds horrific, and it was, especially because I was reading this at the beach where there are a lot of body parts exposed to view. Anyway, as I read dramatic depictions of all non-Christians being sent screaming into the flames, I thought to myself, *What if Islamic fundamentalists in Saudi Arabia published a book that pictured American Christians being thrown into hell? How would I feel about that?*

Wouldn't I be worried that this kind of literature would fan the flames of
terrorism and perhaps even inspire fundamentalists to look forward to the
day when people like us would be destroyed? I don't know why, but I just
couldn't shake that thought. It almost ruined my vacation.

"Then, a couple of weeks ago, at our church—I go to Grace Bible,
where Gil and Nancy Zeamer have been going since they left PCC—Dr.
Roads (I think you know him) gave a sermon on Revelation 19. It was that
passage where Jesus is portrayed as King of Kings and Lord of Lords. He
comes on a white horse, leading a huge army, and it says he slays all nations. And Dr. Roads got quite worked up about the coming of judgment
and how Jesus would personally destroy everyone who didn't believe in
him. At one point, he says, 'You have a choice: Do you want to be in the
army of Jesus, bringing judgment on unbelievers? Or do you want to be
one of the unbelievers under judgment when the King of Kings comes on
his mighty white horse? I know which group I want to be in!' And as I sat
there, a chill ran up my spine. I mean, I physically squirmed in my seat. I
thought about how I'd feel if some mullah somewhere were saying this sort
of thing to Muslims, and I almost had to walk out of the service."

I interrupted, "Yes, I'm very familiar with the passage, but it says the
sword he uses comes out of his mouth. So it obviously refers to a nonlit-
eral sword—to his word or his message convicting people of their evil. It's
not an actual massacre—that would violate everything Jesus stood for. It's
a classic figure of speech from the genre of Second Temple Jewish apocalyptic literature."

"Second what? I'm not familiar with that. All I know is that Dr. Roads
prides himself on his literal interpretation, so I don't think he'd go in for
any of that figure-of-speech stuff. But what I wanted to say was this: the
whole congregation seemed to really affirm what he was saying—you know,
some amens, even some laughter. I got this strange feeling that they actually were glad that all these people were going to be destroyed. I know that
Dr. Roads is a true man of God and a great expositor of the Scriptures, so
I don't mean to criticize him, but then he talked about how in heaven, we
will actually share God's joy that unbelievers are defeated and receiving retribution. After the service, a lot of people, including my own wife, said they
thought the sermon was inspiring. I was almost sick to my stomach."

He paused for a few moments and then said, "I couldn't sleep. I wasn't
sure if there was anyone I could talk to about this. A few days later, I saw
Gil Zeamer at the home improvement store, and standing in the garden
section there, I decided to take the risk of telling him how I felt, what I
was thinking, why I felt so uneasy with the sermon. And the strangest
thing happened. He told me that his wife had had a similar reaction, and

he could see our point, and if I needed to talk to somebody about it, he recommended that I talk to you."

My shock must have been visible on my face, because he continued, "I know, I was surprised too. At first I thought he was joking or suggesting that I was becoming a heretic of some sort. I said, 'You're kidding.' He said, 'No, Dan's a good man. Even though I've had my disagreements with him, he's a thoughtful person, the kind of person you could talk to about this sort of thing. And I know he doesn't hold a grudge.' So that's what brings me here. According to Gil, you've struggled with this whole issue of hell and damnation yourself, and you can help me. Look, Dan, I don't want to become a universalist or anything like that, but I can't shake this feeling that something's wrong with what I've always considered the orthodox doctrine of hell. Can you share with me your thinking on the issue of hell?"

Gil Zeamer recommended he come see me? I was still so surprised that I hesitated for several seconds, my thoughts racing, and I began shaking my head in disbelief. This must have made Chip nervous, because he said, "Look, if you'd rather not talk with me, I can't blame you, considering what role I almost had in your life and ministry. I wouldn't have come if Gil hadn't convinced me . . ."

"No, I'm happy to talk about this with you," I said. Then the thought flashed across my mind: *Wait. What if this guy's a spy? Maybe Gil's still out to get me. How do I know he's sincere?*

TO GOD, ALL ARE ALIVE

Love moved me, which compelleth me to speak.

—*Inferno*, II.72

I WAVERED FOR ONLY a second. I decided to trust Chip and be vulnerable and open with him.

We talked for nearly three hours. He pulled out a PDA and took notes on a number of occasions, but more often, he sat forward on my couch, attentive, serious, a little tense.

At one point in our conversation, I was explaining how hell could be used to control people by instilling fear in them. "Our problem is that we use the idea of hell precisely the way the Pharisees did, exactly the opposite of the way Jesus did. We say everyone not of our elite party—the party of people who believe in certain doctrines, however they're defined—are excluded and will face not only our rejection in this life but also God's eternal rejection and scorn forever. We use hell to instill compliance through fear and—"

Chip interrupted: "Fear—so much of my life is about fear. Lately, I've felt afraid to bring up any of my questions to even my closest friends at BEF. I can't trust them. And I'm sure some of my friends feel the same way about me. I hardly know you, but I feel safer with you than I do with people I've known for years. So much of my religion is about fear—which is why it feels so good, like such a relief, to be talking openly with you now."

Later Chip had a specific question, about an interchange between Jesus and the Pharisees and Sadducees in the Gospels. I pulled a Bible off my shelf and found the passage. In Luke 20:27–40, the Sadducees create a trap for Jesus with a story of a woman who is married and then widowed by each of seven brothers: Will she have seven husbands in the resurrection? They felt they could force Jesus to side with them in denying the afterlife or else make a fool of himself by picturing a morally abhorrent situation in the afterlife. Jesus says they don't understand what life in the resurrection is like: it will not involve marriage.

"Isn't Jesus confirming the Pharisees' view of heaven and hell then?" Chip asked. "It sounds like he's siding with them instead of the Sadducees."

I replied that first of all, the question is about resurrection, not heaven and hell, and Jesus never brings up hell at all. If anything, he implies that only the worthy will be raised, leaving the others in the grave. And if he sides with the Pharisees here, it's the only place he does so. I thought it was more likely that he's not siding with either, that he was taking things to a higher level. But the most interesting and important part of the passage, I felt, came at the end, when Jesus says, "In the account of the bush, even Moses showed that the dead rise, for he calls the Lord 'the God of Abraham, and the God of Isaac, and the God of Jacob.' He is not the God of the dead but of the living, for to him all are alive."

I explained my conclusion: for Jesus, the key was that *to God, all are alive.* Everyone—in this life and beyond it—lives related to God. So people shouldn't think of their destiny in relation to heaven or hell, which aren't the ultimate reality, but in relation to God—God the compassionate Father, God who loves the poor and the weak and the vulnerable and cares when they're mistreated, God who values both personal morality and public justice, God whose will is peace and justice for all.

Poor Chip looked shocked at this point. "Am I overwhelming you?" I asked. "Should I stop there?"

"I am overwhelmed. And a little scared. I've read the Bible all my life, and I've always seen it a certain way. I assumed that anyone who didn't see it my way just didn't respect the Bible. But here you are, showing great respect for the Bible, yet you see things so differently. And I wonder how I'm going to—how I'm going to trust myself to be sure of anything again."

I suggested we walk out to a bench in front of the church and get some fresh air. The bright October sun had taken the chill out of the cool morning. Somehow, sitting side by side on the bench seemed to make it easier for Chip to talk.

"All my life, when I've preached the gospel, it has always been the good news about how to get to heaven, about how you can be sure you're going to heaven. It was all about heaven."

"Well, I'm certainly not trying to undermine anyone's assurance of ultimate salvation," I said. "We're all going to die someday, so it's important to ask where we stand with God and to have assurance that we'll be with God. It would be terrible to take away people's confidence about that. I hope that's not what you think I'm—"

"No, no, not at all," Chip said. "But I'm wondering how you preach the gospel in this, this different understanding of things."

"I tell people God loves them, God accepts them, God isn't holding their sins against them, God wants them to follow his way. I ask them to rethink their lives, to be ready for a new beginning. I tell them how God sent Jesus to invite us to follow him and live in the way God wants us to live. I tell them that Christ died for their sins and that the Holy Spirit can enter their life and begin transforming them. I tell them they truly can be transformed. I invite them to make their first priority to seek God's kingdom and God's justice."

Chip's eyebrows raised at this point, so I quoted Matthew 6:33, where Jesus links God's kingdom with justice. "True, most English Bibles use the word *righteousness* instead of *justice*, but the original word was *justice*, as is clear in other languages. By our unfortunate translation, we make Jesus say something more pleasing to us: 'seek first God's kingdom—which means religiosity. Seek first to pray a lot or read your Bible a lot or use polite language or whatever.' These may be good things, but they're not the priority Jesus commands.

"To seek God's kingdom and justice means, as the Lord's Prayer makes clear, to seek for God's will to be done on earth as it is in heaven. God's will means God's desire for how things should be. How should things be? Just! Compassionate! Peaceful! Reconciled! But justice on earth is of less concern to us if we're preoccupied with evading justice after this life and seeking refuge in a private, isolated, personal piety in this life."

Chip shook his head. "You may be right, but this sounds kind of, uh, liberal. I've always seen the New Testament as being about justification, not justice. How does your emphasis on justice fit in with justification?"

I turned sideways on the bench to face him: "When God forgives, God justifies. We don't earn it. Forgiveness is, by definition, a gift, not something we earn." I took a moment to figure out where to go next. "If we're seeking to evade justice after this life, all we care about is personal forgiveness, our own justification. But even in the Lord's Prayer, Jesus won't let us do that; he makes us link our forgiveness with our pursuit of reconciliation with others—you know, forgive us as we forgive others. If we're seeking justice in this world, a justice that includes reconciliation, then seeking forgiveness is an important first step. If I want God's will, God's justice, to come on earth now, I must admit how often I fail and frustrate that justice. So I need the assurance that God forgives me. That, of course, sets me up to forgive others as I have been forgiven, which leads to reconciliation, which in turn leads to a reduction of injustice by breaking the offense-revenge cycle.

"So forgiveness is not an evasion of justice or an exception to justice—it's an essential element of God's healing, reconciling justice. This comes to the heart of Jesus' message and his quarrel with the Pharisees. For them, God's justice is merciless, unforgiving, heartless, cold. For Jesus, God's justice, God's perfection, is more perfect than theirs: God's perfection is compassionate, merciful, healing, restoring. God's justice justifies; it forgives. That's what a story like the Prodigal Son makes so clear. God's door is open. God wants to welcome us all home, younger wild brothers and older tame brothers alike."

At that point, Chip spoke up. He told me that he had recently visited South Africa to vacation at the home of one of BEF's former board members who had moved to Cape Town. En route, he had stopped in Johannesburg, where he had been given a private tour of the Apartheid Museum. His tour guide was a young Xhosa man who recounted many of his own experiences of racism growing up in Soweto. When they came toward the end to the exhibit that explained Nelson Mandela's release from prison and his leadership toward reconciliation, not revenge, the young man began to weep, and Chip said he began to weep too, and the two of them stood embracing and weeping in the museum for some minutes. "What you're describing," he said, "reminds me of what I felt with that Xhosa guide. That truth and reconciliation should be the last word. That the goal is *shalom*."

I'd never been to Africa, but I began recounting to him what I'd learned from my friends Neil and Markus about how the modern colonial gospel, the gospel of the evasion of justice for the few, had been advised to empower racism, colonialism, environmental degradation, and perhaps even genocide. This world will soon end, so why worry about justice *here and now*? All that counts is where you will end up *then and there*, in the afterlife. Your status there depends on religious piety—on prayer and Bible study and worship, not deeds of compassion and social justice. So if you want to steal lands of indigenous peoples, it's OK: first, land isn't that big a deal—what's the real estate of earth compared to the golden streets of heaven? Second, since these people are heathens, they're going to be damned anyway, which somehow diminishes their dignity and makes it easier to rip them off. Besides, we'll give them the gospel, which will save their souls, and they'll give us their land—that sounds like a fair enough trade. And since the earth is about to be destroyed, why not exploit it, since it will all be wasted otherwise? Why not burn the rain forests, since

God says they're going to burn anyway? Besides, whatever mistakes we make along the way will be forgiven.

I felt terrible talking this way and was worried that I had offended Chip, but although he looked pained, he wasn't angry. In fact, he responded with a quote from Desmond Tutu he had heard when he was in South Africa: When the European missionaries came, Tutu said, the Africans had the land and the Europeans had the Bible. The Europeans asked the Africans to close their eyes in prayer. When they said amen and opened their eyes, the Europeans had the land and the Africans had the Bible. But the Africans got the better end of the deal, he concluded, because the Bible then gave them the rationale to ask for their land to be returned and their rights respected.

"So I feel as though God has been preparing me to think some new thoughts, to accept, or at least to entertain, some new ways of seeing things. I never would have been open to what you've been saying if it weren't for reading that *Glorious Unveiling* book and taking this trip to South Africa, where all this is so obvious," Chip said. I replied that it's pretty obvious in our history too, but we just don't see it.

Chip stood up at this point. He walked over to a bright yellow car parked nearby and leaned against it. "If you're right, then we've gotten far, very far, from what Jesus intended. How could this have happened? How could we have gotten so far off track?"

A PART OF ME
AT THE CORE OF MY MIND

Then did a light from heaven admonish us,
So that, both penitent and pardoning, forth
From life we issued reconciled to God,
Who with desire to see Him stirs our hearts.

—*Purgatorio*, V.52–55

I FELT ODD SITTING while Chip was standing, so I walked over and stood beside him, leaning against the hood of the car. I offered a number of factors to explain what I thought had gone wrong with our understanding of the gospel.

By the fifth century, I suggested, Neoplatonic philosophy had become so enmeshed with Christianity that its Jewish roots were in danger of being overshadowed in some ways. In some branches of Neoplatonic philosophy, the material world and its history are unimportant: what matters is the immaterial, nontemporal world of the Ideal. Our concept of God risked having more in common with the Greek *theos* of Plato and Plotinus than the *Yahweh* of Abraham, Isaac, and Jacob.

In this framework, the gospel could become a plan of escape from the sinful material world of history so that our souls could rejoin the timeless spiritual world of eternity. The human predicament grew less and less a historic, social, and personal one and instead grew into a more and more metaphysical, legal, spiritualized one. In that context, the metaphor of court could predominate, with God as angry judge and each individual as guilty defendant. Other metaphors were marginalized or disappeared—such as the metaphor of an epidemic, with God as healing doctor. As long as the legal guilt of injustice was dealt with in the believer's life, the reality of ongoing injustice in the world could shrink into a less vital concern. This shift away from God's will being done on earth was deeply connected, I suggested, to the merging of Christianity with the Roman Empire after Constantine.

Then, during the Middle Ages, with plagues and barbarian invasions, life was so short and difficult that a message of hope about the afterlife was more than enough good news for people to celebrate. Unfortunately, darker motivations may also have been at work: if the church promises to solve a problem after death, it absolves itself of needing to address problems of this life, and it can demand respect and compliance whether or not it is fruitful here and now in this life. After all, when you dispense eternal salvation, you have a lot of leverage.

In more recent centuries, the conflict between Christianity and science encouraged the church in its conservative forms to withdraw from the affairs of this world even more, concentrating on the hope of heaven, minimizing seeking God's will to be done on earth. Politics busied itself with what were seen as "worldly" or "temporal" concerns, while the church focused on "spiritual" or "eternal" matters. As a result, Christian faith become increasingly personalized, privatized, and marginalized.

One of the deepest problems lay hidden in a misunderstanding of what it means to be chosen or elect by God. Many Christians assumed that to be called or chosen by God was a matter of privilege and blessing only, not for responsibility and service. So God chooses some for heaven and others for hell, and we need to acquiesce to God's choice. Biblically, however, God chooses some, not to the exclusion of others but for the benefit of others: they're "blessed to be a blessing."

Chip pushed away from the yellow car, turned, and reached out his hand to me. As we shook hands, he said, "I want to thank you for this time, Dan. I didn't expect you to treat me so warmly after what happened back in 2002. If there's ever anything I can do for you, just ask."

"Actually, there is something," I said. "At the right time, I hope you can help Gil and me to reconcile."

"That might not be as hard or as far off as you think," he said.

Since that day, Chip and I have been meeting every few weeks or so for lunch to continue our conversation. His progress has been slow, with two steps forward, one back—a lot like my own. He has faced a lot of fear, especially about his future with the BEF. Twice he canceled our appointment and said he didn't want to meet anymore, but each time he called back and rescheduled. A few times he has raised his voice with me; once he treated me to some choice profanity. Each time he apologized.

"I understand," I said, and I was telling the truth. I saved a few of his e-mails, which say something about Chip's honesty, intensity, and integrity.

Dan—
I need to change our breakfast meeting from this Thursday to next if possible. Since our meeting in your office, I've been feeling a mixture of elation and fear—elation because I'm finally facing some of my questions and doubts, and fear because I'm not sure where it leads. But something needs to happen, because I am an irrelevant Christian desperate to be relevant to a world that is desperate for good news.

Unless I hear from you, I'll assume we're on for next Thursday at 7:30 at Just Eggs Restaurant.
Chip

Dan—
Just writing to confirm our lunch meeting Tuesday at 12:30 at Bluebird Grill. Our breakfast meeting last month was deeply disturbing to me. I have felt as if my mind were on caffeine ever since—intellectually jittery, unable to rest. I don't know whether to say thank you or to tell you to jump off a bridge.

Please be gentle with me when we meet. I love Jesus, Dan, and I have built my life upon and around Him. It feels like all my foundations are being shaken. If you were to shake my belief in Him, I would be losing my whole reason for living, my whole orientation for life. The results would be disastrous for me. I'm not sure why I'm telling you this, but you told me you wanted me to be completely honest with you. I'm terrified about meeting with you.

At the same time, I want to tell you that I need to meet with you. I need to explore, to think, and you have given me a safe place. Safe but scary at the same time. Thank you, or curse you, or whatever.
Chip

Dan—
Thanks for the lunch yesterday. The food was great, and I came home feeling so different from last month. As I was driving home, this picture came to my mind. I feel as though I have spent my life as a fisherman on a small island. A storm of questions struck and blew me off course so I was lost

at sea. Then I saw your boat, hoping that you would lead me back to my familiar little island. Instead, you've led me to a huge continent that I never knew existed. I think I will spend the rest of my life exploring this new land. Thank you. Thanks also for your little chart on modern versus postmodern. I'm going to save that placemat. Maybe I'll frame it. I also appreciated your circle diagrams picturing the self, the church, and the world. That rang true.

Chip

Dan—

Thanks for our breakfast this morning. Your biblical story in seven episodes was one of the most meaningful things I've ever heard. It puts everything in a new light. As I was driving back to my office, a thought hit me.

In my way of telling the gospel, what you call the modern Western way, there were always two key questions:

1. If you were to die tonight, do you know for certain that you'd go to be with God in heaven?

2. If Jesus returned today, would you be ready to meet God?

Jesus is important because he paid for your sins when he died on the cross, so if you die tonight, or if Jesus returns today, you'll be forgiven and can enter heaven.

But in this new understanding of the gospel, two very different questions come to mind:

1. If you were to live for another fifty years, what kind of person would you like to become—and how will you become that kind of person?

2. If Jesus doesn't return for ten thousand or ten million years, what kind of world do we want to create?

Here Jesus is important because he leads you and forms you to become a better and better person, and the kind of people who truly follow his way will create a good and beautiful world.

The first set of questions, which used to satisfy me, don't anymore, at least not on their own. I'm realizing that both sets of questions have validity, and the second may be more important. I guess that's obvious to you, but it's just dawning on me.

Chip

Dan—

Sorry you haven't heard from me. Here's what's happening, inside and outside. Inside, the choice I face is whether to take the new insights you're helping me with and add them like fine print to the conventional conservative contract I've always lived by—OR should I rewrite the whole contract? Outside, do I stay in leadership in the BEF and try to bring the others around, or do I quietly disappear? That's what I'd like to talk about next time we meet. Also, I'll be on airplanes a lot next week. Do you have any good books to recommend?

Chip

Dan—

I'm writing from Colorado Springs. Thanks for suggesting I reread *The Great Divorce,* which I read on the plane. It's clear, just as you said: hell, for Lewis, is not an imposed consequence where God gets vengeance on us for mistaken or inaccurate beliefs or retaliates for misdeeds we have done. Instead, it's the outward expression of what we have become. So a person who has become greedy and envious is incapable of being happy when others are prosperous in ways he is not. People who are filled with lust are incapable of being happy when they can't consume whatever pleasure presents itself to them. People who have become proud can't be happy in the presence of others who outshine them.

If to be in the presence of God is to be in the presence of others who are happy and blessed in a million different ways, where there are pleasures beyond what one person could ever consume, and where one is in the presence of glories that make pride ridiculous and pathetic, God's presence then is a place some people would find intolerable. They have become incapable of enjoying the highest good, having formed their affections around smaller, meaner, less noble or less glorious ends. So I've asked myself, what would it mean to be saved—not only from guilt but actually from becoming and being that kind of person?

In that light, Jesus' 'Follow me' isn't a command; it's an invitation to liberation. As you said, the Kingdom of God becomes a way of living, a network of relationships in which one is formed to be the kind of person who can enjoy the highest, noblest, most glorious ends, in this life and forever. This is starting to make sense, Dan. In fact, I'm more motivated by this understanding than I ever was by the old one. Strange. Who would have guessed?

Chip

Dan—

On the plane home late last night, I was staring out the window looking down at the lights, thinking of the millions of people below me in houses, in cars on the highway, in shopping centers. Suddenly, a wave of emotion came over me. I guess it was love. I think I felt, for just a few seconds, a tiny fraction of what God feels when he looks at our world. I loved everybody. I thought about how small they were, how tiny, how fragile. I was struck by how insignificant the differences were between the richest and the poorest, the best and the worst, the smartest and the stupidest. I thought about how small this whole planet would look from a billion miles away yet how precious it would be to God.

Then it was as if my perspective changed, like the camera in my head that I was looking through came out of me and then took me into view. Instead of seeing the lights spread out like diamonds on black velvet, I somehow saw myself looking out the window down at the earth. And I realized that I was taken in by that greater perspective, that the one who was looking at me felt the same affection for me that I felt for the people below me on the ground. I felt this kind of assurance that I was truly and completely loved.

It sounds a little silly and trite, I know, but I think you'll understand. Even though I've preached about God and worked for God all these years, before last night, I don't think I ever truly felt so loved by God. For a second, I felt that I might break, like literally split apart, because the intensity or size of the feeling—or maybe realization is a better word—was so strong and big. All my life, I think there's been this part of me at the core of my mind that was still afraid that God would reject me, that I would somehow in the end be lost forever and condemned. But ever since that moment last night, right to this moment, that fear is gone. I thought of the story of the Prodigal Son, and this thought came to me: *no one who wants to come home will ever be turned away.* I couldn't think of anyone else who would understand this. I just felt I had to share it. Your kindness to me made me susceptible to this kind of moment. Thank you.

Chip

29

THE LAST, BEST WORD

. . . many times the word comes short of fact.

—Inferno, IV.147

A FEW MONTHS AFTER my initial meeting with Chip, Carol and I were driving south on Route 95 in a steady, gentle rain. I reached over and took her hand and said, "I'm so glad we didn't give up these last few years. I'm so glad we survived. There's so much we would be missing now. Thank you for hanging in there with me." The windshield wipers beat their rhythm for a few seconds before she answered.

We were returning from my second gathering with the circle of seven, which was now a circle of eleven because we had added four new members, one of whom was Carol. This year, we had gathered in Camden, hosted by Father Dominic and The Little Flower. We couldn't have chosen a setting more different from Father Scott's cabin. Yet the time was no less rich. Carol and I had stayed in the home of a black family in the neighborhood, Undray and Chantal Washington. We were the first white people they had ever welcomed into their home as guests; they were the first inner-city black family we had ever visited for a meal, much less for a three-day visit. Carol, whose background as a Georgia Southern Baptist was even more conservative than my own, had surprised herself and me as well; she felt so at home with everyone she met at The Little Flower, and they loved her no less. Every time she sat down, it seemed that one of the Washingtons' four small children was climbing into her lap. I'll never forget the sight of my upper-middle-class wife sitting on the stoop of a row house in Camden just the previous night, her pale face smiling and laughing in conversation with Chantal and some of her neighbors, kids playing ball in the street, Chantal's youngest child lying back on Carol as if she were part of the family, which I now realize she truly was.

"Yes," Carol said, "it's hard to believe times that were so bad could give way to times that are so rich and good." Then Carol squeezed my hand: "Dan, I tried to be supportive through those times, but I was truly afraid. I knew Gil and the others were wrong, but I wasn't sure that you were right either. I wish . . ."

"You couldn't have been more supportive," I said. "We were both doing our best. I guess that's what faith is about: not understanding what's happening, not being sure, yet pressing on, doing our best, even if that's not very good sometimes, trusting God to guide us through."

"Well, one thing's for sure," Carol replied. "I've never felt more alive. And Lord knows, I've never been so excited about the Bible. How could I have missed so much for all these years? I guess I'm still a traditionalist— what do you call it, exclusivist?—when it comes to hell. I can't get my mind around all those other views. But I realize that even if that view is the right one, the correct one, it can really be misused. It can have a very bad effect." I asked her what she meant by that. "Well, I suppose you can think about the hereafter in a way that makes you take the here and now less seriously. But you've helped me see that the hereafter sheds its light on the here and now. So even though I don't get all the theological stuff you worry about, I think it's put things in a new light, not just for me but for everybody at PCC."

She was right. Our people were responding to the gospel as never before. I realized they had had pent-up energy to make a difference all along, but they didn't know what or where or how. As I began preaching the passages of the Bible that dealt with injustice, people discovered exciting ways to make a difference in the here and now.

Several small groups in our church had linked up with The Little Flower in Camden, and some discovered that there were similar groups at work in Washington and Baltimore. A few small groups had picked a nation in the world—Honduras, Burundi, Sierra Leone, and Afghanistan among them— and had begun a fascinating process of caring for their chosen country. They educated themselves, prayed, met immigrants and refugees, formed links with local pastors there, sought to influence U.S. foreign policy where they could through writing letters and visiting congressional representatives, and even began planning mission trips to their chosen countries.

Our own small group built a relationship with small groups in three other churches. We set up "blind dates" for groups of people for dinner— one individual or couple from each church would host dinner for another individual or couple once a month. The hosts were to share their life story, including their spiritual journey. Dinner groups from Fire-Baptized Pentecostal Holiness Tabernacle in Baltimore, Saint Gregory's Greek Orthodox Church in Catonsville, Iglesia del Verbo in Washington, D.C., and PCC in Gaithersburg met, mingled, dined, and became friends. The experiment was a huge success, and we began inviting others to join us in our "spiritual blind date" project.

In a sermon before Christmas, I had shared the quote Markus had given me—the one about God's love for the world—and the congregation responded so warmly that a women's group created a quilt with the quote stitched into it. The quilt was mounted and hung on a wall by the exit of our sanctuary so that people would see it every week as they left worship. All around it was displayed a growing collection of photographs and small maps that expressed our concern for God's kingdom, God's justice, and our desire to see God's will done on earth as in heaven.

Furthermore, greater numbers of people we call "spiritual seekers" had begun attending. One young man wrote me a letter that expressed what I heard from several people over the course of the year:

> Dear Dan,
> I want to thank you for PCC and the part you have played in making it the community that it is today. I've been somewhat stagnant in my spirituality for a long time, and I would have loved to find a church like this years ago. But the churches I visited and the Christians I met seemed so out of touch, so angry, and so elitist that I didn't want to be associated with them. When they would say the name *Jesus,* my skin would crawl. I never knew that Christians were people who want to make the world more beautiful and good; I only thought they wanted to make it more religious and more to their tastes, which usually meant conservative. Since coming here, the name *Jesus* now inspires me. I'm learning how wonderful Jesus was and is. I'm not sure I want to be a Christian in the old sense, but I know I'm becoming a follower of Jesus in some new way through the influence of PCC. Thank you for all you've done for me and now several of my friends.
>
> Gratefully,
> Steve Stone

Along with the exciting things happening at PCC, we had our share of personal excitement too. Every calendar in our home had September 18,

2005, marked as the big day. Every plan we made as a family was made in reference to The Wedding. No wonder the year passed so quickly. It was not only the first double wedding at which I'd officiated; it was also the first I'd ever seen.

Ashara looked stunning in her Indian sari, emerald and red with rich gold designs, with a deep cobalt blue sash around the middle and a scarlet cloth draping from her head back across her shoulders like a veil. Even now, I can close my eyes and look slightly to my left, recapturing the scene as the wedding party assembled at the front of the church: Ashara's brown skin, her bright eyes, her radiant smile, her gaze to her right, where Neil stood tall and trim, not in a traditional tuxedo but instead in a hand-tailored black suit and hand-sewn white silk shirt with black buttons made of seashells—gifts from Neil's cousin, a tailor, from Jamaica.

If in my imagination I turn to my right, I see Kincaid, his long blond hair not in the usual ponytail but braided in long braids with beads like Casey's, the work of some of Neil's nieces who flew in from Jamaica for the wedding. He's smiling at me, winking, subtly giving me the thumbs-up sign, almost bouncing in his shiny black shoes. And to his right, holding his arm, is Jess, my only daughter, and her face is so peaceful, so confident, so beautiful that my closed eyes fill with tears now, just as they did on that day.

If I look beyond Jess in her traditional white gown, I can see Carol beaming, eyes focused on our beautiful daughter. Since I am officiating and can't sit beside her, and since Cory and Trent are also in the wedding party, beside her sit Kincaid's father and his wife and beside them our friends Pat and Chloe, right there in the front row, the first time either of them have ever ventured out of the back row at church since they began attending more regularly in the last several months. Chloe has a camera, and Pat holds a black portfolio that holds a poem she will read during the ceremony.

Next to Pat and Chloe sit Ky and Leticia, Ky's hair flopping down into his eyebrows, Leticia wearing a stylish hat, both of them leaning forward from the edge of their seats and smiling broadly.

In the front row on the other side, I can picture Ashara's widowed mother, short and thin and dignified in her scarlet and gold sari, smiling in her gold half-glasses, looking happy but a bit tired, having flown in from Trinidad for the event. And beside her sit Markus, Milagros, Ruth, and Casey, along with some of Neil's friends from Ecuador—Maricel, who can't stop crying, and Glenn, a suntanned biologist in an open sport shirt who told me, "I've never once worn a tie around this virgin neck." Filling the rest of the seats are Jess and Kincaid's friends and classmates, many leaning this way and that to take pictures, everyone erect, attentive, smiling. Father Scott stands beside me, co-officiating the wedding. He gives me a nod, and I begin, "Dearly beloved, we are gathered together in the presence of God to witness and bless the joining together of this man and this woman in holy matrimony."

If I replay those moments in my mind, I can also turn back to the right side, behind Carol, and see Chip and Jane Granger, who have now become our close friends, Chip looking genuinely happy even though he was recently run out of the BEF and vilified by his former friends there. Beside them sit Nancy Zeamer and Clarissa, and yes, even Gil has come. Before the ceremony, I can recall Gil coming up to me in the foyer, looking nervous yet coming to shake my extended hand.

"I'm happy for you, sincerely, Dan," he says. "Jess is a beautiful young woman, and I know you're getting a first-rate son-in-law, in spite of his long hair." He winks to let me know he was kidding. "It's good to be here at PCC again. It was kind of you to invite us after all that."

"I'm so glad you've come. You're always welcome here, Gil," I say.

"Maybe we'll stop in again for a visit sometime," he says, and then clears his throat. "Chip and Jane have been telling us great things since they began attending, and we haven't really settled in at Grace Bible yet, and as good as Dr. Roads is, we still miss . . ."

"We'll always be glad to see you, Gil," I say. "The door here is always open wide to you."

I can fast-forward in my memory, through the readings and prayers, the songs and homily, the vows and rings, the candle lighting and benediction, to the kiss—so long that the congregation actually begins to laugh and clap, and then to the recessional—with Milagros playing a Scottish fiddle tune and the congregation clapping wildly, both couples stopping to give high five's down both sides of the aisle—through the reception, with its toasts and dances and photographs—to later that evening, when the last guests leave and the atmosphere grows quiet. Some friends are still cleaning up the fellowship hall, and the caterers are just pulling out of the parking lot. Kincaid and Jess have left for their honeymoon suite at a hotel near the airport. Father Scott sees me standing alone by a water fountain, catching my breath, reflecting on the day. He comes over and leans next to me against the wall and in a soft voice quotes lines from Pat's poem: "This is the end to which all things tend, the end which makes all things new." Later that night, after Carol has gone to bed and I'm standing at the front door, looking out over the quiet street, I pull out the program from the ceremony and read the last stanza from which those lines came:

Scripture ends in a marriage.
This is the end to which all
Things tend, the end which makes all
Things new. Marriage unites, but
In its fire, true love does not
Consume. Selfishness burns. All
That mars love ignites, makes ash.
But faith, hope, love survive. Love
Is the last, best word, the end
Into which all will bend, and
Then begin again. The next
Word and the new will be love
As well: for love never ends
And in love all are made, yes,
Friends.

Kincaid and Jessica Poole-Ellison left for their extended honeymoon the next afternoon. It wasn't any tame honeymoon they'd planned: it was a fifteen-week adventure in Australia, the home of Kincaid's mother and grandparents. They promised to e-mail us at least once a week, and they almost kept their promise—I think it was more like once every two or three weeks. In December, just before Christmas, we received this short but memorable message.

TO: dancarolp@backhandspring.net
FROM: jcssnkaid@yahoo.com
SUBJECT: News from Tas
DATE: December 23, 2005

Dear Mom and Dad—
We're in Tasmania, enjoying the summer weather at my uncle's home. We were planning a backpacking trip over Christmas in a national park here, but Jess was feeling a little sick, so we decided to stop by the hospital in Hobart before we left. So I hope you're sitting down, because we have some major news: JESS IS PREGNANT! Mid-June is our due date. We're terrified, excited, thrilled, and amazed. We already feel so much love for a tiny human being we have not yet met. God is amazing. What a miracle. Jess sends her love, although she says she feels like barfing at the moment. We love you!
Kincaid
P.S. Will you let Neil and Ashara know?

I called Neil immediately. "Hallelujah!" he said, and after asking Ashara to pick up the other phone so I could tell her the news, Neil said, "Well, actually, Daniel, we have some news too."

COMMENTARY

I gave myself
Weeping to Him, who willingly doth pardon.

—*Purgatorio* III.119–120

BECAUSE THIS IS A WORK of creative nonfiction rather than scholarship, it didn't seem appropriate to include footnotes in the text. Instead, you'll find references and other commentary chapter by chapter in this section.

Introduction

On the idea that some elements of theology are "for mature audiences only," consider Paul's teachings on the gospel, which tempted the immature to say, "Let's sin more and more, so grace can abound more and more!" The apostle Peter noticed this tendency of "the ignorant and unstable" to twist and distort the teachings of "beloved brother Paul" (2 Peter 3:16), yet he didn't blame Paul for their misinterpretations. Rather, he warned others not to follow their bad lead. See also my book *A Generous Orthodoxy* (Emergent/YS/Zondervan, 2004).

Book One: The Last Word

Chapter 1: Something Serious

The first lines from Dan's journal entry obviously reflect the opening of Dante's *Divine Comedy*. Much of what we think we know from the Bible about heaven and hell actually comes from the poets Dante and John Milton (*Paradise Lost*). The epigraphs from Dante Alighieri's *Divine Comedy* that introduce each chapter come from Henry Wadsworth Longfellow's 1865 translation, available online (www.everypoet.com/archive/poetry/dante/dante_contents.htm).

The issue raised by Dan's daughter, Jess, in this chapter reflects a similar issue raised by one of my sons in an episode I recount in *A Generous Orthodoxy*.

The C. S. Lewis quote comes from *Mere Christianity* (HarperSanFrancisco, 2001), pp. 208–209.

Dan admits to avoiding the subject of hell. It is instructive to look at important theological works in recent decades and notice the number of pages they devote to the subject. It truly is the "elephant formerly but no longer in the room" that almost nobody is talking about.

For a summary of four approaches to hell (literal, metaphorical, purgatorial, and conditional), see William Crockett, ed., *Four Views on Hell* (Zondervan, 1992). For a defense of the conventional view, see Robert A. Peterson's *Hell on Trial: The Case for Eternal Punishment* (P&R Publishing, 1995). For a gentle, humble critique of the conventional view, see *What Does the Bible Really Say About Hell? Wrestling with the Traditional View*, by Randy Klassen (Pandora, 2001).

John Sanders, in *No Other Name: An Investigation into the Destiny of the Unevangelized* (Eerdmans, 1992, p. 215), offers a pithy definition of inclusivism: "Briefly, inclusivists affirm the particularity and finality of salvation only in Christ but deny that knowledge of his work is necessary for salvation. That is to say, they hold that the work of Jesus is ontologically necessary for salvation (no one would be saved without it) but not epistemologically necessary (one need not be aware of the work in order to benefit from it). Or, in other words, people can receive the gift of salvation without knowing the giver or the precise nature of the gift."

On conditionalism (annihilationism, conditional immortality), see Edward Fudge's monumental and important work, *The Fire That Consumes: A Biblical and Historical Study of the Doctrine of Eternal Punishment* (Backinprint.com, 2000), or Edward Fudge and Robert Peterson, *Two Views of Hell: A Biblical and Theological Dialogue* (IVP, 2000). See also www.edwardfudge.com.

Two recent books make the case for Christian universalism, which should be clearly distinguished from Unitarian Universalism. One is Philip Gulley and James Mulholland's *If Grace Is True: Why God Will Save Every Person* (HarperSanFrancisco, 2003). Its Appendix 2 includes quotes from across the centuries that show the presence and persistence of this minority report in Christian history. From a Reformed perspective, Jan Bonda, *The One Purpose of God: An Answer to the Doctrine of Eternal Punishment* (Eerdmans, 1993), is an equally strong critique of the conventional view but manifests a somewhat higher view of Scripture. When in this chapter

Jess refers to hell as "a kind of unexpected plan B that God couldn't antic-ipate and is now stuck with," she is anticipating the issues Bonda deals with directly, responsibly, and faithfully.

Dan's fear of being labeled a universalist reflects the anxiety that haunts many religious circles. Sometimes, fearmongering by people in power re-veals the unacknowledged fragility of their own position; it can only be maintained by social threat. Whether or not you agree with Gulley and Mulholland or Bonda, the strength of their arguments and the depth of their concern for an honorable understanding of God should not be un-derestimated. And whether or not they are right, people should not be in-timidated or threatened for honest inquiry into what they're saying. It has been said that anyone who is not a universalist should be at the very least a universalist sympathizer; since Scripture says God is not willing for any-one to perish, neither should we. For ongoing dialogue on Christian uni-versalism, see tentmaker.org, gospelfortoday.org, and savior-of-all.com.

At the end of the day, I share Lesslie Newbigin's discomfort with the conventional categories regarding salvation and hell. (Note that he uses the word *pluralist* in place of *universalist*.)

> It has become customary to classify views on the relation of Chris-tianity to the world religions as either pluralist, exclusivist, or inclu-sivist. [My] position is exclusivist in the sense that it affirms the unique truth of the revelation in Jesus Christ, but it is not exclusivist in the sense of denying the possibility of the salvation of the non-Christian. It is inclusivist in the sense that it refuses to limit the saving grace of God to the members of the Christian church, but it rejects the inclu-sivism which regards the non-Christian religions as vehicles of salva-tion. It is pluralist in the sense of acknowledging the gracious work of God in the lives of all human beings, but it rejects a pluralism which denies the uniqueness and decisiveness of what God has done in Jesus Christ. [Lesslie Newbigin, *The Gospel in a Pluralist Society* (Eerdmans, 1989), 182–183].

It should be noted that no character in this book advocates a relativist view that would say all religions are the same or it doesn't matter what you believe as long as you're sincere. As tragic events in our recent history make clear, it matters a great deal what you believe. For example, it mat-ters a great deal (to the rest of us, at least!) whether you believe in a God who might tomorrow inspire you to violence and genocide or to military conquest and domination as opposed to a God who calls all humanity to reconciliation and peace.

Chapter 2: Flare-Up

Dan's theological problem is entwined with a relational problem. I think it is important to remember how truth and love are linked in the gospel and how our pursuit of truth affects our relational life in various communities.

PCC uses adjectives like *open, mainstream,* and *progressive* to modify *evangelical.* The need for modification reflects the broad range of views currently huddling under the same umbrella. Some believe (and I am sometimes among them) that the term has been captured (here in America at least) by the "religious right" and so is of little use to anyone else. Others believe (at this moment, I am among them) that the term is too rich in history to be thrown away or surrendered to the most strident voices who reside under the big evangelical umbrella.

There is no Biblical Evangelical Fellowship that I am aware of, although the sentiments associated with it do seem to exist in the Evangelical world. (On "big *E*" and "small *e*" evangelicals, see *A Generous Orthodoxy*).

For more on the modern-postmodern issue, see my books *A New Kind of Christian* (Jossey-Bass, 2001) and *The Church on the Other Side* (Zondervan, 1998).

Chapter 3: Poet in a Trench Coat

Neil's cryptic allusion to Bonda refers to *The One Purpose of God,* referred to in the Chapter One commentary.

Pat is modeled on a kindhearted lesbian poet I met in England in 2003. I made Pat intersexual here based on my belief that if we can have honest, informed, and compassionate dialogue on how intersexual people should be treated, we will be better prepared to address the challenging subject of people with intractable (and to all appearances at least, inborn) homosexual orientations. For more information on intersexuality, go to healthyplace.com/communities/gender/intersexuals or dir.yahoo.com/health/Diseases_and_Conditions/intersexuality.

Regarding homosexuality and the polarization it is causing in the Christian community, I would ask two sets of questions, one of each side:

• If you take the "conservative" position, assuming you are right, how do you believe homosexual people should be treated? Should they be constantly shamed? Made to live in secret or hiding? Deprived of basic human rights, equal pay, housing, and so on? Accepted, but on some second-class

COMMENTARY

status that would treat them differently from other people? And if you cannot accept homosexual people in your midst, can you accept those who do, or must you reject (on some level) both homosexual people and those who accept them?

• If you take the "liberal" position, assuming you are right, how do you recommend we decide what is right or wrong sexually? Does "anything go," and if not, how do we decide how to identify any sexual behavior as wrong—on what basis? What are the personal and social consequences of a lack of moral clarity on sexual issues, and how can those consequences be avoided or dealt with? And if you accept and affirm gay people, how will you deal with those whose consciences will not allow them to do so? Does your acceptance of gays require a rejection of those who do not agree with you, and if not, how will the difference be dealt with?

I don't think that either side will be able to listen to the other until they come to the table equipped with well-considered answers to these kinds of questions.

I decided to identify Pat's father as a Nazarene pastor because the International Church of the Nazarene (go to www.nazarenecentennial.org) has such a rich story behind its name. Phineas Bresee, the key figure in the formation of the denomination, intentionally chose the name *Nazarene* because in Jesus' day, it suggested a despised, outcast, rejected people. Instead of choosing a name that indicated an elite form of governance (like Presbyterian or Episcopal) or identified a distinctive practice (Baptist, Anabaptist) or claimed an elite spiritual status (Pentecostal Holiness), he chose an evocative name that associated the denomination with outcasts and rejected people. Pat's father failed to fully live up to that identity, as all of us who bear the name Christian do.

Chapter 4: Party in the Living Room, Torture in the Basement

Carol's pain is an important part of this whole trilogy. I hope it draws attention to the question of how churches treat their pastors—and pastoral spouses and children.

Chapter 5: Playing Hardball

Casey's offer to photocopy relevant articles for Dan echoes an experience of mine that played a part in the development of this book. Several years ago, Todd Hunter, then a leader in the Association of Vineyard Churches, invited me to join a well-known theologian and author in providing some mentoring for young Vineyard leaders. Although I felt completely unworthy to be paired with this theological giant, I readily agreed—hoping that I, along with the young leaders, would receive some mentoring. After one of our sessions, a bright young pastor asked my colleague what areas he felt most needed rethinking in our theology. My colleague answered, "Our doctrine of atonement, doctrine of Scripture, and doctrine of heaven and hell." Later Todd announced, "I think for our next gathering, we'll address the three areas identified tonight as doctrines needing rethinking." Then he assigned the doctrine of atonement to my colleague, suggested another noted theologian to address the doctrine of Scripture, and added, "Brian, I'm giving you hell."

I felt very much as Dan does in this section: it's a subject I had wanted to study but kept putting off. Todd's invitation foreclosed on my procrastination. Todd's kind assistant did for me what Casey did here—provided a thick file of photocopied articles, theological dictionary entries, and so forth. My notes for the presentation, gleaned from that folder of photocopies and additional research, provided the basis for Casey's list of quotes in Chapter Sixteen.

Chapter 6: I Don't Know

The "hell's door is locked from the inside" argument is given a very cursory dismissal by Neil. Dallas Willard gives it a much more thorough and thoughtful treatment in *Renovation of the Heart* (Navpress, 2002), as these quotes make clear:

> To be lost means to be *out of place,* to be omitted. "Gehenna," the term often used in the New Testament for the place of the lost, may usefully be thought of as a cosmic dump for the irretrievably useless. Think of what it would mean to find you have become irretrievably useless. . . . [Hell] is a place they [the hell-bound] would, in the end, choose for themselves. . . . Whether or not God's will is infinitely flexible, the human will is not. There are limits beyond which it cannot bend back, cannot turn or repent. . . . The fundamental fact about them will not be that they are there [in hell], but that they have become people so locked into their own self-worship and denial of God that *they cannot want God* [pp. 55–58].

C. S. Lewis seems to follow this approach as part of his larger inclusivist approach: those who are in hell actually choose to be there and sustain themselves there by their own choice, rather like a child who has been told he can have dessert as soon as he apologizes to his sister for smacking her but would rather miss fudge and ice cream than apologize. In *The Problem of Pain* (Centenary Press, 1940), Lewis suggests that the act of closing in on the self and rejecting God causes souls to shrink or decay into something less and less human, which may suggest that their capacity for suffering decreases. This thought perhaps brings some comfort in the face of eternal suffering. Yet the question remains: If they are holding the door shut from the inside, might at least some ever be willing to open it and join the joy in heaven? *The Great Divorce* (HarperSanFrancisco, 2001) seems to hold out that option, which in its full-blown expression would suggest the view that hell is potentially at least purgatorial for some people; after suffering sufficiently, some, perhaps, would be purged of rebellion and be able to repent, unlock the door, and leave their self-imposed exile from God.

Jonathan Kvanvig, in *The Problem of Hell* (Oxford University Press, 1993), takes a philosophical rather than a biblical path into the subject, although he keeps biblical concerns in view. He rightly, I think, identifies why Christians are hesitant to abandon the traditional doctrine, even though many are uncomfortable with it: "It is central to Christianity that the person and work of Jesus have a point; humanity is in need of something that Christians maintain God has provided in Christ" (p. 170). Remove hell, he suggests, and the person and work of Jesus lose their point. Yet he realizes that "inferring the traditional argument of hell from the need for some such account would be an extraordinarily bad argument" (p. 170). In other words, the fact that Christianity thinks it needs the doctrine doesn't make it true. (I would add that we are in pretty bad shape if getting people out of hell is the only point of the person and work of Jesus that we can think of.)

Kvanvig calls the conventional view "the strong view," which consists of four theses: (1) some people are consigned to hell, (2) anyone consigned there exists there, (3) no one can escape from hell once consigned there, and (4) hell is retributive—one is being punished there for wrongs committed here in this life. He demonstrates how the alternate views try to soften the strong view by dropping one of its theses. Universalism drops thesis 1, making the others moot. Annihilation or conditional immortality drops thesis 2. Purgative or "second chance" views of hell drop thesis 3. He sees problems with each of these alternate views. For example, universalism denies free will: all are forced into heaven. If by nature they have come to hate God and their neighbor, how can they be happy in heaven? And if we picture them unhappily in heaven, might that experience actually be hellish? As for a purgative view, he says that "second chance doctrines are even more problematic, for what problem a second chance is supposed to solve is not clear. . . . Second chance doctrines then quickly become infinite chance doctrines, and infinitely delayed consequences for sin are no consequences at all" (p. 170). His reasons for rejecting annihilation are more complex, and in fact annihilation does have a place in his proposed solution.

As for the strong view, Kvanvig calls it "irremediably objectionable on both moral and epistemological grounds" (p. 169), which he demonstrates in the first part of the book. Moreover, he asserts, "Our understanding of hell must be rooted in an acceptable portrayal of God, . . . [and] the portrayal of God's character that Christians should accept makes God's love his primary motivational characteristic" (p. 136). So a Christian must portray hell "as flowing from the same divine character from which heaven flows. Any other view wreaks havoc on the integrity of God's character" (p. 136). How could a view of hell be seen as flowing from the love of God?

Rejecting both the conventional "strong view" and its common alternatives, he posits what he calls a composite account. Rather than dropping one of the first three theses, he strategically replaces thesis 4, the retribution thesis, with a self-determination thesis, similar to the "locked from the inside" view of Dallas Willard and C. S. Lewis. People remain in hell only because they stubbornly continue to refuse the company of God. However, he argues, the imploding choice of refusing the company of God can be seen as a self-disintegrating, self-destroying, self-annihilating act, and the longer and harder one persists in it, the more surely one progresses toward nonbeing: "The alternative to presence in heaven is nothingness" (p. 146). So hell is "a journey beyond death toward annihilation, but with the possibility that the journey is never completed" (p. 168). In other words, unlike annihilation (which includes the annihilation of freedom along with existence), this view makes annihilation a possibility that could be chosen or accepted but not a certainty imposed on one against one's will. In this way, hell remains "as bad as anything can be," yet God always acts in the most loving way possible in regard to the person who rejects God, including (if I understand Kvanvig correctly) offering the disintegrating being the postmortem possibility of using its freedom to end its existence.

Along the way, Kvanvig makes it clear he is an inclusivist (pp. 159–161), and his final position is not unlike Lewis's position in *The Great Divorce*, but Kvanvig supplies the possibility of nonexistence as the end of one's end.

Personally, while I believe these reflections are valuable, I lean toward the conclusion that they are trying to answer questions that aren't the best questions to ask, even though these questions do inevitably energize our curiosity. The language of hell, in my view, like the language of biblical prophecy in general, is not intended to provide literal or detailed fortune-telling or prognostication about the hereafter, nor is it intended to satisfy intellectual curiosity, but rather it is intended to motivate us in the here and now to realize our ultimate accountability to a God of mercy and justice and in that light to rethink everything and to seek first the kingdom and justice of God.

Chapter 7: The Architecture of the Bible

People trained as I was in the context of systematic theology find it hard to see the Bible as an evolving production whose architecture reflects the evolving and diverse styles, thought forms, language, genres, and assumptions of many cultures over many centuries. Although nearly all our seminaries train people (some would say overtrain them) in ancient languages, too few, I think, help them develop the kind of narrative literacy this chapter hints at.

Dan believes that the latest books of the Hebrew Scriptures were written about 450 B.C., as many evangelicals would. Others, of course, would date the latest books much later. If the latter are right, the point is made even more strongly: belief in hell is a very late development in Jewish thinking.

As for the idea of an afterlife in the ancient Jewish world, the situation is a bit more complex than Dan and Neil realize. Philip Johnston's *Shades of Sheol: Death and Afterlife in the Old Testament* (Intervarsity, 2002) takes into account beliefs of neighboring cultures, archaeological data (such as whether ancient Jews put food in the tombs of their dead, which would indicate some level of belief in an afterlife), and odd biblical passages (such as Saul's conference with the seer of Endor) to present a more nuanced view. Even so, it is clear beyond doubt that the conventional detailed conceptions of heaven and hell held by Christians today were nowhere to be found among pre-Exilic Jews. Even the idea of an immaterial soul was unknown to them, according to Johnston: "In Israel there was no clear distinction between body and soul" (p. 236).

The most that can be said is that certain Hebrew Scriptures funded later thinkers and writers with evocative poetic passages that could be used to support new understandings, imaginations, and beliefs as they developed. Johnston summarizes (*Shades of Sheol*, p. 65):

> Both the lack of obvious religious rites at burial and the lack of interest in graves confirm that Israelite life and faith were centered on the present life and relating to Yahweh in the here and now. Death was

the end of this life, not the start of the next, so religious ceremony was of little significance, and further sustenance was futile. In words attributed to Hezekiah:

Those who go down to the Pit cannot hope for your faithfulness.
The living, the living, they thank you, as I do this day. (Isa. 28:18–19)

Old Testament hope, in other words, was generally historical, not posthistorical, with the very few exceptions presenting themselves in the form of "glimpses" rather than detailed formulations.

For most Israelites, hope remained firmly anchored in the present life. But a few seem to glimpse some form of continued communion with God beyond it. [p. 217]

Johnston acknowledges a few glimpses of something like resurrection (as in Isa. 26:19 or Dan. 12:2), but the rarity of those glimpses is more significant than what they elucidate:

Death is a complex subject which elicits a wide variety of responses. And the Hebrew Bible reflects Israel's religious views over many centuries, in many different social and political contexts. Given these two major impulses towards diversity, it is hardly surprising that a belief in resurrection should emerge in some places. What is surprising is rather the opposite, that it emerges so little! [p. 218]

In his scan of Old Testament passages dealing with the afterlife, Neil doesn't mention two of the most frequently cited, Isaiah 26:19 and Daniel 12:1–3. The former, it seems most likely to me, is a poetic way of saying that the impending exile will end—using language not unlike Ezekiel's dry bone language. The latter reflects later Jewish apocalyptic writing. (For an accessible survey of Jewish apocalyptic literature, see Craig Hill's excellent book *In God's Time: The Bible and the Future,* Eerdmans, 2002.) Both provide exactly the kind of material later Jewish writers (especially those influenced by Hellenic thinking) would use to develop belief in afterlife—an innovative and "liberal" syncretistic development, of course, which the conservative Sadducees rejected.

Chapter 8: The First Two Threads, and
Chapter 9: The Third and Fourth Threads

My main sources for these chapters were Alice Turner, *The History of Hell* (Harcourt, 1993), Alan Bernstein, *The Formation of Hell: Death and Retribution in the Ancient and Early Christian Worlds* (Cornell University

Press, 1993), and Neil Gillman, *The Death of Death: Resurrection and Immortality in Jewish Thought* (Jewish Lights, 1997). Neil and Dan's conversation should be seen as a very general sketch of a very complex and fascinating subject which Turner, Bernstein, and Gillman together take well over 950 pages to describe.

Along with these resources, I am indebted to N. T. Wright's many works, most notably *The Resurrection of the Son of God* (Augsburg Fortress, 2003) and *The Challenge of Jesus* (IVP, 1999). I also highly recommend CDs of Bishop Wright's lectures, available through Regent College, Vancouver, British Columbia, and elsewhere.

In Chapter Nine, Neil labels Zoroastrianism a dualistic religion. Zoroastrians themselves (there are an estimated 140,000 still practicing the religion today) understand it as more accurately monotheistic, with Ahriman a subdominant personality who will be defeated by Ohrmazd.

Chapter 10: The Scapegoat Factor

Elaine Pagels, *The Origin of Satan* (Vintage, 1995), served as a main resource for this chapter. On the book's last page, Pagels says, "For the most part . . . Christians have taught—and acted upon—the belief that their enemies are evil and beyond redemption. . . . I hope that this research may illuminate for others, as it has for me, the struggle within Christian tradition between the profoundly human view that 'otherness' is evil and the words of Jesus that reconciliation is divine" (p. 184). Whether one supports her argument through the book or not, I think this insight is powerful and valuable, ignored at our own (and others') peril, and it has important connections to our ideas about hell.

If there are "two purposes of God"—heaven and hell (in contrast to Jan Bonda's thesis, that ultimate reconciliation is God's single purpose), then it is always tempting to say that some people (sons of hell, the hell-bound) are irreconcilably different, ontologically other and hence inferior, and ultimately disposable. The social consequences of this belief are easy to imagine; in fact, we don't need to imagine them because our history is replete with atrocities that show their effects. (For more on Christian atrocities, see my *A Generous Orthodoxy*, Emergent/YS/Zondervan, 2004.) Or for more nonimaginary examples, one only needs to visit a demonstration against gays or abortionists and witness the "God hates fags" signs and associated hellfire rhetoric.

Contrast this view of "otherness" with the example of Jesus in John 8:1–11 or the vision of Jesus reflected in Luke 15 or in his Sermon on the Mount (Matt. 5–7): that God's gracious love welcomes the sinner home, doesn't condemn, and waters the fields of the evil farmer as well as the good one. Since God loves even those who oppose God, so should we be predisposed to love, serve, and seek to reconcile with our enemies rather than damning, labeling, rejecting, killing, or torturing them. It is embarrassing that something so obvious even needs to be said, but it does.

As for the etymology of the word *Pharisee,* Alice Turner (*The History of Hell,* p. 43) says, "The word *Pharisee* is thought to refer to Persia, just as a Bombay Zoroastrian is a Parsi." I have not yet found other documentation to support this assertion, and guessing about etymology is hazardous, but Turner's assertion seems to fit the facts.

Again, for the complex development and diversity of Jewish beliefs about the afterlife during the period of the Second Temple, which is the historical context in which Jesus would speak, see N. T. Wright's 817-page masterpiece, *The Resurrection of the Son of God* (Augsburg Fortress, 2003).

Chapter 11: Better Than We Realized

When Neil says that "God is even better than we thought, that the gospel is better than we realized," he is making the point that I hope all readers will share as they complete this book, whatever their persuasion on hell.

Chapter 12: Something like a Straight Answer

Neil's discussion of scientific models has ramifications on how we approach not only the issue of hell but also the whole challenge of biblical interpretation. For more on this subject, see Dave Tomlinson, *The Post-Evangelical* (Emergent/YS/Zondervan, 2003), Chapter 7, "The Truth, the Whole Truth, and Something Quite like the Truth." Neil's terms *truth-depicting* and *truth-conveying* come from that chapter. For a more nuanced scholarly discussion, see Stanley J. Grenz and John R. Franke, *Beyond Foundationalism: Shaping Theology in a Postmodern Context* (Westminster/John Knox, 2001).

Chapter 13: End in Embrace?

Neil's "friends" who compile some quotes from the early church fathers about ultimate reconciliation would be Gulley and Mulholland, in *If Grace Is True* (pp. 212–218).

Chapter 14: Piano Lessons and Lumpy Hands

If, when reading the quote from Hitler's physician, you feel a concern rising in you regarding whether the church in America could similarly be seduced into complicity with a rogue government during wartime, I hope you will not suppress it. Along similar lines, we should similarly be concerned that "faith-based initiatives," for all the good they offer, also threaten to make recipients hesitant to speak prophetically to our government. In other words, they could easily become a kind of bribe to ensure support—religious pork, one might say. That's not to say they're wrong—just dangerous.

The story of Shirley's father was inspired by Alberto Dal Bello, a kind man whom I had the privilege of knowing for many years and whose memorial service I officiated while I was writing this chapter. At the memorial service, I heard the moving story of his hands being beaten while in a prison camp in World War II. I never would have guessed that such a gentle man would have endured such torture.

Some readers may object to the inclusion of Dan's reaction to the pile of shoes in the Holocaust Museum. They may argue that it constitutes a kind of "inadmissible evidence" because Dan's reaction is emotional and visceral, and theological matters should be evaluated only in light of rational analysis of the biblical text. I would respond with a few questions: Could the kind of emotional intelligence Dan demonstrates possibly be a God-given faculty along with intellectual intelligence? Might Jesus be relying on a similar kind of emotional intelligence in a passage like Luke 11:12–14? Might our refusal to read with other intelligences beyond analytical intelligence be a symptom not of our conscious commitment to the Bible but of our unconscious commitment to Enlightenment rationalism, the Cartesian method, the methodology of high modernism?

Chapter 15: You Have a Tough Job

The few hours that pass in this chapter echo some of the tough times all pastors share, times when we feel totally drained dry and then five more demands come our way. I once wrote a song to express the strength—which I am not hesitant to call supernatural strength—that can come seemingly from nowhere in such times of bone-weary weakness:

> There's love enough. It won't run dry.
> You think it's gone; you think you've drained dry your supply.

There's love enough and love to spare.
When you stop running, you will find love waiting there, waiting
there.
A few small fish and a couple of loaves of bread.
So little here—how can these many mouths be fed?
When you give all that you have, you'll be surprised
How much your little multiplies.

I always hope that my writings will help people in some small way understand how hard it is to be a good pastor in these strange times. (I realize that it may be disproportionately easy to be a mediocre or poor one.) My goal isn't self-pity or sympathy, just greater understanding among church folk for our brothers and sisters in pastoral ministry.

The guidance that comes to Dan, Nancy, and the others through the time of prayer conveys, I hope, the gentle intervention of the Holy Spirit that we may experience at key junctures on our journey. It's no wonder that the Spirit is called the Comforter, especially in light of the root meaning of *comfort*: the Spirit comes to us "with strength." Much of my writing has dealt with conceptual issues and perhaps as a result has not given me the opportunity to sufficiently emphasize my belief that God is indeed active in our experience. I hope that this lack is to some degree redressed here.

The BEF doctrinal statement that appears in this chapter is meant to suggest that much of what is now called Evangelicalism is really Neofundamentalism. For this reason, my friend Jim Wallis identifies himself as a "nineteenth-century evangelical." What is called postevangelicalism may be an attempt to recapture the spirit of prefundamentalist or nineteenth-century evangelicalism.

As is clear in this chapter, Carol never wavers from her conventional view of hell. I hope she represents all the good people who "can't just go rethinking things all the time" but who have such big hearts that nobody would want to argue with them. I am reminded of the preface to *Mere Christianity*, where Lewis writes, "There are questions at issue between Christians to which I do not think we have been told the answer. There are some to which I may never know the answer: if I asked them, even in a better world, I might (for all I know) be answered as a far greater questioner was answered: *What is that to thee? Follow thou Me.*" I hope that readers—of whatever persuasion—will take this approach, rather than an argumentative one, regarding the questions raised in this book.

Carol also represents the many good people who do rethink the conventional view on hell and in the end reaffirm it or a mildly modified form of it. They do so for good reasons and in so doing preserve several treasures that ought to be preserved, including a deep understanding of the horror of sin; a strong sense of God's moral freedom, integrity, and holiness; and an unquestionable commitment to Scripture. It is important to say that I respect these people and hope they can extend the same respect to me and others who have not been able to remain satisified with either the conventional view or mild modifications of it, even as we seek to preserve the treasures they rightly value.

Chapter 16: All over the Map, and Chapter 17: Deconstructing Hell

The commentary on Chapter Five tells the story behind Casey's notes here. Several of the unattributed quotes come from the *U.S. News and World Report* article noted in the chapter. However, sources referred to as "Maundet" and "Berton and Chase" are completely imaginary. The quotes attributed to these fictitious scholars reflect opinions and conclusions drawn from my own readings and research.

Chapter 18: Proposal, Plan, Implementation

Sadly, the honesty that characterizes the council's conversation in this chapter is too rare. Patrick Lencioni, in *The Five Dysfunctions of a Team* (Jossey-Bass, 2002), suggests a better way, as does Ephesians 4:25.

Walter Brueggemann coins the term *inherency* in *Struggling with Scripture,* by Walter Brueggemann, Brian Blount, and William Placher (Westminster/John Knox, 2002).

Chapter 19: Homework Assignment

The table presented in this chapter may seem overwhelming, but I would encourage diligent readers to do a similar study on their own. It is much easier to label one's received, preconceived, unexamined views as biblical—and to condemn other views as unbiblical—than it is to actually grapple with the biblical texts themselves, in all their wildness, diversity, and vitality.

Book Two: The Word After That

Chapter 20: How Can I Hurt Him?

Dan's reconciliation with Gil does not happen neatly or all at once. But the outworking of reconciliation drives the plotline of the whole story.

Chapter 21: Nice Walleye Fishing Charters

Neil's "posse" here seeks to redress a weakness that several people, most notably my friend and colleague Keith Matthews, pointed out to me: Neo/Neil in the previous two volumes seemed too independent to be believable. Also, the "group of five" in this second part of the book reflects my own rich experience with several groups of friends, most notably my friends in emergent, whom I have "known with" in ways that have made my writing possible. The predominant racial "otherness" of the group expresses my belief that the church in the West needs to come to the table of our brothers and sisters from the global South, not so that we can continue our colonial project of controlling them, patronizing them, or dictating to them but so that we can learn from them in dialogue and know with them in friendship, as we work with them to seek the Kingdom of God. (I sometimes fear that the word *postcolonial* really means *post-Euro-colonial,* which is another way of saying that we may be entering a period of *American neocolonialism.* I hope and pray this will not be the case.)

Tony Jones's cabin in Minnesota inspired the cabin in these chapters. Thanks to Doug Pagit for teaching me to speak Minnesotan so nicely, now.

If you would like to find or form a group in real life that could become like the fictional group in this chapter, you'll find some resources at www.emergentvillage.com.

Chapter 22: Wolves in Lawyers' Tuxedos, and Chapter 23: Up Toward the Stars

My friend Andrew Jones (tallskinnykiwi.com) invented the term *deep ecclesiology* that is so important in this chapter. (I hope he will someday soon write more on the concept.) Thanks to Spencer Burke (www.theooze.com) for the "opt-out" language regarding salvation.

As this chapter makes clear, the solutions to our problems with various doctrines of hell—and the concepts of God that are associated with those doctrines—are not just theological and intellectual; many of them are spiritual, practical, and relational. We can't merely think our way into better ideas; we need to relate (or love) our way into a better life. True, grappling with these issues intellectually can help us move out of ugly, distorted concepts of God, but we won't move into a more beautiful knowledge of God without spiritual practices such as prayer, confession, worship, fellowship, and service. We aren't going to wrestle to the ground the truth about God in a logical assault any more than Jacob could pin down the angel in Genesis 32; we will receive it "on winds that blow / From beyond the rim of all we know."

Chapter 24: A Colorful Breakfast

Dan and Casey realize they're being invited into the "circle of five." I hope that through this book you will feel yourself being invited into the possibility of a similar kind of friendship or fellowship. Again, for more information, go to www.emergent.info.

Chapter 25: A New Kind of Christianity

Thanks to Dallas Willard and Keith Matthews for the Louis Evely quote, which was included in their Fuller Seminary class notes.

The character Milagros is a composite of many fine people I have met who are part of the Christian Community Development Association (www.ccda.org) and other similar groups. The Little Flower has many real world counterparts, such as Harambee in Pasadena (www.harambee.org) or Camden House in New Jersey (www.camdenhouse.org), Rutba House in Kentucky, and Simple Way in Philadelphia (www.thesimpleway.org), who are banding together in a promising movement called the "new monasticism."

Chapter 26: Second Thoughts

The network I mentioned earlier, emergent (www.emergentvillage.com), has identified four practices that give it shape. One feature of what is sometimes called the "emerging church" is a turn from doctrines to practices; unity is built less around a list of things one professes to believe and more around how one pursues truth and puts beliefs into action through practices. In this way, churches and other similar organizations (the distinctions are less important in a deep ecclesiology) see themselves as communities of practice. For more on this turn, see my friend Diana Butler-Bass's book *The Practicing Congregation* (Alban, 2004).

Chapter 27: To God, All Are Alive

The character Chip was inspired by a few people I have met who had the courage to raise questions and say, "I'm changing my mind on some things." *The Glorious Unveiling* and *Left in Flames* are imaginary titles.

Chapter 28: A Part of Me at the Core of My Mind

Dan's summary regarding the engagement of Christian thought with Neoplatonic philosophy is very broad and is easily abused. A simplistic "Jewish equals good" and "Greek equals bad" equation does justice neither to the important contributions of Greek thought to Christian theology nor to the important missionary challenge for the early church. Just as thoughtful Christians today must take seriously the currents of modernity and post-modernity in our culture, Christian leaders in our first millennium coura-geously, honestly, and deeply engaged with the thought forms of their world. The depth of their engagement should inspire us, even when we see, in ret-rospect, ways in which we might wish they had been more discriminating. Who are we to judge when we haven't proved that we will do half as well in our milieu as they did in theirs?

Dan refers to ecological carelessness late in this chapter. Two of my fa-vorite groups that combine spirituality and care for creation are the Au Sable Institute (www.ausable.org) and the Evangelical Environmental Net-work (www.creationcare.org).

Thanks to my friends Claude and Kelley Nikondeha, Graham Codring-ton, and John Benn; to Evariste, Justine, and Solomon; and to so many oth-ers for being my hosts and friends in Africa in the summer of 2004. Much of the content of these final chapters grew from my time there, learning from them and the new friends they introduced me to.

Chip refers to a chart that contrasts modernity and postmodernity. My books *The Church on the Other Side* and *A New Kind of Christian* present this information. He also refers to circle diagrams, which can be found in *A Generous Orthodoxy,* and to a seven-episode overview of the biblical story, which is presented in *The Story We Find Ourselves In* (Jossey-Bass, 2003).

Chapter 29: The Last, Best Word

The mission groups described in this chapter are inspired by the work of Church of the Savior in Washington, D.C. (see www.seekerschurch.org), by innovative mission agencies like International Teams (www.iteams.org) and International Justice Mission (www.ijm.org), and by my own home congregation, Cedar Ridge Community Church in Spencerville, Maryland (www.crcc.org).

A final word: Many of my friends and acquaintances who have read parts of the manuscript of this book or who have heard me speak on this material have told me about the deep and positive effect it has had on them. Many of them have struggled greatly with the view of God that aris-es from the conventional view of hell, and they have felt an overwhelming sense of liberation and worship as they read these pages. Their hearts have been filled with a greater love for God and their neighbors, and I pray and hope that this will be your experience as well. Yet I know that some good people will read this book and find it disturbing or unsettling. If you are in the latter category, I hope you will feel free to ignore whatever does not seem right to you and profit by whatever does. Let the chaff blow away, and cherish whatever grains of truth remain, however few, however small. Even if the alternative views presented here do not win your confidence, I trust that you will have benefited from entering into this important conversation about matters of ultimate concern.

THE AUTHOR

BRIAN D. MCLAREN graduated from the University of Maryland with degrees in English (bachelor of arts, summa cum laude, 1978; master of arts, magna cum laude, 1981). His academic interests included medieval drama, Romantic poets, modern philosophical literature, and the novels of Dr. Walker Percy.

After several years' teaching and consulting in higher education, he left academia in 1986 to become founding pastor of Cedar Ridge Community Church, an innovative nondenominational church in the Baltimore-Washington area. The church has grown to involve several hundred people, many of whom were previously unchurched. In 2004, he was awarded a doctor of divinity degree (honoris causa) from Carey Theological College in Vancouver, British Columbia, Canada.

McLaren has been active in networking and mentoring church planters and pastors since the mid-1980s and has assisted in the development of several new churches. He is a popular speaker for campus groups and retreats and a frequent guest lecturer at seminaries and conferences, nationally and internationally. His public speaking covers a broad range of topics, including postmodernism, spiritual formation, biblical studies, evangelism, apologetics, leadership, global mission, church growth, church planting, art and music, pastoral survival and burnout, interreligious dialogue, ecology, and social justice.

McLaren's first book, *The Church on the Other Side: Doing Ministry in the Postmodern Matrix* (Zondervan, 1998, rev. 2000), has been recognized as a primary portal into the current conversation about postmodern ministry. His second book, *Finding Faith* (Zondervan, 1999), is a contemporary apologetic, written for thoughtful seekers and skeptics. His third book, *A New Kind of Christian* (Jossey-Bass, 2001), further explores issues of Christian faith and postmodernity and won *Christianity Today*'s Award of Merit in 2002. His fourth book, *More Ready Than You Realize: Evangelism as Dance in the Postmodern Matrix* (Zondervan, 2002), presents a refreshing approach to spiritual friendship. *A Is for Abductive*, written with Leonard Sweet and Jerry Haselmeyer (Zondervan, 2002), and *Adventures in Missing the Point*, written with Anthony Campolo (Emergent/YS, 2003), explore theological reform in a postmodern context. He is one of five authors of *The Church in the Emerging Culture* (Emergent/YS, 2003). His 2004 release, *A Generous Orthodoxy* (Emergent/YS/Zondervan), is a personal confession and has been called a "manifesto" of the emerging church conversation.

The second release in the *New Kind of Christian* trilogy, entitled *The Story We Find Ourselves In* (Jossey-Bass, 2003), seeks to tell the biblical story in a new context. *The Last Word and the Word After That* completes this trilogy.

McLaren has written for or contributed interviews to many periodicals, including *Leadership, Sojourners, Worship Leader, Christianity Today,* and *Conversations.* His work has been featured in *Christian Century, Christianity Today,* and *Time,* and he has appeared on numerous radio and television broadcasts, including *Larry King Live.* In 2005, *Time* magazine named him as one of the twenty-five most influential evangelicals in America. Many of his articles are available at www.anewkindofchristian.com. He is also a musician and songwriter.

He is on the international steering team and board of directors of emergent, a growing generative friendship among missional Christian leaders (www.emergentvillage.com), and has served on several nonprofit boards, including Sojourners and Off the Map, an organization helping people cultivate a practical spirituality (off-the-map.org); International Teams (www.iteams.org), an innovative missions organization based in Chicago; and Mars Hill Graduate School in Seattle. He has taught at several college seminaries (including Fuller Seminary in California, Biblical Theological Seminary in Pennsylvania, and Western Seminary in Oregon) and is currently an adjunct faculty member at Mars Hill Graduate School (www.mhgs.edu).

McLaren is a principal in a new leadership coaching and organizational consulting firm, ILS (www.ilscc.net), which seeks to provide assistance to churches and organizations dealing with a variety of change- and growth-related issues. His personal website and weblog (www.anewkindofchristian. com) provides access to numerous articles, reviews, interviews, links, FAQs, reading lists, and other resources.

McLaren and his wife, Grace, have four children. He has traveled extensively in Europe, Latin America, and Africa, and his personal interests include ecology, fishing, hiking, kayaking, camping, songwriting, music, art, and literature.

HOW IT ALL BEGAN

In this excerpt from the beginning of A New Kind of Christian, *the first book in the trilogy, Pastor Dan Poole and his new friend, Neil Oliver (Neo), meet for coffee and bagels—and a very interesting conversation about why Dan is burned out in his role as church leader.*

○

THE NEXT WEEKEND when I met Neo, we enjoyed a few bagels and cups of coffee (much better than the rec center brew), talked about my daughter's chances for a soccer scholarship, and reviewed our summer travel plans. (He had put on a lot of miles already that summer—including a trip to Seattle, where his parents now lived, and then a two-week stint escorting his church youth group to Guatemala for a short-term mission trip.)

When I turned the subject to life as a high school teacher, though, he put up his hand and said, "Just a minute, Dan. Before we go there, you must tell me more about why you're thinking of leaving ministry. I'd hate to be aiding and abetting a Jonah, you know, fleeing the work of the Lord. I think the church would be impoverished to lose yet another leader like you."

"'Yet another' leader? What do you mean?" I asked.

"It's just that, well, I have heard of quite a few pastors quitting in the last few years. It would be a shame if you left too, unless it was absolutely necessary," Neo replied. "Do you really feel you have no option but to leave your career, your calling?" He was looking right at me. We had both stopped eating.

I saw no way of getting the information I wanted without a partial disclosure, so I decided to let a little air out of the balloon I was holding inside. Just a little though. I told him I was tired, tired of all the church politics, tired of the constant criticism, tired of having to fight for every little change, tired of working for so many people who think they could do what I do better than me, who just don't understand. "I guess I sound like I'm feeling sorry for myself," I said.

"It's understandable. Your problems remind me of the story of Moses," Neo replied. "Leadership is hard. But I think there must be even more to it than that."

Neo apparently saw through my partial disclosure. At that moment, I remember deciding, "OK, I'll just let go. . . . I'll just let the pent-up balloon of emotion inside me escape." I leaned forward and spoke quietly, almost whispering: "You're right. Leadership is hard, but it's next to impossible when the leader isn't sure of where he's going."

"Yes?" he said, intoning a question.

I answered his question with a question. "What does a pastor do when he's having questions and doubts of his own? Can he stand up in his pulpit and say, 'Brothers and sisters, for the past three months, God hasn't seemed real to me. I have faith that God will seem real to me again in the future, but to be honest, God doesn't seem real to me today'? What does a pastor do when he questions the stock answers he's supposed to be convincing others of?"

Neo pressed his lips together, squinted his eyes, and nodded his head, as if to say, "Go on."

And then it all flowed out: "Remember when I told you—at the concert, out on the front step—that I felt like a fundamentalist? Well, I feel like a fundamentalist who's losing his grip—whose fundamentals are cracking and fraying and falling apart and slipping through my fingers. It's like I thought I was building my house on rock, but it turned out to be ice, and now global warming has hit, and the ice is melting and everything is crumbling. That's scary, you know? I went to seminary right out of college, and it was great, and I thought I was getting the truth, you know, the whole truth and nothing but the truth. Now I've been a pastor for fourteen years, and for this last year or so I feel like I'm running out of gas. It's not just burnout. It's more like I'm losing my faith—well, not exactly that, but I feel that I'm losing the whole framework for my faith. You know, I keep pushing everything into these little cubbyholes, these little boxes, the little systems I got in seminary and even before that—in Sunday school and summer camp and from my parents. But life is too messy to fit. And I'm supposed to be preaching the truth, but I'm not even sure what the truth is anymore, and—that's it, really—I just feel dishonest whenever I try to preach. I used to love to preach, but now every time—well, maybe not every time, but quite often—when I start to prepare a sermon, it's agonizing and . . . and people come to me with their problems and I used to be so sure of what to say but now I try to act confident but I don't know. The only thing I'm confident about is that I don't have all the answers anymore. I'm sorry. I'm not making any sense."

"No, you're making more sense than you realize," he said, and then he started working on me. I felt like I did when I'd gone to a chiropractor a few years before. He was probing here, pushing there, poking, stretching. *Are you feeling depressed, maybe suicidal?* Not seriously, not at all. *Is your marriage OK? Are you having moral problems?* No real problems there, thank God. *Are you working too many hours? How many?* Maybe fifty, fifty-five—that's not really it. *Are you afraid to tell your people what you're really thinking?* Yes, I feel that all the time. *Do you feel trapped by your profession, like you have to choose between your own personal pursuit of truth and the requirement to give an orthodox sermon every Sunday?* Yes, yes, exactly. *Do you sometimes feel that your seminary professors are looking over your shoulder and scolding you?* Every day. *Are you struggling with some specific doctrines or theological positions?* Yes, several. *Do you have anyone to talk to about all this?* Well, there's my wife, Carol. But it really upsets her to see me questioning. *Anyone else?* No. Nobody.

After about ten minutes of this kind of rapid-fire questioning, he said, "I think I understand your problem."

THE STORY CONTINUES

In this excerpt from The Story We Find Ourselves In, *Neo and his friend Kerry, a scientist, are hiking in the Galápagos Islands and discussing God, evolution, and the book of Genesis.*

○

AT THIS POINT, Kerry interrupted Neo again. She told him about her youth group leader, Steve, and his either-or ultimatum about God and evolution. It didn't sound like Neo was a biblical literalist. How did he reconcile God and evolution?

Neo laughed. "Kerry, believe me, I've been in a lot of debates about all of this back in my career as a teacher. Back in the early '90s . . . well, that's another story for another time. Let me just answer your question. I think that the literalism of many of my fellow believers is silly. I don't mean them any offense, and I'm sure many of my opinions are no less silly than theirs. But still . . ."

Kerry replied, "Well, to me, believing in God at all seems pretty silly sometimes. Why does their literalism seem sillier to you than your own belief?"

This section of the climb just below the rim was the steepest yet. Neo needed another rest. Finding a chair-sized rock, black, porous, obviously volcanic, Neo sat, beads of sweat forming on his coffee-brown forehead, and leaned forward with his elbows on his knees. He took a couple of deep breaths and continued talking. "All my own silliness aside, do they imagine God literally saying, 'Let there be light'? In what language? Hebrew? Latin or Arabic maybe? Or maybe English, but if so, which accent—American, English, Aussie, or Jamaican? And where did the air come from to propagate the sound waves for God's literal words; and for that matter, where do the vocal cords come from for God to say those words? And as for the business of the six days, assuming that you're not a flat-earther, you have to acknowledge that when it's day on one side of the globe, it's night on the other. So when Genesis says that the first day begins and ends, from whose vantage point does it mean—Sydney, Australia, or Greenwich, England?"

Kerry laughed and said, "You're being very wicked."

Neo replied, "Actually, St. Augustine raised some of those kinds of questions long before I did. He too was bugged by Christians who seemed to be know-it-alls. But please don't misunderstand, Kerry. Like the staunchest literalist, I believe in the story of Genesis, but I think I believe it more in the way that ancient Semitic nomads huddled in their blankets around a winter fire would have believed it, as they told it and retold it, generation to generation, feeling the poetic rhythms—'and there was evening and there was morning, a second day, a third day, a fourth day . . .' I believe in it as a story that gives us something so much more important than textbook-style so-called objective facts and newspaper-style information— two things that we moderns value far more highly than our ancestors did. For me, it is a story that gives us *in-formation* . . . a story that *forms* us *in*-wardly with truth and meaning—something that we moderns seem to value far less highly than our ancestors did."

"So, Neo," Kerry interjected, "you see it as a myth, right? It's just another creation myth."

Neo replied, "No, no, no. I didn't say that. In fact, the more I interact with the story, the less I want to carve it down to fit in any modern categories, whether 'myth' or 'fact.' And I certainly don't want to reduce it with a *just* into anything less than fact. No, Kerry, to me, it's far more than 'just myth' or 'just fact.' To me, it's the beginning of the story we find ourselves in, right here and right now." As he said those last words, with one hand he patted the rock he was sitting on, and he lifted the other hand in a sweeping gesture. Kerry shook her head, whether in disagreement or frustration or just from being overwhelmed, neither she nor Neo could tell for sure.